The
Economic Writings
of
Du Pont de Nemours

ALSO BY THE AUTHOR:

Unemployment in West Virginia and Its Solution

The
Economic Writings
of
Du Pont de Nemours

James J. McLain

Newark
University of Delaware Press
London: Associated University Presses

Associated University Presses, Inc.
Cranbury, New Jersey 08512

Associated University Presses
Magdalen House
136-148 Tooley Street
London SE1 2TT, England

Library of Congress Cataloging in Publication Data

McLain, James J
The economic writings of Du Pont de Nemours.

Bibliography: p.
Includes index.
1. Du Pont de Nemours, Pierre Samuel, 1739-1817.
2. Physiocrats. I. Title.
HB93.D86M3 1977   330.15'2   76-14769
ISBN 0-87413-114-6

PRINTED IN THE UNITED STATES OF AMERICA

Contents

Preface

In recent years contemporary economic thought has come under increasing attack by those who argue that the accepted theories are losing their power to explain the behavior of economic activity. Of the three traditional factors of production, namely, labor, capital, and natural resources, contemporary theory has emphasized the importance of capital in relation to labor in its production theory. The third factor of production, natural resources, has been taken for granted, generally "held constant," for simplicity. Of course, economists are quite capable of building theories incorporating all three factors as variables. But the fact is that at a time when the economy's crucial dependence on natural resources has finally become obvious to all, economic science approaches present problems with a heritage biased against an emphasis on natural resources as an integral part of theory. It is imperative, then, if economics is to retain its scientific honesty, that it consider placing greater emphasis on natural resources within economic theory, both for descriptive and analytical purposes.

This study of a half-century of economic thought and writing by a French physiocrat is offered in the hope that the story of his success in his earlier years in the physiocratic school and his attempts in his later years to interpret and revise in physiocratic terms the arguments of the English classical school might encourage a reassessment of our own theories from a natural-resource point of view. Another important reason for studying Du Pont's work is that, to the extent that contemporary economics is faulted for neglecting to consider social and political institutions within the scope of its models, Du Pont's economics is of interest for its continual emphasis on social, cultural, and political institutions. As noted in the conclusion of this work, in 1817 Du Pont demonstrated that physiocratic theory, though rejected by younger economists, could serve as a powerful engine of analysis even in the new industrial era. His major disagreement with the classical economists, over the appropriate scope of economic science, offers an alternative view for consideration by those who find the scope of contemporary economic theory too restrictive.

I am indebted to the following persons for assistance and advice throughout the preparation of this work: Ronald L. Meek of the University of Leicester; Richmond D. Williams, John B. Riggs, Harold F. Williamson, B. Bright Low, Ann M. Aydelotte, and Carol B. Hallman, all of the Eleutherian Mills Historical Library, Greenville, Delaware; Mark Perlman, Jacob Cohen, Gilbert Shapiro, Herbert Chesler, and the late Carter Goodrich, all of the University of Pittsburgh; and two anonymous readers who were particularly helpful in pinpointing errors and inaccuracies.

I wish to acknowledge the vital support of the Eleutherian Mills Historical Library for a nine-month research grant during 1970 and 1971. I also wish to thank the Department of Economics and Finance of the University of New Orleans for administrative aid in the preparation of the final manuscript. My wife receives particular praise for receiving M Du Pont into our family these many years. Finally, I acknowledge the permission of the publishers and of the holders of rights to unpublished sources, particularly the Eleutherian Mills Historical Library, to reproduce passages that appear in this work.

The decision to translate quotations into English and omit the original French, rather than to include both the French and the English was a difficult one but was necessary for reasons of cost. The author will be happy to supply copies of the original French passages to serious scholars upon request. The author is indebted to Jacqueline Davila for professional translations of most of the passages, although quotations from

Say are taken from readily available, if sometimes awkward, nineteenth-century translations of his work, and two passages from Du Pont's letters have been translated by this author. Following Ronald Meek's work I have referred to the *produit net* as the "net product" throughout, and I have otherwise attempted to standardize the translations of other physiocratic and general eighteenth-century terms according to modern scholarly usage, but the reader should be aware that, during nearly sixty years of writing, the same French words often acquired new shades of meaning. Thus, for instance, *commerce* might more often be translated as "trade" in the writings of the 1760s but would more fittingly be rendered as "commerce" in later writings (but *échange* would always mean "trade" in the sense of a two-way exchange of goods).

Another victim of cost constraints has been Du Pont's *Table Raisonnée*, a monumental organizational chart of moral, political, and economic society, much of it in fine print and comprising over two square meters in area. Even if it had been translated and divided into quadrants, like enlarged sections of a roadmap, it would have filled over thirty pages whose interrelationships would be as incomprehensible as a dismembered input-output table. Its full-scale publication remains an unattained landmark in the history of economic thought.

This book is a revised version of a doctoral dissertation written under Mark Perlman of the University of Pittsburgh. Portions of a paper, "Du Pont as a Historian of Economic Thought," presented at the 1974 History of Economics Society Annual Meeting at the University of North Carolina, Chapel Hill, have been incorporated into one chapter. Expanded sections from an unpublished paper, "Du Pont as an Economic Heretic," have been added to the presentation of Du Pont's relations with Malthus and Say. The bibliography is limited to those sources actually cited in the text and should not be taken as a complete listing of publications on physiocracy or as a complete guide to Du Pont's works, many of which dealt with topics other than economics.

The
Economic Writings
of
Du Pont de Nemours

I.

Introduction

Some men take their place in the history of economic ideas as progenitors of new modes of thought. Such a man was François Quesnay, whose *tableau économique* extended the thought forms of the Enlightenment to the pursuit of economic reasoning. Others play a less dramatic role in the history of economic thought as transmitters of new ideas or as preservers of old ideas in periods of social revolution. Such a man was Pierre Samuel Du Pont de Nemours whose career bridged monarchy, despotism, and restoration in eighteenth-and-nineteenth-century France.

Du Pont's economic biography was written in France in 1888; in 1965 his general biography was published by a historian; and from time to time aspects of his career have received attention from students of economic ideas. Nevertheless, a full evaluation of his contributions to economics, based on a comprehensive study of his papers, is long overdue. The present inquiry is addressed to the purpose of providing such an assessment.

By his twenty-fifth birthday Pierre Samuel Du Pont de Nemours had joined the physiocratic school; by his fiftieth year he had become the major physiocratic spokesman in the revolutionary National Assembly; and by his seventy-fifth, as secretary-general of the Provisional Government of France, Du Pont had accepted the resignation of Bonaparte. As these quarter-century signposts indicate, Du Pont was a colorful, if secondary, figure in the events of eighteenth-and-nineteenth-century France. His varied activities spanned a range including, but stretching far wider than, economic matters. Nevertheless, he was an active member of the first economic school, and it is his physiocratic thought that is the primary concern of this inquiry.

An interpretation of the development and influence of Du Pont's economic thought can hardly be effected in total disregard for the other activities of his life. More generally, the development of the economic thinking of such an *homme engagé* can hardly be assessed without an awareness of the social background and intellectual climate of his lifetime and the years immediately preceding his birth in 1739. Thus, in the first section of this introduction, it is appropriate to consider briefly the political, economic, and social events of eighteenth-century France. Although the debate over the question of whether events influence ideas or ideas influence events will not be joined in this work, it will be recognized that social events do not occur in the total absence of ideas, nor do ideas flourish but in a climate of socially favorable conditions. Accordingly, the ideas current in eighteenth-century France will be discussed briefly in the second section of this introduction. Such an artificial separation of events from ideas does not do justice to the importance of their mutual interplay. Nevertheless, an exposition of the development of their reciprocal effects into a synthesis of forces in the eighteenth century is beyond the modest scope of this introduction.[1]

A. Social and Intellectual Background

1. *Government Finance*

The reign of the Sun King, Louis XIV, was at its zenith fifty years before the birth of Du Pont de Nemours. The relative impoverishment of the Italian courts following the Thirty Years' War (1618–48) had conferred the prerogative for European cultural leadership upon the French court, which under Louis's leadership carried the cultural movement of the Renaissance to its extreme development in the extravagant embellishments of the baroque style. This style required the greatest detail in craftsmanship and was profusely liberal in its use of gold in its decorations. Both the extravagance of this style and Louis's conspicuous leadership in his effort to establish the dominance of French culture throughout Europe led the monarch to spare little in the way of expenditure that might augment the grandeur of his reign. Consequently, the country's public finances were tailored to the King's cultural and other expenses, rather than the more responsible opposite set of conditions, namely, expenditures tailored to the resources of the fisc.

Besides support of the court, other expenses included the maintenance of the strongest military force in Europe. Between 1688 and 1714 France fought two more wars. The relative peace of the mid-eighteenth century began only in 1714. Thus, the government not only found it necessary to replenish its military strength expended during the Thirty Years' War but had to finance two more campaigns as well toward the end of Louis's sumptuous reign, adding to the strain of public requirements on the national economy.

By the end of the Sun King's reign in 1715, the court's extravagance and the continued military expenditures had heavily strained the sources of public revenues in an economy not fully recovered from the requirements of war. The young Louis XV came to the throne in that year to reign over a half-century of surface calm in France. But the government's credit rating had already been seriously impaired by the financial machinations of his predecessor.

To say that government finances did not improve during the reign of Louis XV (1715–74) is to overlook two balancing sets of facts that through their countervailing forces neither permitted improvement in the government's finances nor drove the country over the brink of bankruptcy into political chaos until later in the century when one of the forces gave way. One of these sets of forces consisted of the complex institutional arrangements by which the country was governed and in spite of which taxes were raised. France was divided haphazardly into several overlapping sets of political jurisdictions at the regional level. A major source of government revenue, the salt tax, or *gabelle*, was assessed differently in different areas. Altogether, there were four kinds of *gabelle* districts, ranging from the provinces of the *grande gabelle* to those of the *petite gabelle*. Quite different jurisdictions, the ecclesiastical dioceses and parishes, assessed ecclesiastical tithes, or *dîmes ecclésiastiques*, which were paid by the peasants in money or in kind. Also, the nobles assessed their seignorial dues, although this form of taxation varied from area to area according to the degree to which the medieval relationships of lord and vassal had been maintained. Peasants were also responsible for the *corvée*, or contribution for the upkeep of roads. This payment generally was in kind, with the peasants supplying their own labor on the roads in their parishes.

Another tax, the *taille*, was paid directly to the king's representatives. Again, the level of the *taille* varied regionally according to the relative political influence of the various regions on the central government. To complicate matters, the Tax Farmers, which were private corporations, advanced to the king's government the revenues required for the operation of the government for one year in return for the privilege of collecting several taxes and revenues such as rights of passage and import duties. The Farmers gained a reputation for ruthlessness in collecting as much revenue as they could; their profit was the amount they collected in excess of the sum they had forwarded to the government.[2]

Balanced against these institutional arrangements was a combination of fortuitous events that precluded a total breakdown of the financial machinery until the 1780s. There were no wars on French soil during the greater part of the century. There were no severe winters, droughts, pestilences, or plagues. Indeed, in contrast to the preceding century, there was an absence of natural calamities, any one of which could have brought an abrupt halt to the uneasy flow of funds through the royal coffers and possibly an earlier beginning to the Revolution.

Within these sets of opposing conditions the financial schemes of John Law were followed by successive administrations of desperate finance ministers. In an effort to cope with the enormous debts accrued by the recently deceased Louis XIV, the regent turned to the genius of the financier Law. Between 1716 and 1718 Law established the first Bank of France, consolidated the Indies, Africa, and China companies into one trade monopoly controlled by himself, acquired the farming rights to the Treasury, and began to purchase stock in the Louisiana Company in return for shares in the Bank. The nation soon plunged into a heady speculation in the stock of the Louisiana Company. The panic of 1720, which followed public realization of the discrepancy between promise and reality in the Louisiana venture, affected severely the price of the stocks on which the Bank's (and the nation's) circulating notes were based. Ultimately, many paper and real fortunes were made and lost. Many of the middle and lower classes had had their fingers burned in their initial investments; their saving patterns would be slow to return to ventures of an uncertain nature. Such unstable financial conditions might have caused more serious problems had not the middle of the century been relatively calm within the French homeland. The government continued to cope with its low credit rating, high debt, and normal responsibilities by a return to a specie monetary standard and by increases in the levels of taxation.

2. Government Economic Policy

Government economic policy was highly erratic during the early- and mid-seventeenth century under Armand Jean du Plessis Cardinal Richelieu and Jules Cardinal Mazarin. However, Jean Baptiste Colbert, as finance minister under Louis XIV between 1665 and 1673, reintroduced the mercantilist policies first implemented by Maximilien de Béthune, Duc de Sully in the early 1600s. Following the economic doctrines of the Italian writer Antonio Serra, Colbert sought to improve foreign trade, to rehabilitate existing industries, and to create new ones.

To improve agriculture Colbert attempted to redistribute the burden of taxes from the peasantry to the Church, the nobility, and the bourgeoisie, a move that was strongly resisted. However, he succeeded in establishing research centers for the improvement of agriculture and other temporary improvements in the system. To improve foreign trade he gave monopolies to the French East and West Indies Companies, subsidized shipbuilding, encouraged the development of colonies as sources of raw materials for the mother country, and even attempted to negotiate a free-trade treaty with England. He prohibited the exportation of wool and flax and encouraged the revitalization of several industries and the establishment of new ones. His rules and regulations governing the terms and conditions of manufacture have since become examples for later ages of infamous government control over free enterprise. But the purpose of his controls was to improve the quality of French manufactured goods and thereby to render them increasingly competitive qualitatively as well as through lower wage and resource costs that came as a result of lower prices for agricultural products.

Following his death in 1683, Colbert's economic policies were abandoned, and by the end of the century conditions were worse than they had been before the implementation of his reforms. In the words of David Ogg, France

> was reduced to a state of poverty and misery barely paralleled in the tragic annals of the French peasantry. The taxes were heavier and more inequitable than before. The old opportunities for malversion were re-introduced, and practically all the new industries introduced by Colbert were swept away.[3]

If government economic policy in the seventeenth century could be characterized as rudderless with the exceptions of the administrations of Sully and Colbert, economic policy in the eighteenth century could be described as almost totally without direction. In the 1730s and 1740s the government assumed control of mining and improved the road and canal systems. In the 1760s, under physiocratic influence, exportation of grain was liberalized; however, the free trade in grain coincided with local shortages in several regions, causing a premature end to the experiment and turning popular opinion against free international trade. In the 1770s another finance minister, Anne Robert Jacques Turgot, attempted to reform finances but was defeated and dismissed at the behest of vested interests. Finally, in the 1780s the government attempted to rationalize finances and to liberalize foreign trade, notably through the Anglo-French Commercial Treaty of 1786. But major reforms were to await the removal of reactionary political and institutional obstacles in the Revolution.

3. Economic and Social Conditions

The economy that supported an increasing burden of taxation was overwhelmingly agricultural. Even Colbert's policy of industrialization in the last century had concentrated on the development of manufactures for luxury markets and for export rather than heavy industry. Unlike Britain, the major impetus for industrialization came if anywhere from government rather than from merchants and businessmen. Also unlike Britain, there had been no significant enclosure movement nor rapid improvement in agricultural productivity that might have supported a reallocation of resources by an active middle class from agricultural production to manufacturing.

Indeed, the middle class seems to have played no leading role in developing manufacturing in France. The government was the only significant entrepreneur on the scene. If anything, the relative domestic peace of the century brought to the comfortable classes an urge for romantic idealization of a pastoral way of life, which had never existed but which nevertheless turned their attention and energies away from the paths of commercial and industrial activities, which their British counterparts were exploring, to the escape of a simpler, happier way of life in some nonexistent, French, agricultural Shangri-La.

In sum, the bulk of the eighteenth century revealed a slowdown in government emphasis on manufacturing from the Colbertist period, exhibited no forceful movement on the part of a middle class for economic development in any particular direction, and resulted in a heavy burden of taxation on an agricultural sector that accounted for the bulk of economic activity in the country. The consequent slow growth of the agricultural sector only increased the gap between its true condition and the idealized view of the pastoral life so dear to the middle and upper classes of the nation.

4. Condition of French Agriculture in the Eighteenth Century

According to Henri Sée's researches,[4] by the middle of the eighteenth century approximately 25 percent of French land was owned by the nobility. Another 6 percent was owned by the Church. Most of these lands were divided into plots too small for economically efficient farming. The *métayers*, or sharecroppers, who farmed these plots turned 50 percent of their profits over to the landlords. In addition to this land that was the outright property of the noble or ecclesiastical landlord, the greater part of the remaining land surrounding their property was also encumbered with dues and taxes owed to the local landlords, primarily the Church. These payments, such as the *dîmes*, or tithes, were holdovers from the medieval period. The landlord generally incurred no obligation to the peasants in return for these payments. Only a very small percentage of the land was owned by peasants in a state of total unencumbrance from feudal dues. However, by the middle of the century this pattern was slowly making way for a new type of agricultural operation: that of the middle-class entrepreneur who rented lands near cities or in the North of France, where institutional arrangements were more amenable to the establishment of large-size, efficiently operable farming enterprises. Such businessmen were termed *fermiers*.

By and large, 90 percent of the owners of land in France were peasants, but for the most part their holdings were too small to support their families. As the pattern had been in much of medieval Europe, the size of holdings decreased as they were successively divided among a growing number of heirs. Consequently, the majority of peasants had to supplement their own lands' earnings by hiring themselves out for work on larger holdings.

The rate of population growth increased in the early part of the century in response to the renewed peace and to a lack of natural checks early in the century. An increasing number of peasants were forced from the land into beggary and vagabondage. As a consequence of the population pressure on the already limited holdings of land, the peasantry conscientiously sought to limit the sizes of their families. The rate of growth in the population fell to between .04 and .05 percent and remained at that level for the duration of the century. Some peasants, however, were able to escape the general condition of poverty. Those peasant landlords who were sufficiently wealthy to live in comfort were known as *laboureurs*.

Thus, French agriculture in the eighteenth century, unlike its English counterpart, did not benefit from an enclosure movement that welded small holdings together into large estates and forced the rural proletariat into the cities, and, unlike Eastern Europe, France did not experience a strengthening of the power of local nobles over the peasantry. Instead, the responsibilities of the local lords lessened, their authority stagnated in the face of rising control by a centralized national government, and the misery of the nominally independent peasant increased, at least in comparison to that of his city cousin. The only other trend in evidence was the minor move on the part of the bourgeoisie, which came to own one sixth of the land in the North. Some historians interpret the evidence as indicating that, in spite of widespread mendicancy and vagrancy, the peasants modestly improved their economic position during the century.[5] All seem to be in agreement that their economic position worsened in comparison to those employed in the towns, and all agree that the adverse weather conditions and poor harvests of the last decades of the century abruptly reversed any modest improvements in living standards that may have occurred in France during the greater part of that century.

Techniques of production on the small holdings had hardly

improved since the Middle Ages. Indeed, some authorities argue that practices actually deteriorated between the fifteenth and eighteenth centuries in France. In the words of one authority,

> French agriculture was at this time quite backward, especially if we compare it with English agriculture. The methods of cultivation remained very primitive, and progress was very slow, except in the richest and most fertile regions. The farm-buildings were poorly arranged, and the implements were unsatisfactory and quite primitive, being hardly superior to those employed during the Middle Ages. Intensive cultivation was practically unknown almost everywhere. The system of fallow land was used [almost] universally. . . . The peasants, prompted by the spirit of routine and having but little capital, devoted no great care to cultivation.[6]

Such was the condition of eighteenth-century French agriculture, the largest sector of the economy, and a sector that supported the commercial sector. As already noted, however, the commercial sector was characterized by little industry of the type that was developing at the same time across the Channel.

5. *Intellectual Background of Eighteenth-Century France*

Much of the intellectual movement in France during the 1700s originated with the philosophical movements of John Locke and others in England during the late 1600s. Although the specific antecedents of physiocratic thought are to be discussed in detail below, it is appropriate to note that the publication by Montesquieu of *Esprit des Loix* in 1748 marked the high water of the absorption of English ideas into the French intellectual setting of the Enlightenment. The period was ripe for ideas that placed man's responsibility for the composition and direction of his society squarely on the shoulders of mankind rather than on a divinely appointed ruler. By the middle of the century Montesquieu's attempt to synthesize the studies of social action into one social theory was promptly followed by an outburst of intellectual activity.

It was in this setting that Denis Diderot and the other

philosophes began publication of the *Encyclopédie*, that Voltaire unleashed his cynicism upon society, and that Jean Jacques Rousseau developed his own version of the contractual theory of society. It was also in this setting that the first school of economic thought, the physiocratic school, developed.

B. The Physiocratic School

Physiocracy, as the theory of the first school of economic thought, is summarized in nearly every work on the history of economic analysis. The story of the development of the school, though perhaps less well known, is by no means a forgotten tale. The relationship of the disciples of the founding physiocrats—to each other, to its theory, and to the leaders—has received less emphasis in comparison to the school and its development. Accordingly, it is appropriate to summarize here the development of the school only briefly, to devote considerably more attention to the roles of the disciples and of Turgot to the school, and to conclude with some comments on the influence of the school both on economic policy and on economic theory.

1. Physiocratic Theory

The essential feature of physiocracy is its natural-resource theory of value. Value and, consequently, wealth, which is the total stock of valued products, originate with the products obtained from the land and the water. It follows, according to this theory, that only the primary activities of agriculture, fishing, and in some instances mineral extraction are truly productive activities. On this proposition is based the physiocratic class system: a productive class of farm workers (and fishermen, etc.); a "sterile" class of artisans and tradesmen who transport, refashion, and exchange the products raised by the first class; and, finally, the landowning class, including the Church and the king himself.

Quesnay's well-known *tableau économique* illustrates the mutual interdependence of these three classes in what was the first grasp of the economy as a circular flow. The landlord rents his land to the agricultural worker and forwards him his working capital. The agricultural worker combines this capital with his own labor and with the land to achieve a result that is possible in no other economic activity. The land produces goods whose value shows an excess above the total value of capital and labor put into the land after all costs have been considered. Such net product, or *produit net,* is paid to the landlord, who either reinvests it as capital improvements in the land or spends it on consumption goods. The function of the sterile, or artisan, class is both to purchase and to consume the products of agriculture as well as to fashion the implements required for agriculture and agricultural investment; the artisan class also refashions the primary wealth of nature into consumer goods for the population in general.

The landlord's position is uniquely important, for embodied in his function is the decision as to what proportion of the net product is to be reinvested in agriculture, and upon this capital-investment decision rests the rate of economic growth in the economy. And the rate of accumulation of wealth through economic growth was of paramount importance to the physiocrats. Thus, all three classes have necessary economic roles.

However, physiocracy is more than a theory of the economy. It is a theory of society, and, specifically, of an ideal society. The primary functional link between the economic and the political institutions of physiocracy is to be found in the concept of the single tax, or *impôt unique.* Although most economic functions are carried out in a system of free markets, some functions, such as the provision of transportation networks, defense, civil order, and justice, are to be provided by the government. There is only one ultimate source of wealth in the economy, the net product, which in the end must bear the full burden of any taxation. Direct taxation of this source of excess wealth avoids the distortion of markets through indirect taxes, and both simplifies the process and lowers the expenses of collection. Consequently, the needs of the state are met through a single tax on the net product.

Physiocratic economic theory rested in the political and

moral cradle of natural law, a doctrine whose acceptance secularly had been on the wane since the end of the preceding century. With physiocracy there was an order to the universe, part of whose operations were manifest in the provision of mankind's needs by nature. It followed that mankind should cultivate nature assiduously and should trade her products according to the natural laws of market forces. The role of government was to assure, under the guidance of a wise monarch, that man's reason was utilized to its fullest in discerning and understanding the laws of nature. The monarch was also to see that his government protected the property rights that underpin all the economic functions, especially those of the landlord, and that the government protect free-market operations from distortion through monopoly or government interference.

Besides the single tax on the net product, other economic policies followed from physiocratic theory. In concert with economic growth high grain prices would permit a higher net product and, consequently, higher rates of growth. Improved techniques and internal transportation systems, both possible functions of government, would obtain the same end of fast growth through lower agricultural costs. Free international trade would open new markets and permit the purchase of goods wherever their prices were lowest.

All in all, the superstructure of natural law and enlightened despotism was useful but not totally necessary to the economic framework of physiocracy. If the exclusive productivity of nature, or natural-resource theory of value, is accepted as a premise, then all their other conclusions as to the means of achieving economic growth follow from it independently of the political setting. Consequently, it was possible in later years after the eclipse of their school for physiocrats, including Du Pont de Nemours, to alter the accepted but unnecessary political conditions of their doctrine without retreating from its economic tenets.

2. Development of the Physiocratic School

Georges Weulersse, in his classic work on the physiocratic

school,[7] Ronald Meek, in his *Economics of Physiocracy*,[8] and Joseph Spengler, in his article on physiocracy in the *International Encyclopedia of the Social Sciences*,[9] have all related the story of the conversion of Mirabeau the elder to physiocratic thought by Quesnay in the latter's entresol rooms at Versailles.

François Quesnay, son of a wealthy farmer, was a genius. By twenty he had taught himself the fundamentals of medicine, and by twenty-six he was a practicing physician of some renown near Paris. By 1756, at age sixty, he was the personal physician of Madame de Pompadour and was a familiar figure in the court at Versailles. There were in those years many individuals, highly respected in historical retrospect for their intellectual agility, who visited Versailles and frequented the salons of Paris. Hume, Smith, Turgot, Franklin, and others associated with stages in the development of political and economic thought were to be seen mixing with one another in the 1750s and 1760s. Consequently, in the absence of any statement from Quesnay himself, it is impossible to describe the means by which he hit upon the concept of physiocracy.[10] Its formulation clearly reflects his own agricultural background, just as its circular flow reflects the eighteenth-century physician's knowledge of the body's circulatory system. Its trappings of natural law were clearly an idea that was in disfavor among the rationalist thinkers about him. But the concept of natural law fit well with another idea, that of *laissez-faire*. The brilliant administrator Jean Claude Marie Vincent de Gournay was a close acquaintance of Quesnay, although the two did not agree on either the question of the exclusive productivity of nature or the doctrine of natural law. Gournay was a strong proponent of laissez-faire commerce, a trait that he passed on to his disciple Turgot and an idea that Quesnay made an essential part of physiocracy.

It was in the year 1757, two years before Gournay's death and six years before Du Pont was attracted to the school, that the school was formed by Quesnay's conversion of Mirabeau. Mirabeau had just written the extremely popular treatise, *L'Ami des hommes*, in which he expressed the populationist view that accumulation of labor was the key to economic growth. With Mirabeau's mind won over to physiocracy, the school now had a vehicle on which it could travel from the doctor's intimate circle to the wider audience of Mirabeau's admirers. As of that moment the only publications on the topic of physiocracy consisted of two articles, "Fermiers" and "Grains," written by Quesnay for Diderot's *Encyclopédie*. The first of these articles outlined Quesnay's views on the importance of modernization in agriculture; it was only the second article that introduced the concept of the net product. But by the time that Quesnay had converted Mirabeau, the master's system was worked out in his mind, at least in its fundamentals. In December of 1758 he printed copies of the *tableau économique* on the king's personal printing press. Legend has it that Quesnay presented the idea of the *tableau économique* to Louis XV as a problem in typesetting and successfully persuaded the monarch to set the type himself, thus assuring that Louis would at least have read the *tableau* and studied its composition in the detail required for setting up its complicated combinations of brackets and lines. If the legend is true, Quesnay's efforts were successful only in obtaining proofs of a *tableau* struck by the hand of the king of France. The exercise did not influence the sovereign's mind sufficiently for him to institute political or economic reforms of a physiocratic bent. Quesnay's *tableau économique* was never published in its original form, owing to the doctor's reticence to publish anything himself that might compromise his position at court. The proofs were lost for over a century until Stephan Bauer discovered in 1890 a copy of what has come to be called the "first edition".[11] Copies of a second edition are also in existence.[12] And a third edition, recently rediscovered by Marguerite Kuczynski in 1965 in the Eleutherian Mills Historical Library, has just been published in English.[13]

Although subsequent events in the eighteenth century obscured the *tableau économique* from popular reputation, its complicated circuitry was quite impressive to the followers of Quesnay. Mirabeau, who lacked the patience necessary to follow through its patterns without painful concentration, was nevertheless so convinced by the ideas behind Quesnay's *tableau* that he included a modified version of it with commentaries in one of the later "books" of his *L'Ami des hommes*.

More important, in 1760 Mirabeau published his *Théorie de l'impôt* under Quesnay's careful guidance. In this work Mirabeau informed the king that his subjects were a gang of ragamuffins and, further, that the king was to blame for their pitiable condition. Mirabeau's solution was to impose the single tax on agriculture's net product and to abolish all other forms of taxation. Louis's reaction, however, was not to revise the tax system but, rather, to imprison the Friend of Mankind. Mirabeau's imprisonment was soon commuted to house arrest, but the effect on the physiocratic movement was significant. From late 1760 until early 1763, when a pamphlet entitled *Réflexions sur l'écrit intitulé: Richesse de l'Etat* was published by a young unknown named Du Pont, Quesnay thought it best to speak of his theory only in private. The pamphlet by Du Pont, which expressed ideas strikingly similar to those of Quesnay himself, was permitted to circulate without censorship or action against its author. Quesnay saw the pamphlet's unobstructed circulation as a sign that physiocratic ideas could once again be publicly aired with impunity. And both Quesnay and Mirabeau saw the work's author as a potential convert to physiocracy.

However, before Du Pont's admission to the physiocratic circle in 1763, Quesnay and Mirabeau had already attracted another disciple to the school, Louis-Paul Abeille, whose jealousy of the new disciple Du Pont was partly responsible for Abeille's rejection of the physiocratic school and its doctrine in 1768.

The other major disciples attracted to the school following Du Pont's conversion in 1763 included Mercier de la Rivière, a government official and onetime intendant of the island of Martinique. Following his conversion Mercier published in 1767 the theoretical work *L'Ordre essentiel et naturel des sociétés politiques*. This work refined much of Quesnay's theory but did not differ from it in its fundamentals. But because of its highly theoretical nature, the book was found lacking in popular appeal. Du Pont's *De l'origine et des progrès d'une science nouvelle* was primarily a popularized version of Mercier's difficult treatise.

Another important disciple was the Abbé Nicolas Baudeau, who was converted to physiocracy by Du Pont in 1765. Baudeau was editor of a journal entitled *Ephémérides du Citoyen*. Following his conversion, his journal was at the disposition of Quesnay's group and was edited for five years by Du Pont until its suppression in 1772. When Turgot came to power as finance minister in 1774, Baudeau revived the *Ephémérides* until it was proscribed once again with the fall of Turgot. Finally, in the 1780s Baudeau again revived the publication, but his physical and mental health, already in rapid decline, soon brought about its permanent cessation through his death.

Other faithful followers of the school occasionally wrote tracts and articles, but these persons are too numerous and their individual contributions generally too insignificant in their differences from the central writings of Quesnay to merit consideration here. It is notable, however, that some of these included crowned heads of Europe, such as Leopold II, grand duke of Tuscany and later to become emperor of Austria, also the margrave of Baden, and King Gustavus of Sweden. The margrave of Baden was the only one of these royal physiocrats to implement actual agricultural reforms in a consistent plan. Between 1770 and 1792 the margrave operated three estates, including their villages, on physiocratic principles. Tax rates were decided locally, raised locally, and collected from the net revenues of agriculture. These royal physiocrats were more important for their encouragement of writers such as Du Pont than for their own contributions to the literature.

Anne Robert Jacques Turgot himself was not a physiocrat. Some say he was. He didn't consider himself a member of *any* school. He disdained organized disciplines, which, he felt, restrained the mind from free thought. He also disagreed with many of the physiocratic tenets, including the one that the source of all value is in the very act of production of agricultural goods and raw materials alone. He also saw room for taxes on commerce and industry, although he was in strong favor of tax reform in general. Turgot held firmly to the laissez-faire doctrine of Gournay and was aware of the causes behind the creation of value through the process of exchange itself. His foremost economic treatise, *Réflexions sur la formation et la distribution des richesses*, agrees with the physiocrats over the desirability of improving agriculture, of simplifying the national tax structure (though not so far as to agree with the single tax on the net product), and of free domestic and international trade in the absence of monopolies and government restraints. Major contributions by Turgot to the aims of the school occurred first during his period as intendant of Limoges, when he successfully implemented fiscal and commercial reforms, and, second, during his brief tenure as minister of finance, when he similarly freed trade in grains and attempted to simplify the national tax structure. Both his offices brought to the physiocrats their only real hopes of reforms sympathetic to their principles.

By the time of Turgot's accession to the Finance Ministry, all the important works of physiocracy had been written. Quesnay had long since turned his interests away from active consideration of economic science toward the realm of pure mathematics and was less than a year away from his death. Mirabeau was in the midst of family problems that have since supplied the grist of many historical and biographical studies. Louis XV had been succeeded by the much less experienced (and some say less intelligent) Louis XVI, who would be even less capable than his predecessor of controlling the reactionary nobility and the impatient liberals. Du Pont himself was in Poland, establishing a national education system, and he would shortly be called to assist Turgot in the Finance Ministry. The other physiocrats were similarly dispersed. The momentum of their doctrine and their writings was on the wane. And when Turgot finally fell from power in May of

1776, their death knell as a unified force was sounded. The Tuesday evening meetings held at Mirabeau's house in Paris would no longer serve as a focus for intellectual attention and popular curiosity. Before long the activities of the Revolution and the ideas of Adam Smith would both obscure the theory of physiocracy and, ironically, realize many of its goals.

3. Influence of the Physiocratic School

The influence of the physiocratic school was two-fold: it influenced economic policy down through the Napoleonic period in France, and it influenced the subsequent development of economic thought. Each of these two channels of influence is considered here in turn.

a. Influence on Economic Policy. Although physiocratic theory was never accepted as a basis for working policy by any major government, the physiocratic school did generate from within its own membership a tremendous outpouring of writings on economic policy. These writings in turn stimulated non-physiocratic and antiphysiocratic writers to publish their alternative views. Although few attempts at reform in French economic policy were successful prior to 1789, the Revolutionary assemblies had a large selection of writings from which to choose their programs, as a result of the stimulus of physiocratic thought during the thirty years preceding the Revolution. Consequently, many of the physiocratic and non-physiocratic studies of public administration, transportation, agriculture, and even financial structures were adopted or modified for adoption by the first French Republic.[14]

b. Influence on Economic Thought. Although Adam Smith may have been influenced to some extent by his meetings with the physiocrats in Paris, it is generally agreed now that Smith had already conceived his views of the economic mechanism before his stay in France.[15] Nevertheless, as Spengler points out, physiocratic theory was influential in shaping the arguments in the more famous debates over economic theory in early nineteenth-century England, including those concerned with underconsumption and overpopulation.[16] From that time till the present, as economists have continually revised their interest in macroeconomic analysis, they have continued to draw inspiration from this early and often neglected view of the economy.

Notes to Chapter I

1. The material for this social and intellectual background was drawn from many secondary sources that are listed in the bibliography. Volumes 6, 7, and 8 of the *New Cambridge Modern History* were particularly useful in tying together the diverse elements of this period into one thread with which to connect the other sources.

2. For an excellent account of the relationship of the Tax Farmers to the administration of government finances in later eighteenth-century France see J. F. Bosher, *French Finances, 1770–1795: From Business to Bureaucracy* (New York: Cambridge University Press, 1970). See particularly chap. 5, "Private Enterprise in Public Finance," pp. 92–111.

3. David Ogg, *Europe in the Seventeenth Century*, 8th ed. (New York: Collier, 1962), p. 287.

4. Henri Sée, *Economic and Social Conditions in France during the Eighteenth Century* (New York: Crofts, 1927). See particularly chaps. 1 and 2. The data included in the next two pages come largely from this source.

5. Differing positions on this historical point are presented in the provocative anthology, Ralph W. Greenlaw, ed., *The Economic Origin of the French Revolution: Poverty or Prosperity?* (Boston: Heath, 1958).

6. Henri Sée, *Economic and Social Conditions in France during the Eighteenth Century*, cited in ibid., pp. 51–52.

7. Georges Weulersse, *Le Mouvement physiocratique en France de 1756 à 1770* (Paris: Félix Faulcon, 1910).

8. Ronald L. Meek, *The Economics of Physiocracy: Essays and Translations* (Cambridge, Mass.: Harvard University Press, 1963).

9. Joseph J. Spengler, "Physiocratic Thought," *International Encyclopedia of the Social Sciences* 4: 443–46.

10. V. Foley has recently provided information explaining Quesnay's longstanding interest in agriculture and taxes, as well as his intense political awareness, developed during political maneuvering earlier in his career between the physician and surgeon guilds. See V. Foley, "An Origin of the Tableau Economique," *History of Political Economy* 5, no. 1 (Spring 1973): 121–50.

11. Henry Higgs, *The Physiocrats* (New York: Macmillan, 1897), p. 42.

12. Meek, *The Economics of Physiocracy*, p. 118.

13. Marguerite Kuczynski and Ronald L. Meek, eds., *Quesnay's Tableau Économique* (London: Macmillan for the Royal Economic Society and the American Economic Association, 1971). This third edition had been discovered by Schelle in 1905 but had since been lost.

14. Du Pont's own work on committees of the Revolutionary government, discussed later in the text, bears out this point in his case.

15. See, for instance, Ronald L. Meek, "Smith, Turgot, and the 'Four Stages' Theory," *History of Political Economy* 3, no. 1 (1971): 9–27; also Eduard Heimann, *History of Economic Doctrines: An Introduction to Economic Theory* (New York: Oxford University Press, 1964), pp. 78–80.

16. Spengler, "Physiocratic Thought," p. 445.

II.

Economic Biography of Du Pont de Nemours

In 1961 the Longwood Library, founded in 1955 by descendants of Pierre Samuel Du Pont de Nemours, was merged into the Eleutherian Mills-Hagley Foundation to become the Eleutherian Mills Historical Library, a new major depository of archives and research center in economic history and the history of economic thought. Documents and publications relating to Du Pont de Nemours constitute an important portion of the holdings of the library. Since 1961 these valuable holdings have been sorted and systematically organized for scholarly use.

It would be folly to overlook, and thoughtless to ignore, the first significant utilization of Du Pont de Nemours's papers, by the American historian Ambrose Saricks. Saricks used the library's archives for his biography of Du Pont, published in 1965.[1] Following his dissertation research on Du Pont's political involvement in the French Revolutionary assemblies, Saricks returned to Eleutherian Mills in the early 1960s to complete an amply documented and conscientiously written history of Du Pont. The comments in the present economic biography reflect both this author's own study of Du Pont's papers and Saricks's able reconstruction of Du Pont's life and career.

Gustave Schelle, a Frenchman, published the first study of Du Pont's economic works in 1888.[2] Although he did make use of transcripts of some of Du Pont's correspondence, sent

35

to him by the physiocrat's grandchildren, Schelle did not have the opportunity to inspect Du Pont's papers firsthand. The fact of availability further limits the usefulness of Schelle's work. It is in French and is rarely found in American libraries. The other biographies and biographical sketches of Du Pont de Nemours that have appeared (mainly in French) do not add to the information provided by Saricks's and Schelle's works.

Thus, although the present writer has himself dedicated over a year to the study of Du Pont's economic writings, he cannot help but be indebted to the useful work of Saricks's general biography and Schelle's early ground-breaking study.

Because of the breadth of Du Pont's interests and career, the present biographical sketch excludes many of the fascinating events and personages of Du Pont's life but includes those factors that the writer believes bear on Du Pont's economic thought.

A. Childhood and Youth

Du Pont was born December 14, 1739 in Paris, the elder child of a watchmaker. His father's family were Protestants who had secretly maintained their religion through the persecutions of the previous century. His grandfather is known to have owned at least two properties in Rouen, where Du Pont's father was raised. Du Pont's mother was born into a family related to the minor nobility but was raised by another family who promptly set her free when she came of age without a dowry. She took employment in her brothers' shop in Paris, close to the shop where Du Pont's father worked. They met soon thereafter.

As a young child Pierre Samuel was sent to live in the country with a peasant family who were paid to raise the child in a supposedly wholesome rural setting. Such boarding was common practice among the city-dwelling bourgeoisie. The enterprising peasant, however, attempted to maximize his profits by minimizing the costs of feeding and clothing young Pierre and, furthermore, made a habit of taking the child on his rounds of the local drinking houses. The boy was found to have stunted growth, imperiled health, and a surprisingly early proclivity for brandy, after a year in the country. His mother insisted on his return to the city.

Du Pont's father, by all descriptions, was a strong-willed and narrow-minded man who saw no usefulness in education beyond the level necessary to be a successful horologist and a good Christian. His mother was equally strong willed concerning the desirability of higher education, especially as the son soon proved to be a bright pupil.

At his mother's insistence, Du Pont's apprenticeship was delayed and his education extended. He proved to be one of the brightest students of his tutor, who operated a small school near the university section. Seeing the young boy's brilliance, his tutor had Du Pont memorize several classical works in their entirety. After young Du Pont astounded an audience of 400 with his erudition, the twelve-year-old prodigy was encouraged by his schoolmaster to broaden his knowledge of the classics in preparation for a performance before an even larger and more important audience in the heart of the university community in Paris. The performance was suddenly canceled, supposedly at the insistence of the university rector, who felt that his own position would be threatened by any such brilliant demonstration of learning on the part of a young man who had never attended the university. Both the young Du Pont and his tutor were forced to forego all fame when the performance was canceled.

Following this blow to the young scholar's dignity, Pierre's father insisted that the boy undertake his apprenticeship without further delay. But Du Pont received another respite when his mother announced that Pierre would study religion in depth prior to his confirmation in the Protestant faith. Du Pont studied religion and philosophy with the Swiss-educated chaplain to the Dutch embassy in Paris. These studies only succeeded in making Du Pont skeptical of Christian doctrine, but they did not take from him his belief in the concept of a benevolent God.

Another influence on Du Pont in his formative years was his involvement in the séances of a seer with whom his mother was acquainted. Du Pont became deeply involved in this woman's circle, but after several months his reason conquered his fascination, and he repudiated the circle's spiritual conjurings as outright quackery.

When Du Pont was seventeen his mother died, and he had no choice but to take his place at his father's workbench. But the young man insisted on stealing away whenever possible to the salon of a popular young lady, where his penchant for versification could find an audience. Eventually, Du Pont was turned out of the house by his exasperated father, who saw no good in a boy who rejected hard work and practical study for the frivolities of the idle classes.

However, during his abortive apprenticeship with his father, Du Pont had been permitted to study mechanics, trigonometry, and other mathematical skills. He became interested in engineering and contemplated a career in the Army Corps of Engineers. Such a career would provide an escape route from horology and would offer one of the few opportunities for a middle-class youth to obtain a military commission and thereby entrée into the upper classes.

Du Pont read deeply in the works of the famous military engineer Sébastien Le Prestre, Marquis de Vauban, one of whose most popular treatises was the *Dîme Royale*, published at the turn of the century. This book constituted an eloquent plea for a simplified system of taxation. Thus, Du Pont was well aware, while still in his teens, of the controversies over the cumbersome national tax system.

When Du Pont left his father, he shared his new rented quarters with a young man who soon contracted smallpox and other illnesses from which he eventually died. During his roommate's protracted illnesses Du Pont became interested in medicine and gave the attending doctor no rest during the man's frequent visits. The doctor eventually planned a program of study for him, and before long Du Pont was devoting his spare time to volunteer work in the hospitals. After several months of part-time study and practice in the medical field, Du Pont concluded that he was unfit for a career in medicine because it would have required him to watch helplessly as many of his patients died in spite of his best efforts to nurse them back to health. Instead, he turned to the task of conquering the skills of watchmaking, and thereby proving his abilities, if not his preferences, to his father by becoming apprenticed to another horologist. Through his new master he eventually became acquainted with the encyclopedist Denis Diderot and others of his circle.

In early 1763 Du Pont presented his father with an extremely complicated watch mechanism as proof of his abilities and as a token of their reconciliation. From that time onward the two Du Ponts were friends, if nothing more, and from that moment on Du Pont renounced horology for other pursuits. He did admit in later life, though, that the study of horology had been very useful to him for its insights into mechanics and even the orderly nature of the universe.

By this time the young man of twenty-three had read extensively in the classics, religion, philosophy, the military arts, and the more recent writings popular in Diderot's circle, including those of Locke, Hume, and Voltaire. By this time he was also interested in the condition of agriculture, whose problems were made known to him at a very early age, and which seemed to be tied up with the problems of government finances for which Vauban had tried to suggest a solution. Du Pont had become an amateur medical practitioner as well. Moreover, he believed in a benevolent God, and he appreciated the orderliness of the universe, which seemed to work at least as accurately as a watch mechanism. Clearly, such a young man would be easily disposed to accept the theory of physiocracy—if he were only aware of it.

B. Career in Pre-Revolutionary France

When Du Pont wrote his first pamphlet in the spring of 1763, in response to another pamphlet on the national tax system, it attracted the attention of the Marquis de Mirabeau, who in turn introduced Du Pont to François Quesnay and to physiocracy. The impact of physiocracy on Du Pont was energizing: his own ideas concerning nature, the problems of society, the weaknesses of government, and the nature of the universe were all galvanized before his very eyes into a uniformly logical system that could seemingly provide the practical solutions to all the problems of mankind.

Quesnay promptly set the young *économiste*, as the physiocrats were called in their own age, to work assisting the intendant of Soissons, who had Du Pont undertake agricultural surveys of his intendancy, a task Du Pont carried out with relish. Between 1763 and early 1765 Du Pont wrote, under the guidance of Quesnay, a careful study of the likely results of the liberalization of the grain trade upon French agriculture, utilizing the information he had collected from his study of the Soissons region. Later during this period Du Pont first made the acquaintance of Turgot, who was then the intendant of Limoges. Du Pont assisted Turgot in his own research projects, and the two of them together assisted Daniel Trudaine and his son in projects dealing with the actual liberalization of the grain trade, which the Trudaines were working on in the French government.

Early in 1765 Du Pont was selected to become editor of the *Journal de l'Agriculture*, which had come under physiocratic control. The journal floundered and failed in 1766, partly because of the discontent of subscribers who resented the monopolization of its pages by physiocratic writings, which Du Pont subsequently resumed along with his agricultural studies. In 1768 Du Pont again became editor of a physiocratic organ. The editor of the *Ephémérides du Citoyen*, Nicolas Baudeau, was converted to physiocracy and brought his journal into the camp, but he soon became unable to continue the editorship.

For several years, from 1768 to 1772, Du Pont edited this publication, which appeared three times a month. Although it contained nonphysiocratic and antiphysiocratic writings as well as contributions by members of the school, Du Pont insured that any views antithetical to physiocratic doctrine were prefaced, annotated, or appended with physiocratic commentaries provided by himself. The *Ephémérides* contained translations of some of the latest English and American writings on political economy, as well as reports on conditions in agriculture, government, and culture throughout the world. Under continual pressure of deadlines for producing copy for each issue, Du Pont published every bit of whatever writing he could cajole from his physiocratic colleagues; he also wrote many articles himself, generally under pseudonyms or coded initials; and he printed selections from travelogues, ancient works, and even popular narrative poems, whenever these could be suitably footnoted to emphasize the physiocratic lessons allegedly contained in their contents.

However, by 1772 Du Pont had become overburdened with the journal, and interest in physiocracy had begun to wane along with the publication's subscriptions. A convenient act of proscription by the government brought the publication to an end.

Du Pont continued to write private reports on political and economic events for the margrave of Baden and the king of Sweden, for which he was compensated. He soon received the consent of the French king to become a personal advisor to the margrave, who was then beginning to reorganize his lands along physiocratic lines. Du Pont also became tutor to the margrave's son, a position he would hold through correspondence lessons for many years.

In June of 1774 Du Pont was offered a permanent post as tutor to the children of the Polish royal family and chairman of the newly established national committee for education in Poland. The lure of a highly paying permanent position of such stature was too much for Du Pont to refuse. Just after he left for Poland, Louis XV died, and the new king, Louis XVI, appointed Turgot as his minister of finance. Turgot immediately requested Du Pont to be his assistant, but Du Pont was loath to resign so abruptly a post he had only just accepted from a head of state. Finally, Turgot arranged to have Louis XVI personally request of the Polish king Du Pont's release; the request was accompanied by the offer to Du Pont of ample funds in compensation for the salary he would forego by resigning his position in Poland.

Anxious for such a suitable justification to return to France and serve with Turgot, Du Pont speedily accepted the offer. With some of the funds he purchased an estate near Nemours, only a few miles from Mirabeau's own residence. The thought of having his own experimental farm on which to practice physiocratic principles while assisting Turgot in the mission of reorganizing the tottering fiscal structure of the country brought Du Pont back from central Europe in the dead of winter. His assumption of the post of inspector of manufactures was sobered by the news that he had missed by days the passing of his old master Quesnay. Nevertheless, Du Pont set out to serve his new master Turgot, actually by functioning as Turgot's personal secretary, as faithfully as he had served Quesnay.

It is difficult to discern which of the financial projects in Turgot's administration were prepared by Du Pont and which by Turgot himself, as their ideas on administrative reform of the fisc were so closely allied. Du Pont's later writings always deemphasize his own role in Turgot's administration, although it is clear from his correspondence with Turgot that there was an extremely high degree of collaboration between the two men. But the collaboration lasted only seventeen months before Turgot was dismissed from office in May of 1776, after his enemies at court, fearful of his reforms that would have weakened the position of the nobility, had convinced the king that Turgot was disloyal. Du Pont fell from power with him; he retained his title of inspector of manufactures but not the duties of the office.

For the next few years Du Pont, now thirty-six years of age, retreated to his country estate and continued to send memoranda to Turgot's sucessor and to seek payment for his supposedly continuing position. Although much of Du Pont's time was occupied with thoughts and writings on natural science, political theory, philosophy, and a translation of the Italian narrative poem *Orlando Furioso* into French, he still continued to attend sporadically the Tuesday meetings held by Mirabeau in Paris. Nevertheless, his spirit was depressed over the loss of what he saw as the greatest opportunity to obtain critically needed financial and economic reform, which the Turgot administration had promised for France.

In 1779 Du Pont was recalled by the acting finance minister, Jacques Necker. Du Pont undertook a variety of studies concerning the French economy and other countries' controls over their own economies. Following publication in 1781 of Necker's famous *compte rendu*, which was the first accounting of the sources and amounts of the government's income and the disposition of its expenses, Necker fell from office through political intrigue. He was eventually followed in his position by Charles Alexandre de Calonne, who held the office from late 1783 to early 1787. Throughout this period Du Pont not only retained his post but, partly through the efforts of Charles Gravier, Compte de Vergennes, the foreign minister and a close associate of Du Pont, was given increasingly important duties in the Finance Ministry.

Du Pont's acquaintance with Benjamin Franklin, the Moravian leader James Hutton, and French officials (including Vergennes) who were sympathetic to the American cause during the American rebellion against Britain, led Du Pont to increase his liking of America and his disliking for Britain, a disposition that he had earlier exhibited in his offer to go to America as a French agent against Britain in 1776. His further studies, during this period, of British regulation of its own trade only increased the intensity of his feelings against the British commercial and the political systems, which he saw as the source of its restrictive policies. Such feelings were often to color his economic writings.

From 1781 to 1783 Du Pont carried out research that eventually led to the creation of the free port of Bayonne in 1784. Du Pont also had the opportunity to draw deeply during this period on his experience in assisting Turgot, who had actually balanced the national budget for a time. This experience was useful in his increasing responsibilities in advising the government concerning its critical financial condition. However, it cannot be said that Du Pont played a significant role in guiding fiscal policy during these years.

From 1783 to 1789 Du Pont served as chargé d'affaires for the government of Baden in Paris. In late 1783 Du Pont was raised to the nobility by the king. Noble rank would enhance Du Pont's ability to function effectively in an administration composed almost exclusively of nobles. Despite the death of his first wife in 1784 and the consequent increased parental responsibility he now assumed for his two teenaged sons, Eleuthère Irenée and Victor, Du Pont continued to involve himself deeply in public administration. He worked on projects to improve the quality of agricultural products, to free internal commerce, and to encourage freer international trade. During this time he prepared several policy papers as a member of the government's newly established agricultural committee, whose function was to advise officially on all government policies affecting agriculture.

His position in Calonne's administration rose further when he became a member of a committee headed by the Marquis de Lafayette to liberalize French-American trade. Moreover, Du Pont is thought to be the primary composer of the French position in the Anglo-French Commercial Treaty concluded in 1786. The ministers of state and finance, Vergennes and Calonne, were the officials responsible for the Treaty. Definite manuscript documentation is scanty on the question of the degree to which Du Pont's own ideas influenced the final form of the Treaty.[3] Between the implementation of the Treaty in 1787 and the outbreak of the Revolution in 1789 Du Pont devoted much attention to convincing public opinion, especially among the merchant class, of the ultimate benefits of the Treaty.

C. Du Pont and the French Revolution

In 1787 Calonne convinced the king that the government's financial crisis was so critical that new fiscal programs of a radical nature had to be introduced. Such programs could never overcome the opposition of the vested noble interests at Court. Consequently, Calonne persuaded the king to convene the Assembly of Notables, a vestigial legislative body that had not met for 160 years. Du Pont was active in the preparation of Calonne's reports and programs for presentation to this body; Calonne's suggested reforms bore a remarkable similarity to the reforms attemtped by Necker and Turgot. Again, it is sometimes difficult to determine which parts of the programs were written by Du Pont and whether Du Pont had significant influence over the selection of their contents. Nevertheless, several of the proposals for tax reform definitely were written by Du Pont and reflect his own attitudes on the questions. The Assembly of Notables' opposition to Calonne led to his downfall in early 1787, and his eventual successor, Lomenie de Brienne, acted to restrict Du Pont's activities. Brienne had sought to dismiss Du Pont outright, but Du Pont's popularity and obvious capacity for mental work rendered him indispensable to a generally crumbling administration. Du Pont continued to serve as secretary to the Assembly, but his position as inspector of manufactures was divided into five new bureaus, and Du Pont was made inspector general of only one of them. When Necker was recalled to replace Brienne in 1788, Du Pont became involved in preparations for the convocation of the Estates-General.

Du Pont decided that he could be more effective in bringing about reform as a member of the Estates-General itself rather than as merely a functionary of the administration proposing to that body. Consequently, he ran for office as a delegate from Nemours, the jurisdiction in which his property was located, as a member of the Third Estate, which was composed mainly of commoners. His role in this body, which soon transformed itself into the National Assembly, has been detailed by Ambrose Saricks.[4] Du Pont's economic writings in connection with his activities in this body are discussed in the critique of his writings found in the present work. As a reformist, Du Pont's ground moved from left to right as the Revolution became increasingly radicalized. At one point Du Pont found himself personally defending the king from a mob by gathering together a band of loyal guards and fencing with the protagonists in the palace grounds. In 1791 Du Pont established his own press and newspaper, *L'Historien*, to publish his views. Finally, in early 1793 he was forced to flee Paris for his own safety. His son Irenée carried on the work of the Du Pont press. Until his own arrest in 1794, the father worked on his never-completed autobiography and practiced medicine in the countryside. When imprisoned in La Force he organized his fellow political prisoners for a final defense of their cells and lives against an expected massacre by the prison guards. Such dramatics were not uncommon occurrences during the Revolution. Although his close friend, the Marquis de Lafayette, was merely imprisoned, others of Du Pont's friends and acquaintances including Antoine Laurent Lavoisier, under whom Du Pont had sent his son Irenée to study chemistry, were executed, or in the cases of Turgot, Mirabeau, and Vergennes, had already succumbed from natural causes before the Revolution.

By September 1794 Du Pont was free again and returned to his country estate where he remained until 1795. From this period until the last decade of his life political thought replaced economic thought as his primary intellectual interest. Although much of his correspondence in his later years was with political leaders such as Thomas Jefferson, James Madison, James Monroe, Francis Walker, and Charles Maurice de Talleyrand-Périgord, the correspondence emphasized personal matters, the art of politics, or theoretical political and social frameworks for physiocratic systems rather than economic theory itself.

With the establishment of a constitution in 1795 Du Pont became a member of the nearly powerless Council of Elders (*Conseil d'Anciens*), where he busied himself with committee reports and speeches. He used his seat in this body as well as his own newspaper as vehicles for the expression of his own views concerning the proper operation of the government, views that did not agree with the actions of the Directory. In the coup d' état of 18 Fructidor (1797) Du Pont was again arrested, and his printing press was wrecked. Several persons obtained Du Pont's release from prison the following day.

D. First Visit to America

After this incident Du Pont turned his efforts away from reform of French government and society and began to draw up plans for the establishment of an agricultural community he proposed for the wilderness of Kentucky. The community would be composed of Frenchmen and other Europeans and would, of course, practice physiocracy. He raised subscriptions for the company and went to America with his sons and their families in 1799. Victor had resided in America before as a consular representative for the pre-Revolutionary French government, and he was familiar with the customs and language. Irenée's knowledge of the practical arts would be useful for selecting lands and erecting necessary structures in the settlement. The entire Du Pont family had completed the crossing by early 1800. Eventually, it was found that the proposed land settlement idea was financially infeasible partly because land prices were much higher than had been advertised in the popular press. Consequently, the three Du Pont men sought to repay their investors' confidence and capital by establishing an import-export firm in New York City. Unfortunately, the new firm contracted to provision the French expedition sent to quell the insurrection of the Haitians on Santo Domingo. Bonaparte was infuriated by the failure of the expedition to put down the revolt, and his government refused to honor the claims of the fledgling Du Pont firm. For this and other reasons, Du Pont, now past sixty, decided to return to France in 1802. He hoped to calm his own creditors' fears concerning the company's solvency and to obtain payment from Napoleon through direct petition or through the influence of his acquaintance Talleyrand. Homesickness for his native country was also part of his decision to return. Du Pont spoke little English, found the sound of the language harsh to his ears, and thought the Americans' crudeness to be an unfortunate heritage of their British past. He did not return to America until 1815. During his absence his son Irenée closed the import-export firm in New York and established a gunpowder factory on the banks of the Brandywine River in Delaware.

E. Return to France

During his final thirteen years in France Du Pont pursued several miscellaneous activities, few of which relate to his economic writings. Upon his return to France Du Pont acted at the request of Jefferson in an unofficial capacity to smooth the negotiations between France and the United States for Louisiana and (it was mistakenly thought at the time) the Floridas. Following the successful conclusion of the Louisiana Purchase Du Pont devoted several years to seeking financial restitution from the new French regime for the debts owed the Du Pont company over the Santo Domingo affair. Other duties, none of them notable from the viewpoint of the history of economic thought, occupied his time during these years. Early in 1803 Du Pont became a director of the Banque Territoriale, a land bank that accepted mortgages in return for loans to owners of the mortgaged properties. Partly because the paper notes it issued were declared illegal along with all other circulating notes issued by private banks, the Banque Territoriale failed shortly after Du Pont's appointment. He was active in the negotiations surrounding its final dissolution, but the surviving documents offer no insights into his economic thought.

Du Pont was elected one of fifteen members of the Paris Chamber of Commerce following its reestablishment by Napoleon in 1803. He served as its secretary until 1807 when he was elected its president, an office he held until 1810. Much of his energy in connection with these offices was expended in attempting to convince Napoleon of the advantages to be gained by substituting free trade for his policy of blockade. As in so many of these activities of his final years, Du Pont was not successful in persuading the Emperor that laissez-faire would aid in his efforts to conquer Europe.

It was not until 1807 that Du Pont once again took up arms in the field of economic thought. In that year he wrote a review of Malthus's *Treatise on Population (Traité de la population)*. In the following years he edited the writings of Turgot, a task that was not completed until 1811. In the remaining years between the publication of his *Oeuvres de Turgot* and the exile of Napoleon to Elba in 1814, Du Pont expanded his work on *Education in the United States*, which he had originally written in response to a request from Jefferson for a memorandum on the subject. He continued to participate in the proceedings of the National Institute and was active in several other cultural and philosphic organizations.

In April 1814, as Napoleon was about to resign, Talleyrand appointed Du Pont to the administrative post of secretary-general of the provisional government that the first minister was organizing in Paris as a prelude to the return of a government loyal to Louis XVIII. Two weeks later a formal government owing allegiance to the restored Bourbons was established, and the septuagenarian *économiste* returned to private life for the last time.

F. Retirement in America

Already disillusioned with his inability to participate actively in government and in society in restoration France, Du Pont made arrangements for his ultimate return to the United States. These plans were hastily moved forward when Napoleon returned from Elba. Du Pont left Paris the same day Bonaparte entered the city, March 20, 1815. He arrived in Delaware in May.

Du Pont's most significant economic activities during his last 28 months in America consisted of his preparation of a book containing a critique of Malthus's population theory and an extended version of a letter he had written to Jean-Baptiste

Say during Du Pont's crossing to America. Both these commentaries were aimed at convincing the other two economists of the lasting usefulness of physiocratic theory for understanding the economic and social phenomena these men were investigating.

Typical of the frustrations of Du Pont's last years was his trip to Monticello to meet the former president with whom he had corresponded for so long. Jefferson, unaware of Du Pont's approaching visit, had left on an inspection tour of his lands only days before Du Pont's arrival. Du Pont waited several days at Monticello but was forced by the threat of winter weather to return to Wilmington without ever actually meeting Jefferson.

It is fitting that the last event of Du Pont's life typifies his habitual readiness to serve others in need. In July 1817 the Du Pont gunpowder mills, near the family residence, experienced one of their periodic disasters, this time a fire. In the middle of the night the old man clambered after the other family members and employees down to the banks of the Brandywine, where he assisted in the bucket brigade and became thoroughly soaked. He caught pneumonia, which aggravated his other geriatric ailments and led to his demise a few weeks later. He died on August 7, 1817, the year of the publication of David Ricardo's *Principles of Political Economy and Taxation* and the year before the birth of Karl Marx. He was buried in the family cemetery, near the site of the library that now contains his papers.

Although Du Pont left no disciples to carry on the physiocratic tradition, he had in a sense fulfilled the hopes of Quesnay by carrying the physiocratic standard, first raised by the master in 1757, for the greater part of a century. The outpourings of economic writings that came from Du Pont's pen are examined in the following pages.

Notes to Chapter II

1. Ambrose Saricks, *Pierre Samuel Du Pont de Nemours* (Lawrence, Kan.: University of Kansas Press, 1965).

2. Gustave Schelle, *Du Pont de Nemours et l'école physiocratique* (Paris: Guillaumin, 1888).

3. For a detailed study of this question see Marie Martenis Donaghay, "The Role of Physiocratic Thought in the Anglo-French Commercial Treaty of 1786" (Master's thesis, University of Virginia, 1967).

4. Saricks, *Pierre Samuel Du Pont de Nemours*. See also Saricks's microfilmed dissertation on Du Pont's political involvement in the French Revolutionary assemblies, cited in the bibliography at the end of this work.

III

The Early Economic Writings of Du Pont, 1761–64

A chronological, rather than topical, organization of a man's economic writings lends itself to a study of general changes, or lack of such changes, in a man's approach to ideas and events, and, in the present case, imposes a discipline on the otherwise bewildering array of topics handled by Du Pont, while not entirely sacrificing the topical perspective; for a subject, once in the mind or in the public eye, tends to receive concentrated attention within a compact span of time. For these reasons it is well to begin with Du Pont's first economic writings in 1763 and continue chronologically to his final writings in 1817. Later, these chronological studies will be drawn together into a topical summary and conclusion.

A. Du Pont's First Economic Tract

With the dubious exception of a bit of economic advice in the form of verses presented by Du Pont to a nonplussed Finance Minister Étienne François de Choiseul in 1761,[1] the earliest example of his economic thought is his first published work, *Réflexions sur l'écrit intitulé: Richesse de l'Etat,*[2] which was written, as Du Pont noted in his autobiography,[3] and according to secondary sources,[4] as far as can be determined, in the absence of any contact with the physiocratic school. Still, this pamphlet, composed in response to Roussel de la Tour's *La Richesse de l'Etat*,[5] exhibits in its reasoning and argument some similarity to physiocratic doctrine. Roussel had argued in his work for replacement of the complicated system of French taxes by a single progressive capitation tax to be augmented only by continued export and import duties. Du Pont countered, in his maiden pamphlet, that if anyone should pay a single tax, it should be the class of landowners. It is important at this point to investigate Du Pont's initial publication in more detail because it is the only example, at least in *prose*, of his economic thought before, according to his own memoirs, he came under the influence of Quesnay and Mirabeau.

Roussel's *Richesse de l'Etat* was an appealing revision of tax-reform proposals first suggested by Vauban in 1707.[6] Roussel estimated that two million of the French population of approximately sixteen million were persons with taxable wealth. His suggestion was simple in theory: rank the two million according to wealth, dividing them into twenty groups of one hundred thousand. Each person in the first, or poorest, bracket would pay a fixed low amount of revenue to the government; similarly, each person in the twentieth, or wealthiest, bracket would pay the highest amount. A schedule of progressive assessments applied to the twenty groups.[7] This capitation tax would replace all but import and export duties as the source of government revenues.

Du Pont's first objection to Roussel's scheme was to note that the total amount of government revenue to be attained through the proposed tax exceeded the actual net product of the kingdom by 25 percent.[8] He did not think that an increased level of income would result in increased expenditures by the government to the benefit of the *"bien public,"* which he announced in the first sentence of his pamphlet to be his chief concern. The attitudes expressed in his first work indicate that less than enough investment was being directed into agriculture. In all likelihood, he feared that increased taxation would lead to further impoverishment of agriculture. But none of this is spelled out in support of his criticism of

Roussel's sizable projected revenue. Perhaps the statement was considered self-evident to Du Pont's contemporaries.[9]

Du Pont's foregoing objection was not so much to the internal logic of Roussel's scheme as to the fact that Roussel offered it as a means for the government to realize more revenue than it did at the time: Du Pont questioned the assumption made by Roussel that there existed in the economy an extra 25 percent potential revenue that might be diverted to government use without further harm to the already impoverishing system.

For the lower classes were indeed impoverished by the system, as described in the introductory section of this study. Roussel's system would have the second, or next to the bottom, group of taxable persons paying approximately 30 percent more per capita than the first, or bottom, group. The third group, in turn, would pay in excess of 100 percent more than the second group. Du Pont appealed to the readers' common-sense knowledge of their country in noting that the second and third groups of poor persons were virtually as poor as the bottom group, and that Roussel's tax schedule would consequently place a disproportionate burden on many of the poorest. Under existing conditions, it would be uncollectable as well.

Du Pont also criticized Roussel's assumption that as many as two million out of the sixteen million Frenchmen Roussel assumed to make up the population were potentially taxable. Again, Du Pont's counterproof came from an appeal to the readers' intuitive knowledge of the social structure. Du Pont argued that each taxable farmer, artisan, merchant, and city-dwelling landowner supported at least 50 and in many cases 300 or more persons (farm hands, servants, other employees, and their families), and that Roussel's 1:8 proportion seemed to be excessively optimistic.

But Du Pont's observations go deeper than that. He observed that if Roussel's system were to be effected, the tax burden on the typical agricultural worker would indeed be less than under the present system.[10] Thus, to Du Pont's mind, if

Roussel's system could be instituted, it would theoretically shift the burden of taxation away from the lowest class of agricultural workers. However, since taxes were in fact paid on behalf of these workers by their employers, the city-dwelling landowners, the system, in Du Pont's view, would not achieve such a shift in the tax burden unless institutional changes were made to channel that income, representing exploitation of agricultural labor, away from the proprietors to be distributed to the workers, so that they might pay their taxes themselves from their income and keep the difference for themselves.

However, Du Pont's interest was not in pursuing these points; his thoughts lay in a different direction. He stated that a great number of proprietors in fact kept their agricultural workers at subsistence levels of income. Consequently, he saw no reason, given existing social structures, why proprietors under Roussel's system would be likely to turn over voluntarily the fruits of their exploitation of the workers. At best they would turn over just enough to cover the taxes imposed on the workers. Du Pont saw the alternative of the landlord's returning profits to the workers so that the workers could pay the taxes instead of the more direct route of having the landlord pay the taxes himself as only creating additional difficulties for collection agencies. Du Pont did not acknowledge realization of the fact that since the landlord would be taxed at a higher rate than his poorer workers, his income after taxes would indeed be higher through Roussel's system, and he would indeed have an incentive to return to the workers what in fact would be a lesser amount than that which he would have to pay otherwise, under a progressive tax system.

The direction of Du Pont's thoughts led him to assert without evidence, other than the readers' knowledge of their society, that the "intermediate classes" carry too light a tax burden. He thereafter equates "intermediate classes" with landowners, and he adds a cryptic assertion that he knows what it is that could increase agricultural revenues, over and above improved management.[11] These statements seem almost out of place in what is otherwise a well-reasoned critique of Roussel's reform proposal. On the one hand, the suggestion by Du Pont of a means of improving agricultural output hardly helps discredit Roussel's plan. On the other hand, if Du Pont had in mind a plan for the improvement of agricultural production, and felt moved to mention it in this publication, why did he not spell it out? Answers to these questions are but speculation: perhaps he had heard of the physiocratic school and wanted to attract its attention; just as likely (and more in character) he might have thought that his critique would be widely read and would lead to a popular demand for elaboration in print of his ideas for the improvement of agriculture.

Finally, Du Pont criticized Roussel's proposed maintenance of import and export duties, without, however, revealing the sources of his prejudice in favor of free international trade.

B. Du Pont's "Pre-Mirabeau" Economic Thought

Thus, Du Pont's first publication, and his only one before he came into contact with the physiocrat Mirabeau, reveals a firm grasp of the mechanics of the agricultural sector of the economy, a familiarity with figures on taxation, and a happy abandon characteristic of the age in combining appeals to common-sense perceptions of social and economic conditions with scattered facts and deductions, sufficient to present a plausible argument for refutation of Roussel's work, as it turned out, to the great satisfaction of Quesnay and Mirabeau. It reveals a predilection toward the landowner as the critical link in economic transactions as well as a lack of corresponding interest in commercial classes and their functions. It also reveals a lack of any attempt to go beyond what was sufficient to discredit Roussel, such as investigating the proper division of agricultural returns among laborers, landowners, and government; his only steps beyond strict refutation involve his own statement that he possessed a solution to the ills of agricultural production, and by extension, of government finance. Thus, without demonstrating a knowledge of the doctrinal justifications of the physiocrats for their causes, Du Pont nevertheless argued in favor of the principles of a single tax on landowners (hence, on the source of their wealth, i.e., rent) and of unrestricted foreign trade, basic to physiocratic doctrine. It is as if a young man, in 1853, five years after the appearance of the *Communist Manifesto,* were to argue the inevitability of revolt of the urban masses in a capitalist society, the releasing of the means of production, and the withering away of the state, all without reference to, and in apparent ignorance of, the writings of Marx and Engels.

Again, the question of the prior influence of Quesnay's ideas returns to haunt the inquiry. The question of whether Du Pont's ideas developed from his general knowledge of ancient and eighteenth-century classics as well as from his observations of conditions in the countryside, or, at the other extreme of possibilities, came from some prior awareness of physiocratic doctrine, or, between the two extremes, came from ideas circulating at the time, the same ideas that, combining with Quesnay's own experiences and background, led him to hit upon the doctrine of physiocracy, is one that Du Pont's own unfinished autobiography can enlighten, if not completely answer.

Du Pont's autobiography, completed, unfortunately, only to his twenty-fifth year, or 1764, provides information about his early education, the books he read, and his acquisition of ideas from others, from books, and from reflection. Specifically, in 1763, when Du Pont published his *Réflexions,* he had traveled in the countryside, studied medicine (as had Quesnay), and had become personally acquainted with Diderot (publisher of the *Encyclopédie*), whose nimble mind and wit he greatly admired. But, according to Du Pont, he thought of the tenets of physiocracy all by himself, sitting at a table and cradling his head in his arms on the table top. As this may be a bit hard to imagine, his own description of what happened appears in the footnote below.[12]

C. His "Post-Mirabeau-Pre-Quesnay" Economic Thought

In reference to his first publication Du Pont stated in his autobiography that he thought of the ideas which comprise the tenets of physiocracy quite independently of others.[13] He revealed the progression of his acquaintance with political and economic ideas clearly during the period of his first writings and discovery of the physiocrats (or, depending on the point of view, their discovery of him). In March or April of 1763, after publication of his *Réflexions,* he was sent for by the intendant of Soissons to carry out agricultural studies of the province for the intendant. It so happened that the official was closely connected with Mirabeau, who sent along copies of his *L'Ami des hommes* and *Théorie de l'impôt* for Du Pont to read, which the young enthusiast did, and about which he subsequently corresponded with Mirabeau.[14] It was during this period, but before Du Pont's introduction to Quesnay or any of Quesnay's writings (including those articles published in the *Encyclopédie* as early as 1757, if Du Pont's autobiography is accurate), that Du Pont undertook his second published work, *Réponse demandée par Monsieur le Marquis de*** à celle qu'il a faite aux Réflexions sur l'écrit intitulé: Richesse de l'Etat.*[15] This pamphlet is, with one notable exception, a restatement of some of the points in his first pamphlet. Du Pont did elaborate on a point he had made, but had not explained, in the earlier work, namely his opposition to export and import duties, which Roussel had seen fit to retain in his reform proposals for the tax system.

D. Du Pont's Early Views on Trade

It is useful to point out for subsequent comparison with his first book-length work, *De l'exportation et de l'importation des grains,* to be written in 1764 after his exposure to Quesnay, the exact reasons for the desirability of free trade, as expressed by Du Pont in his second pamphlet. According to Du Pont, each state should trade in order to obtain a lower price on products from other countries than it could obtain on the home market and to sell in foreign countries those domestically produced goods that are lower in price than their foreign equivalents.[16] No excursion was made into the causes of differences in prices of identical products among countries, although in Du Pont's subsequent book he was to give a justification of international commerce founded on the twin benefits of expansion of agricultural production and stability of grain prices that would result from free trade.

Rather than justifying at greater length his free-trade position, he chose to attack the mercantilist, or "Colbertiste," position by emphasizing at length three points: (1) the interests of the nation and its merchants are not necessarily identical; (2) a nation must import as well as export to continue trading; and (3) money is not wealth but only a proxy for wealth.[17] His elaboration of these points hardly differed from twentieth-century classroom explanations. What is interesting, however, is that Du Pont expressed them in 1763, before Adam Smith's major works and before the rise of the free-trade movement. A possible source of Du Pont's views on trade was Richard Cantillon's *Essai sur la nature du commerce en général*, published posthumously by Mirabeau in 1755. There is no evidence that Du Pont read Cantillon's book, which breaks with the mercantilist views on trade by calling for free importation of goods. Nor is there any evidence that Du Pont had studied Hume's *Political Discourses*, first published in 1752. Nevertheless, it is quite possible that Du Pont absorbed the idea of free trade from Mirabeau's *L'Ami des hommes*, which expounded on Cantillon's views, or even absorbed it from the circles he frequented before his initial contact with Mirabeau in 1763.

The *Réponse* is his only extant writing during this post-Mirabeau-pre-Quesnay period, as Méliand soon found him work in the Society of Agriculture of Soissons, in its Office of Agricultural Administration. It was only then that Du Pont read the first of the works of Quesnay, namely his *Encyclopédie* articles on grain and agricultural entrepreneurs.[18]

Does the fact that an extended defense of his free-trade sentiments apears in his second pamphlet but not in his earlier one indicate that his views on trade in this work should be attributed to Mirabeau? The answer may lie in the contents of the two books by Mirabeau that were given to Du Pont by Méliand and in the two letters Du Pont reported in his autobiography that he received from Mirabeau during this period.

Although the two letters from Mirabeau to Du Pont, along with the majority of Du Pont's early correspondence, were not preserved, a pamphlet attributed to Mirabeau, *Réponse par Monsieur le Marquis de*** à l'auteur des Réflexions sur un écrit intitulé: Richesse de l'Etat,*[19] may have been the published version of one of Mirabeau's letters to Du Pont, especially since the pamphlet is addressed to Du Pont, is in letter form, and was answered by Du Pont in letter form in his *Réponse.* Mirabeau's pamphlet praised Du Pont's critique of Roussel, set up a "straw-man" defense of Roussel's arguments, using Du Pont's own calculations from his *Réflexions,* and challenged Du Pont to demonstrate the falseness of Mirabeau's supposed defense of Roussel, which Du Pont promptly did in his *Réponse.* Mirabeau did not, however, raise the question of taxes on international commerce, which Du Pont discussed at length in his *Réponse.* Moreover, there is nothing in Mirabeau's pamphlet that can be interpreted as a source for Du Pont's ideas concerning higher and stabler grain prices as presented in his *Réponse.* Mirabeau's books, however, are more enlightening.

In the 1760 (revised) edition of his *L'Ami des hommes, ou traité de la population,*[20] one of the two books given Du Pont by Méliand, Mirabeau wrote of the advantages to be gained for a country's agricultural production by removing restrictions from commerce in general, but in few instances did he touch on international commerce. The wording of his introductory discussion of the benefits of unrestricted commerce, however, is similar to that used by Du Pont in opening his discussion of international trade.[21]

As for Mirabeau's other book, *Théorie de l'impôt,* if, as Du Pont stated in his autobiography, he was as yet unexposed even to Quesnay's articles in Diderot's *Encyclopédie* (despite the many evenings Du Pont spent reading in Diderot's study between 1761 and 1763), then it is highly likely that he was influenced by what he read in this work by Mirabeau. In this two-volume work, Mirabeau's comments on international trade are scattered, diverse, and relatively incomplete as compared to the closely reasoned arguments presented by Du Pont for the abolition of taxes and restrictions on foreign trade, first (in summary form) in his *Réponse,* and the following year (after contact with Quesnay's writings) in much greater detail in his first book-length publication, *De l'exportation et de l'importation des grains.* Nowhere in either of Mirabeau's books nor in his pamphlet did he mention the desirability of higher and stabler grain prices, which were, however, important physiocratic tenets laid down by Quesnay as early as 1757.

Thus, it can be concluded that Du Pont's inspiration for discussing taxes on international trade and grain prices did not come exclusively from Mirabeau, at a time when the proponent of these ideas in France, Quesnay, was supposedly still unknown to Du Pont. It is possible that these ideas, as elaborated by Du Pont, came to him as his head was resting in his arms on a table, as described in his autobiography, but it is also possible, given Du Pont's statements concerning his earlier use of the libraries of Diderot, Méliand, and others, that he had actually read Quesnay's 1757 articles in the *Encyclopédie* and by 1763 may have come to think that the ideas were his own. However, according to Du Pont, when in June of 1763 he was given Quesnay's articles, "Grains" and "Fermiers," form the *Encyclopédie* to read, their impact upon him was like a religious experience, a grand awakening to the realization that others not only held his own views, but also held positions of influence within the government that could make a reality of their implementation.

E. His "Post-Quesnay," or Early Physiocratic, Period

Du Pont's writings of the next eleven years (i.e., from 1764 until he became Turgot's assistant) may be viewed as the gospels of an apostle seeking to spread the teaching of his master, Quesnay.[22] Any deviation at all or any unusual interpretation of Quesnay's doctrine in Du Pont's writing in this eleven-year period would therefore be of interest for revealing the extent to which (1) Du Pont's own thought processes may have altered the master's views, (2) Quesnay's views may have further altered Du Pont's ideas, and (3) events and other men's ideas influenced Du Pont's writings. The importance of such a pursuit is not only to determine the influence of men and ideas on one another during the height of the physiocratic school, but to be able to compare these influences, under the *ancien régime*, with changes in Du Pont's thought fifty years later, after the Enlightenment burst into flames of Revolution and finally burned out in the ashes of Napoleon's empire.

F. Analysis of Du Pont's First Physiocratic Treatise

It remains now to conclude the systematic investigation of Du Pont's works as a protégé of the physiocrats with an interpretation of the contents of *De l'exportation et de l'importation des grains*.[23] This, his first book, was written, according to Du Pont's autobiography, to prove his grasp of physiocratic doctrine. The work is particularly useful for the present line of inquiry because it expands on the ideas of his *Réponse*, defending both free trade and high, stable grain prices. A comparison of this first work of his "post-Quesnay" period with his second pamphlet (the only work of his "post-Mirabeau-pre-Quesnay" period), and with his first pamphlet (the only work of his "pre-Mirabeau" or virgin period) will provide a clearer view of the influences of Quesnay and Mirabeau upon Du Pont's own ideas. The discussion will be useful for shortening the investigation into Du Pont's later writings of this eleven-year period, which will be seen to be largely an effort to defend the truth of physiocracy, as revealed to him, against its detractors.

The entire work *De l'exportation et de l'importation des grains* was devoted to demonstrating the advantages to be gained for a nation from free international trade in grain and other goods. Du Pont devoted the first fifteen pages of this 127-page work to a basic description of the physiocratic conception of the source of wealth, the mechanics surrounding the *produit net*, or net product, and the means by which it may be increased. The argument was stated succinctly, although there was no attempt to go beyond the tenets laid down by Quesnay and Mirabeau, whose works were quoted copiously throughout the introductory section. As with so many of Du Pont's works, especially of this early period, Schumpeter's observation that Du Pont's "talents were those of the pianist and not of the composer" is verified.[24] The bulk of the book consists of a detailed description of the causes of fluctuations in grain prices and a demonstration of the reasons why free international trade in grain would both raise and stabilize French grain prices. A world market for grain would dampen any price fluctuations caused by localized famine or glut. Thus, prices would tend toward stability, and reinvestment of revenue could continue at a steady rate, the country's population could continue to prosper without fear of food shortages or sharp intermittent price disruptions, and, in the long run, stability of prices would lead to stable growth in agriculture with an implicit maximization of the net product. However, in contrast to his final work in 1817, Du Pont did not go so far as to discuss alternative growth paths.

In accordance with Mirabeau's ideas on population, there was in Du Pont's book no concern that demand for grain would fail to match increases in its supply. Thus, Du Pont's analysis of stable prices elaborates on the basic physiocratic position by investigating in greater detail than Quesnay had done the mechanisms behind stability of supply, but his analysis fails to consider the factors necessary for stable demand. In the case of a basic consumption good such as grain, such a failure is not damaging to the analysis, since demand for grain remains as stable as the population within the trading area. However, when the analysis is extended to products whose demand schedule, regardless of its degree of stability, is more elastic, then the physiocratic, and thus Du Pont's own, method of analyzing price changes suffers in effectiveness.

The higher level of grain prices would result from the disappearance of the existing differential between French and the higher English grain prices, with England envisioned by Du Pont as the ideal industrialized recipient of France's agricultural cornucopia. He conceded that higher domestic grain prices would touch off domestic inflation, but he calculated by means of a table and attendant verbal explication a net shift of revenue to agriculture, a net increase in proprietary rent, and consequently a net increase in the all-important net product, and ultimately a net increase in the wealth of the nation, all by means of this very trade-induced inflation. The remainder of the work demonstrated two other advantages to be gained from unrestricted trade. Free trade would enable the country to purchase cheaper foreign goods, thereby conserving the nation's net product from flowing sluggishly through inefficient domestic production and at the same time raising the standard of living in the nation through the availability of a greater variety of imported goods. He also devoted a chapter to the benefits from free trade that would, in his view, accrue to the northern part of France, "the principal granary of Europe,"[25] a plug, no doubt, for the *"fermiers"* idealized in Quesnay's article.

An answer to the question of to what extent Du Pont's arguments for higher and stabler grain prices and other benefits from free trade (e.g., higher standards of living nationally and particularly increased economies of scale in agricultural production in northern France) were his own, or to what extent they were borrowed in whole or in part from Quesnay and Mirabeau, requires further investigation. If they were in some sense his own original thoughts, to what extent did they vary from the masters' views on the topic? As concerns the benefit from free trade of more and cheaper imported goods and the modernization of agriculture, no antecedents are to be found in Mirabeau. As for higher and stabler grain prices, Mirabeau touched on the benefits of stabler prices that would result from removing restrictions from interprovincial trade, but he shed no further light on the problem. The possibility of antecedents in Quesnay, however, is a different matter. His works prior to 1763 were limited, at least in published form, to his two *Encyclopédie* articles.

Quesnay's path-breaking 1757 article, "Grains,"[26] contains a shadowy outline of the physiocratic economic system and deals at length with the benefits to be derived from international trade. It is significant, however, that Quesnay not only mentioned the effects of low grain prices on the wealth of the agricultural sector and thus on the country itself, but also included a reference to what Du Pont was to expand in 1764, namely a discussion of the mechanics of inflation (and deflation) that cause a net redistribution of real wealth to (and from) the agricultural sector. To Du Pont, unlike Ricardo some fifty years later, such a redistribution of wealth to landowners was desirable to increase the base of the nation's economy. However, it must be remembered that Du Pont's book was written under the guidance of Quesnay, who probably approved of Du Pont's redistribution mechanism and perhaps even prompted its description.

G. Summary and Conclusion

It is fair to state, then, that Du Pont's own prior views on the economy coincided remarkably with those of Quesnay, and that the source of their similarities is to be found in their common backgrounds, common events, common ideas, and even in a commonality of prior economic and social writings. But the independent development of Du Pont's views ceased when he became a member of the physiocratic school. After he came under physiocratic influence, his writings came to repeat, elaborate, and build upon the ideas of Quesnay and Mirabeau, wherever his extensions of their theory would strengthen physiocracy. An example of such an extension was the case of the redistribution of income to landlords through higher grain prices, a mechanism not spelled out by Quesnay, but one for which the master's writings had laid the groundwork, and one that reinforced the master's theory. But Du Pont failed to investigate questions not suggested by Quesnay's and Mirabeau's own writings, such as the assumption of stable demand for grain and by implication for all products made from the primary products of agriculture.

In addition to the foregoing reasons, since Du Pont himself admitted that Quesnay oversaw his writing of *De l'exportation*, it is fair to say that wherever Du Pont elaborated physiocratic theory, it was only with the intention of strengthening Quesnay's framework. Du Pont neither sought to question the theory, nor investigated questions that might possibly have displeased his master. Consequently, from his first physiocratic writings Du Pont seems to have accepted the blinkers imposed upon him by the theory. The question of to what use he put this theory as a tool of economic analysis assumes greater importance as further study of his writings reveals that he never sought to contradict, but instead sought to revise, the essential structure of physiocratic economic theory over the remaining 53 years of his career.

Du Pont was appointed editor of the *Journal de l'Agriculture, du Commerce et des Finances* in 1765 and held that post until the end of 1766. In 1768 he was appointed editor of another physiocratically controlled journal, *Ephémérides du Citoyen*, a post he held until the dissolution of the journal by the government censors and through lack of operating funds in 1772. Works of this period can be divided into those that appeared in the journals (including those that were also published separately) and those which were published only outside the journals. Of these two groups it is convenient to begin with the nonjournal publications, for they were written, in some cases, before he assumed editorial positions, and in others, during the interlude between positions, and consequently reflect a greater attention to detail than Du Pont could give his works under the pressures of operating a journal.

Notes to Chapter III

1. Typical lines of his memorandum to Choiseul are:

> Hurry citizens, filled with an ecstasy faithful
> To the best loved king among kings, let us raise an altar,
>   And may an immortal monument
> In the centuries to come consecrate our zeal.
> We shall not change through vain ornaments,
> Of our attachment this beloved proof,
> But the cry from our hearts, the vow of our land
>   Incessantly will be there in lieu of incense.

. . . .

> And you, whose work, active, tireless
> Makes for the happiness of a friendly people . . .(etc.)

[From his autobiography, *L'Enfance et la jeunesse de Du Pont de Nemours* (Paris, 1906), p. 191.]

2. Pierre Samuel Du Pont de Nemours [hereafter DPDN], *Réflexions sur l'écrit intitulé: Richesse de l'Etat* (Paris, 1763).

3. DPDN, *L'Enfance*, p. 201.

4. Cf. Gustave Schelle, *Du Pont de Nemours et l'école physiocratique* (Paris: Guillaumin, 1888), pp. 10–13; and Ambrose Saricks, *Pierre Samuel Du Pont de Nemours* (Lawrence, Kan.: University of Kansas Press, 1965), p. 21.

5. Roussel de la Tour, *La Richesse de l'Etat* (Paris, 1763).

6. Sébastien Le Prestre Marquis de Vauban, *Dîme royale* (Paris 1707).

7. "The number of persons in the Kingdom is estimated at two millions, taxable or non-taxable, who are being considered as subject to an eventual tax proportionate to their wealth. They should be divided into twenty classes of one hundred thousand each, taxed by progression, increasing from one *écu* which would represent taxation of the most indigent class, up to 730 *livres*, for the foremost class, composed of the wealthiest" (Roussel, *La Richesse*, p. 1).

8. Although Du Pont did not cite a source for his population figures, he argued that the population of France was closer to 20,000,000 than Roussel's figure of 16,000,000. Roussel posited his assumption of 16,000,000 on a population survey made by the government at the turn of the century. That estimate had been 20,000,000, which Roussel reduced by one-fifth to obtain his figure for the year 1763, following the general opinion then held that French population was declining over the period. The estimates referred to by Du Pont for government tax collections were, he implies, taken from government sources that he did not, however, cite in his pamphlet.

9. Du Pont's entire statement on this topic is contained in the following sentence: "A first objection, which perhaps should be the only one, would be to ask the author how could public revenue possibly be over one fourth higher than the sum of private revenue" (DPDN, *Réflexions*, pp. 6–7). A footnote to the sentence reads: "The total amount of private revenue, estimated by the *vingtième*, is 581,000,000 *livres.*" Roussel's figure was 740,000,000 (Roussel, *La Richesse*, p. 2).

10. "One objection which will be made to me is that, in reducing so much the number of taxpayers, I must feel that the poorest one among them will be able to pay a rather considerable tax, than that proposed by the author of the *Richesse de l'Etat*, that is what I don't know; but what I am quite sure about, is that there are a great many landowners, running their property by themselves, who often do not cover their expenses, and go into debt mortgaging the property till its entire value is eaten up. It

is true that this is the result of a small indigent cultivation; for poverty, as anything else in this world, tends to multiply itself" (DPDN, *Réflexions*, p. 21, n11).

11. "Does he [Roussel] believe that the 'intermediate classes' have been spared too much? I address myself to him, his intelligence and his humane feelings answer me that he will not dare say yes. But, one will object, the extra tax charges [*frais de perception*], the farms, the employees. . . . I know just like everybody else that there are abuses; the government contemplates correcting them, and simplifying this enormous machinery that we call *finance*" (ibid., pp. 23–24).

12. "My study habits, acquired during the time I lived alone and without a library, do not consist in asking questions or reading but in searching throughout nature and at home, to close myself in, and, sometimes, with my elbows on the table and hands over my eyes, to immerse myself into a state of deep sustained reflection on whatever it is I want to know. This form of interior and solitary meditation is not of any value for the physical sciences; but it works perfectly in metaphysics and ethics, and it is also in this way that one best comes up with mechanical inventions. When I let myself slip into reading, I read too much, I don't know when to stop. When I am given lessons, others' ideas do not enter my head in single file; they handicap one another. Mine, on the other hand, are really mine, and in the very fact that I have conceived them, I understand them clearly, I arrange them in the order which is most suitable to my intelligence, I go straight from the point that I know to the closest one of those which I don't know which leads to the objective towards which all my efforts are directed. The learning procedure that I created for myself is quick and I profit by it; it does not overload my memory, it exercises my judgment and makes me more apt to give myself a new one later. I have taken the trouble to invent several common things already known to everyone; this has almost always resulted in my expressing them more succinctly, more clearly, more simply, than those who knew them before I did.

"I found out by this method, and on my own, that land and water are the sole sources of wealth, all comprised of the crops, and divided then, shared by all men by means of the various works of society, through trading and wages; that whatever may be the constitutions, there never are citizens in the absolute sense, people whose interests are absolutely inseparable from that of the public matters, and whose revenues really contribute to its upholding, that those who gather the wealth and who own the property which produces them, that is to say the landowners; that the interest of these landowners requires the freedom, the happiness, and the immunity of all other inhabitants of the country and of all types of work.

"These bases established in my head seemed to me so important for humanity, that the obligation to spread the knowledge of them and to apply them as much as I could to the governing of nations, and particularly to the happiness of my country, seemed to me a real mission for which I was accountable to God, to humanity, to my fellow citizens. My character then acquired a dimension above vanities which had blinded my youth and above private interest. I dreamed less of fortune and glory, the pursuit of which had first determined my working, than I did of the degree of felicity and prosperity to which I could raise my country. I no longer saw in the ministers the protectors which I found necessary, but rather the instruments I needed so that the useful truths may reign, those truths whose beauty and simplicity touched equally my mind and my heart.

"Such is the belief which has guided my entire life ever since" (DPDN, *L'Enfance*, pp. 183–86).

13. Ibid., p. 201.

14. "Monsieur Méliand [i.e., the intendant] told me: 'You are a true follower of Mirabeau. . . .' The good Intendant . . . gave me on the spot the *Ami des hommes* and the *Théorie de l'impôt*. I devoured them, being unable to contain the pleasure I felt to find myself on the right road. I would get up, clap my hands and cry for joy, if anyone had seen me read they would have thought I was crazy.

"I found myself quite happy to have some ideas in common with the author. . . , and I asked him to please continue helping with my education. He had taught me that 'subsistence is the measure of population': it is the only economic truth which is his idea. He answered my letter obligingly and encouragingly, telling me of . . . another teacher . . . Monsieur Quesnay whom he did not name, and to whom he referred only by the use of the phrase 'Saint John the Baptist.' I have always somewhat resented the prophetic elocution of my teacher Mirabeau when thinking that, should he have written me like any other, I would have become Quesnay's son three months earlier" (ibid., pp. 207–8).

15. DPDN, *Réponse demandée par Monsieur le Marquis de*** à celle qu'il a faite aux Réflexions sur l'écrit intitulé: Richesse de l'État* (Paris, 1763).

16. Ibid., pp. 12–15.

17. "Let us see in what way both import and export duties can facilitate or hamper either operation; first of all, as far as selling is concerned, it is clear that duties on exportation increase the cost of the merchandise, that in order to remain competitive the owner must lower the real value, that this tax therefore, which at first sight, seems to be paid by the foreign buyer, falls twice as hard upon the domestic seller, as much through the diminution of the first hand, as through the advantage afforded other foreigners to cover all markets; and limits every day the extent of his operations. Therefore the duties tended indeed to be bad for trade, to isolate a nation, to force the consumption of the surplus in its territory; which would soon lead to a lack of extra production, and which would daily restrict agriculture, which would become hampered, once it could no longer spill its products all over the world. . . .

"The objection which I just made to import duties consists of three important errors; the first one is the confusion of the interest of the country's nationals in trading with the interest of the nation in trading; the second is the persuasion that one can always sell, and never buy; the third is the idea of wealth being tied to money which is in fact only a symbol of wealth" (ibid.).

18. "I comforted myself very well by reading, following the advice given me by the letters from Monsieur Mirabeau, the articles 'Farmers' and 'Grains' from the *Encyclopédie* into which Monsieur Quesnay had incorporated the first principles of his doctrine, and in which is to be found the true and ingenious observation of the difference which exists between the position of the first grain sellers who have but little to sell at high prices in the years of meager crops and who sell a lot at a low price in years of abundance, and the fate of the consumers who buy it every year in equal quantities and suffer a variation only in price. . . . I was learning to follow the deep thinking of this great man whom I did not yet know, and who was to serve as my father" (DPDN, *L'Enfance*, pp. 210–11).

19. Victor Riqueti Marquis de Mirabeau, *Réponse par Monsieur le Marquis de*** à l'auteur des Réflexions sur un écrit intitulé: Richesse de l'État* (Paris, 1763).

20. Victor Riqueti Marquis de Mirabeau, *L'Ami des hommes, ou traité de la population*, 2d rev. ed. (Paris, 1760).

21. Compare the following quotation by Mirabeau, "Trade is primarily nothing but the art of bartering with advantage" (ibid., 2: 100), with the corresponding quotation by Du Pont, "Trade named duly so, is the exchange that a nation or its members make of their surplus for the surplus of others. The handling of this exchange is reduced to two operations, selling and buying. Nations deal between themselves as do private concerns and he who sells the cheapest, and buys at the highest price, enjoys the most trade. The interest of a nation is therefore to be competitive in both cases" (DPDN, *Réponse*, pp. 11–12).

22. As to the strength of Du Pont's apostleship, it may be noted that he wrote in his autobiography: "Then Quesnay invited me. From then on I stuck to him as to a master, a teacher, a father: he welcomed me and treated me for eleven years as the son and the disciple he loved. His strong soul and his deep genius did not lend

themselves easily to the expression of tender feelings, but yet I had the good fortune of seeing in him many of these towards me.

"I was only a child when he opened his arms; it was he who made me a man" (DPDN, *L'Enfance*, p. 215).

23. DPDN, *De l'exportation et de l'importation des grains* (Paris, 1764).

24. Joseph A. Schumpeter, *History of Economic Analysis* (New York: Oxford University Press, 1954), p. 226.

25. DPDN, *De l'exportation*, p. 95.

26. All references, unless otherwise stated, are to Meek's English translations of Quesnay's works in Ronald L. Meek, *The Economics of Physiocracy: Essays and Translations* (Cambridge, Mass.: Harvard University Press, 1963), pp. 72–87.

IV

Economic Writings during the Period 1765–66

In the fifteen monthly issues of the *Journal de l'Agriculture* edited by Du Pont between September 1765 and November 1766 there appear nearly 500 pages either with contributions by the editor himself (mostly under assumed names) or with lengthy footnotes appended by him to articles by other writers.[1] For the most part his arguments, criticisms, and polemics constitute an outright "propagandization" of the physiocratic doctrine. His writings in the *Journal* may be divided into his views on the methodology of "economic science" (i.e., physiocracy) and his economic theory as revealed in his discussions of economic problems of his time, and the writings will be examined in that order.

A. His Methodology

Du Pont's view of scientific method, or a means of gaining knowledge of the universe, differs from the Newtonian tradition that arose in England in the late seventeenth and early eighteenth centuries.[2] The extreme example of the latter method is found in the Political Arithmeticians who held that all knowledge of universal laws and the way in which man should order his world would become evident from the precise measurement of all phenomena. Du Pont shared their conviction in the existence of natural laws, in both their physical and moral senses, but held that knowledge of these laws and man's proper activities in accordance with them would come, not from endless quantification of phenomena, but rather from public writing, that is, from the airing of all ideas of educated men. He set forth his faith in this method in the first issue he edited:

> Our work falls naturally into three parts; the first historical, the second descriptive, and the third one intended to spread an interest in and contribute to the progress of the *science of economics*, through the example and the help of good and wise Citizens who will be willing to communicate their enlightenment and to use us to publish their writings.[3]

He would seem to respect the inductive method developed during the preceding century in stating that

> it is only through the knowledge of facts that one can give a solid basis to reasoning, since the principles themselves are nothing else but the expression of the natural and physical order which directs the facts.[4]

It was this faith in the airing of ideas acquired through study of facts that, in Du Pont's view, led to a knowledge of the operation of economic phenomena, which, as he said of

> *Agriculture, Trade* and *Finance* come incessantly to sustain one another; that the same principles must guide their administration; that the same means favor all three. That is why the study of these three important branches of human knowledge, of their combination, of their relation, of their reciprocal influence, of the natural and physical order which must serve as their base, forms what is called *economic science*.[5]

But of the few contributions to the *Journal* that did present the results of the measurement of phenomena, the majority were the accounts of agriculturalists, reporting advances in farming. None of these nor any other scientific measurements were incorporated into Du Pont's arguments in the *Journal*. The agriculturalists' reports seem to have been included to fill space in a monthly publication sorely in need of voluntarily contributed articles rather than to be used as data on which to build knowledge of the economy or of economic theory. Thus, it would appear that Du Pont in his *Journal* writings did not place a serious reliance on induction in arriving at the truths of economic science. Indeed, Du Pont, in his only signed article, admitted, or rather asserted, that

> already the source of wealth is known. Already the laws of their natural distribution have been discovered and calculated. Already, a simple but surprising formula, affords the studious mind the means to determine with precision the extent of the effects happy or fearful, which all causes that can influence this distribution must have *of necessity*. Already we know what a *net product* is . . . . Already the great principles of the natural order, evidently the most advantageous to men gathered in a society and to the Sovereigns who govern them, the right to ownership in general, the security of progress in cultivation in particular, the freedom and immunity of trade, find apostles and supporters everywhere; while the small number of men who have the bad luck to let themselves be carried away by private interests, to the point of fighting stubbornly and by all sorts of means against these principles, try in vain to dissemble their lack of power, and seeing that they might quiet one of their adversaries, they would for that reason impose silence on the truth.[6]

This statement that the truths of economic science are already known, written at the end of his editorship in the November 1766 number, may be interpreted as a reflection of his bitterness at losing the post of editor to a less zealous physiocrat than himself, or as a sudden revelation that there was no longer a need to seek further for economic truths. In either case, it is clear that although Du Pont may have paid lip service at the outset of his editorship to the employment of methodology in Newtonian tradition, that is, one in which theory is continually tested against measurable phenomena, he followed, in fact, a more deductive methodology, with both sides of any dialectical argument controlled by the editor. In practice, his approach forswore actual measurement but employed hypothetical statistics, where necessary, to convince readers of the plausibility of the basic physiocratic theory. By the last issue of the journal under his editorship, he had concluded that economic theory had been "*déjà connue*," or already revealed, in its entirety by Quesnay, and that testing was therefore superfluous.

Thus, Du Pont's economic methodology consisted of the deductive method, combined with a tinge of romantic appeal to one's feelings or intuition, rather than a rational appeal to verification. In short, Du Pont was clearly a romanticist rather than a rationalist in his view of the universe.

B. His Economic Thought in the
Journal de l'Agriculture

Though Du Pont expressed conflicting views at different times on the methodology of economic science, he presented them, in individual instances, relatively clearly. In contrast, his ideas on economic theory itself must be gleaned from scattered writings ostensibly on other topics, for he presented no coherent explication of economic theory per se. Thus, Du Pont's thoughts on economic theory as revealed sporadically in the *Journal de l'Agriculture* are organized here for expository purposes into his interpretations of value, exchange, allocation, commerce (both agricultural and industrial), and government policy.

1. *Theory of Value*
Basic to any theory of wealth, whether it be mercantilist national "treasure," Smith's wealth of nations, or modern man's gross national product, is the concept of value. Throughout the history of economic analysis the way in which economic man has made choices among alternative uses of resources has involved some criterion for comparison among choices, in short, for the valuation of goods and services, either absolutely or comparatively. In any view of the economy, the summation of all economic goods, however valued, constitutes the stock of wealth of that economy. It is often said that a prime weakness of physiocracy is its lack of a

well-thought-out theory of value. Du Pont's concept of value is nowhere in his editorial comments or articles clearly set forth, for Du Pont was nowhere writing a comprehensive treatise. His theory of wealth, nevertheless, can be exemplified by a discussion of the following quotation:

> The wealth of an Empire consists in having many products of everyday use which have in a permanent way a great market value [*valeur vénale*].
> This wealth is therefore composed of the quantity of consumption goods of the territory and of the market value of these same products.
> An increase in market value, without a decrease in products, is an increase in wealth.
> An increase in products without decrease in market value, is an increase in wealth.
> An increase in the market value of some products, which only results in a decrease in overall production, destroys wealth; for, in supposing that through this increase in the price of some products, one would still obtain the same sum of numerical value, this would not mean that there would not be a decrease in the use of it, and therefore, a decrease in happiness for humanity, since there would be less opportunity to consume, less production to be consumed.[7]

If a nation's wealth thus consists of the quantity of consumable agricultural goods as measured by the market value of these goods, what of the value of nonagricultural goods? Du Pont says elsewhere in the *Journal* that such goods are exchanged for agricultural goods of earlier seasons according to the familiar operation demonstrated by the *tableau économique*. Consequently, it is likely that Du Pont meant to include by implication the entire market values of all goods, for these represent the accumulated value of agricultural production from previous years. The likely reason for his failure to point out the implicit inclusion of other goods in the wealth of the nation is to be found in his constant striving to demonstrate that such goods have no value in themselves, that they are valueless except for that value which arises from their having been traded, directly or indirectly, at some point for agricultural goods or having been refashioned from agricultural goods by workmen sustained by agricultural products. No creation of value, or addition to net wealth, is involved in such transfers or reworking of materials, according to Du Pont and the other physiocrats. The reader is left to infer such connections from Du Pont's failure to push through explicitly the operations of the net-product theory of value. In the quotation Du Pont states that either an increase in the market value of goods, the quantity of goods remaining constant, or an increase in the quantity of goods, the market value remaining constant, represents an increase in wealth. Since by market value (*valeur vénale*) Du Pont meant value as measured in stable prices and not as a result of changes in the price levels, it is clear that the total market value and the physical quantity of goods are positively related, so that an increase in their product represents, as he suggested in the final sentence of the quotation, an increase in enjoyment and happiness on the part of the consuming public.

Therefore, Du Pont's early theory of value shares with physiocratic thought in general a failure to search beyond market forces for the sources of value. His theory of value reveals an elaboration on, but no variance from, the position held by Quesnay in his original exposition of the school's precepts, an exposition resting on cost of agricultural production rather than on utility or other demand factors to explain value.

2. Theory of Exchange

Du Pont's theory of exchange does not differ from Adam Smith's theory presented ten years later, is consequently familiar to the modern reader, and may accordingly be discussed in brief: If exchange of goods, both within and among countries, takes place in the absence of restrictions, the market in each instance strikes a balance between the costs and quantity of a good on the one hand and the demand for it on the other. For Du Pont the purpose of this exchange mechanism is narrower than Smith's, however. It is to assure that no more resources than necessary are allocated to the production and distribution of nonagricultural goods, because such production and distribution, although useful, merely transforms, but does not add to, the total stock of wealth.

Du Pont recognized that exchange involved the use of money or credit. Their use to him played an essential role in the exchange act: they established goods' prices and a measure of their values; for the economy as a whole, money prices measured all goods and served as a measure of total wealth.[8] Money prices, as noted in the discussion of value, assess the values of all goods under conditions of free trade:

> *Trade* is a natural and indispensable end result of *Agriculture* exercised by men grouped in a society. It is seen that *Trade* divides among all men the products of Agriculture; gives the farmers means to create new ones out of them thanks to the multiplication of outlets; gives a market value to the goods of the land which, with its help, acquire the quality of *wealth*. One can see that it maintains the price of the products above the costs of cultivation, thanks to the competition among buyers; and it secures therefore the existence of the *net product* or revenue which Agriculture creates, which is the only available wealth, and consequently the only base for *Finances* or public revenue which decide the power of States.[9]

Hence, merely by mentioning the fact that buyers (initially) maintain a demand sufficient to support the levels of agricultural prices, Du Pont alluded to, but did not discuss, the underlying physiocratic tenet that a high and stable grain price is advantageous to agriculture and thus to aggregate wealth.

Du Pont was also aware of the distorting effects of government spending. Only occasionally, however, did he go into the nature of money in his writings in the *Journal de l'Agriculture*. One example occurs in a June 1766 issue:

> Certainly a Nation which would spend more than its revenue, would ruin itself and bear all the effects of poverty of which the author has spoken, even though it would not trade with other countries, and though the total amount of currency would remain the same.[10]

Despite the brevity of his comments, it is clear from his early writings that he was fully aware of the monetary mechanisms that were to become an important topic in his later policy writings. Credit, an essential part of the exchange mechanism, played an important role in the physiocratic paradigm. Credit, or seed-money, was essential for bringing about an increase in harvests later in the season and thus essential for bringing about an increase in the net product. This important role of credit in the physiocratic system appears to have been responsible for Du Pont's later interests in credit and banking institutions.

Thus, in summary, Du Pont's view of the mechanism of free-market exchange, and its pricing and credit functions, does not differ in its basics from the ideas later popularized by Adam Smith and Jean Baptiste Say. The purpose of the exchange system in Du Pont's mind, however, was distinctly physiocratic: to assure the proper allocation of resources between and within agricultural and industrial activities.

3. Allocation Theory

Du Pont's comments on allocation are not conveniently disentangled from his views on value, exchange, and commerce. Just as price was the measure of value under free exchange, it was also the allocator of resources within the economy, as Du Pont revealed in his letter against monopoly in the coasting trade in grain:

> I am convinced that one can resist, for a limited time only, the evidence of physical laws which establish a natural level of prices in free trade, and which guarantee in this manner that all which is saved on trading costs (thanks to the effect of competition or otherwise) turns into the profit of the value of the products.[11]

A typical example of his understanding of the operation of the allocative mechanism was his critique of British protection of haberdashery. He observed that free trade in hats and beaver skins might enable English haberdashers to produce hats at lower prices by obtaining beaver skins from a cheaper,

French, source. Moreover, if protection were removed in Britain, not only might Englishmen have cheaper hats as a result of lower resource prices, but the French themselves might find that English hats would then be cheaper than their French-made counterparts. The possibility that hats, or any other goods, might be more cheaply imported than produced at home reflects an implied (or unconscious) assumption about specialization: because other countries specialized in certain products, such as hats, their advantage, either in lower prices or in better quality or both, would be augmented by yet lower costs from free trade. Following Du Pont's assumptions, if France itself were to specialize in agricultural goods such as hides and skins, which yield a net product, France would have its net product and cheaper prices for manufactured goods as well. When, Du Pont felt, men observed the ample profits being made in agriculture under free trade, they would eagerly channel their investments into agriculture. Thus, he argued, free trade in itself would allocate investment into agriculture. If the French realized this truth before other nations did, France would prosper all the more in comparison to the other economies until they too learned to invest in agriculture, after which the entire world would prosper.

Whether or not the physiocratic premises concerning the net product of agriculture are accepted, it is apparent that Du Pont's views of price allocation both of resources and of finished goods reflect an understanding on his part of the allocative mechanism strikingly akin to the classical view of allocation later propounded in England.

4. Commerce and Industry

The allocative mechanism in a free economy is, of course, a determinant of the composition of agricultural and industrial goods produced by the economy. Consequently, Du Pont's views on allocation call for an assessment of his understanding of commerce. According to Du Pont, commerce, both within and among countries, is the generator of exchange activity. Consequently, a vigorous, unrestrained, and unaided commerce—in short, free trade—is the necessary counterpart to the maximization of agriculture's net product and, thus, to the increase of each and all nations' wealth. It is significant that Du Pont changed the publication's title to *Journal de L'Agriculture, du Commerce et des Finances* to reflect the three categories within which he strove to channel public discussion of the new "economic science." Under the category of commerce was subsumed discussion of industry, a relegation that reflects the physiocrats' negative reaction to the financially ruinous policies of a century of Colbertist industrial development.

By *commerce* Du Pont meant both the sale of commodities and industrial goods at their source and the resale of commodities and goods at a different place. The latter involved both transport costs, which Du Pont saw as generally unnecessarily high, and speculative windfalls, which he held to be both unjust and a misallocation of resources. Other aspects of commerce to arise from Du Pont's writings include his characterizations of selling as "passive commerce" and buying as "active commerce," although the only usefulness of such a distinction (other than for filling out certain journal issues) seems to have been in his condemnation of mercantilist policies; but even there it appears less than essential to the argument. Another point that Du Pont dwelt on at length was the fact that, in his view, trade, whether internal or external, was generally not in surplus products. He argued strongly that as long as farmers and craftsmen provided goods for trade, then commerce in these items was necessary to their livelihood and certainly was not surplus; he extended the logic to hold that traded goods as well should not be viewed as in any way superfluous to a nation.

The distinction between industrial and agricultural commerce in Du Pont's writings was explicitly stated only in one article in the *Journal*, his "Réflexions sur le Commerce de pure Industrie."[12] By *industry* Du Pont meant goods produced by workers in workshops.[13] Items so produced were referred to as manufactured goods, or simply as "goods" as opposed to commodities produced by agriculture.

An example serving to show that Du Pont was not of the opinion that investment should take place in agriculture to the total exclusion of industry, but rather that he sought to let the market mechanism indicate its correct allocation, appears in his discussion of the proper commercial activities of French colonies.[14] Having established that supposed luxury goods are not luxury goods at all if they are necessary to a nation, he argued that a colony should not be forced to produce "luxury" goods for shipment to the home country, as many Frenchmen insisted, but, rather, that the free-market mechanism should be permitted to indicate those goods, whether agricultural or industrial, or indeed transport services, that a colony was best suited to provide. The point of his, and physiocracy's, theory was that the composition of commerce between agriculture and industry would be determined by market mechanics, even though physiocracy held industrial commerce to be sterile.

The upshot of Du Pont's views on commerce is clear: although it is true that Du Pont shared the physiocratic distinction between the productivity of agricultural activities and the sterility of industrial and trade activities, he did not permit himself to fall into the dogmatic position that all nonagricultural commerce was unworthy of serious consideration. Rather, he understood, as well as did the classical economists of a later generation, that the free-trade system would establish the best composition of commercial activities for the maximization of national, and indeed, global, wealth.

5. *The Role of Government*

There is one remaining point of importance to be discussed in Du Pont's writings in the *Journal de l'Agriculture*: that of government economic policy. Near the end of his "Lettre aux Auteurs, etc. au sujet du Cabotage des Grains" he recommended particular government action for bringing about free coasting trade.[15] This recommendation for change in government policy is the first time that Du Pont jumps from a general argument to an outright call for specific government policy, something he would come to do many times later when in the government service. This recommendation comes in 1766, only three years after his induction into the physiocratic circle. To say that it was the physiocratic influence which led him in this direction is without foundation. His very first contribution, it may be recalled, was a poem addressed to the government, recommending certain modes of economic behavior; but from the time of his critique of Roussel's tax proposal in 1763 until he made this proposal, he had been more active in criticizing the proposals of others and preaching the theory of physiocracy. Here, then, is the reemergence of Du Pont's instinct to advise and the beginning of his active role in government policy-making. To clarify his idea of the role of government policy in the economy, it must be recalled that Du Pont felt that free trade is necessary, but not necessarily sufficient, to bring about a physiocratic state. For Du Pont saw a need for government policy to encourage positive investment within agriculture through the allocative mechanism of exchange, because man's blindness to the bounteousness of nature must be overcome; man's habit to forget the land, to consider preoccupation with it as either backward (as in the case of the entrepreneur) or unsophisticated (as in the case of the absentee landlord), must be overcome with government encouragement of investment in agriculture.

Thus, Du Pont interpreted the government's desired policy role as one of bringing about the conditions necessary for free trade, and of encouraging men's intelligent economic behavior. Such behavior would automatically bring about the physiocratic economic system.

C. Summary

An overall assessment of Du Pont's comments and articles in the *Journal de l'Agriculture* from July 1765 to November 1766 finds in his writing a keen understanding and analytical use of what was to become, following publication of Smith's *Wealth of Nations* in 1776, classical economic theory. At the same time, an analysis of four subcategories of that theory, namely value, exchange, allocation, and government policy, reveals that Du Pont's conception of economic theory was simply an elaboration of the theoretical framework constructed by Quesnay to justify his view that agriculture was the source of wealth. Value was measured by free market prices; allocation of resources into the various branches of production and commerce was similarly effected by the price mechanism; and, finally, Du Pont shared with other physiocrats and subsequent classical economists a belief in a laissez-faire role for government, but one that was tempered in Du Pont's case by a predilection toward active encouragement of investment in agriculture.

It is worth noting that had Du Pont not been a physiocrat, his free trade theory could still have been a useful analytical tool. He had grasped the internal logic of the system of production and allocation, which is independent of one's views of the source of wealth, whether it be a labor theory of value, a "natural resource" theory of value, utilitarian theory, or no theory at all. It is a fact, however, that he came to this view of the operation of the competitive exchange mechanism through the particular physiocratic emphasis on the primacy of nature. Without the vehicle of physiocracy, his own insights concerning the operation of the economy would have lacked a uniform framework for critical analysis.

Notes to Chapter IV

1. With the exception of his final article, which he signed "Du Pont," the articles authored by Du Pont were signed "M.C." (or "Mr C."), "Négociant de Bordeaux," or with some other pseudonymous designation. That these articles were in fact penned by Du Pont is attributable to several sources: in the volumes of the *Journal* at the Eleutherian Mills Historical Library Du Pont had written his name at the head or following the articles in question; Schelle, who used another set of the *Journal*, likewise included them in Du Pont's bibliography; and Weulersse, who with Schelle was unaware of the presence of Du Pont's handwritten signatures in the copies that had been owned by Du Pont, not only attributed those signed "M.C." to Du Pont but provided a general catalogue of the authors of contributions to the *Journal* according to the initials used for their articles. The key to the catalogue presented by Weulersse had originally been provided by Du Pont in an edition of the *Ephémérides* (4 [1769]: x–xi).

2. For an interpretation of the rise of this method see William Letwin, *The Origins of Scientific Economics: English Economic Thought, 1660–1776* (London: Methuen, 1963).

3. *Journal de l'Agriculture* 2, pt. 1 (September 1765): iii–iv.

4. Ibid., p. iv.

5. Ibid., p. xxx. Du Pont's italics.

6. Ibid., 7, pt. 2 (November 1766): 212–13.

7. DPDN, fn. to Forbonnais's "Observations sur le Mémoire qui traite des Loix prohibitives du Commerce étrange," *Journal de l'Agriculture* 4, pt. 1 (January 1766): 60–61, n5.

8. "Trade is nothing else but the debit of the products of the territory, which is made by means of exchange, be it against other products in nature, or be it against money which is used as a guarantee in order to secure products of equal value to those which were debited, when one is willing" (DPDN, "Préface," *Journal de l'Agriculture* 2, pt. 1 [September 1765]: xxv). [Again:]
"Trade is an exchange; whether one gives money in order to have merchandise equal in value to that money, whether one gives merchandise in order to have money of equal value to this merchandise, or whether one gives merchandise for other of equal value. So, in trading, each one is a seller and a buyer; each one, except in the case of fraud, receives as much as he gives, each one still deals with *assets* and *liabilities*. The exchange of one value for another (although necessary) does not then render richer or poorer those who make this exchange. He who would buy more money than he has merchandise to pay for or who would buy more merchandise than he has money to pay for, would be, it is true, in any of the two cases, the debtor of his seller, because in either case he would have bought more than he could pay; this is what is called credit trade and not liabilities trade. Credit trade does not of itself ruin the debtor, since the latter has received in his very purchase the value of what he owes. In this way, the debtor is not the tributary of his seller . . ." (DPDN, unnumbered ft., *Journal de l'Agriculture* 3, pt. 1 [October 1765]: 69–70). Du Pont's italics.

9. DPDN, "Préface," *Journal de l'Agriculture* 2, pt. 1 (September 1765): xxvii–xxviii. His emphasis.

10. DPDN, editorial postscript to "Réponse à la Lettre de Mr. M. insérée dans le Journal de Mars dernier, par l'auteur des *Ephémérides du Citoyen* [i.e., Baudeau]," *Journal de l'Agriculture* 5, pt. 3 (June 1766): 57.

11. Mr. C. [DPDN], "Lettre aux Auteurs, etc., au sujet du Cabotage des grains," *Journal de l'Agriculture* 4, pt. 1 (July 1766): 178.

12. *Journal de l'Agriculture* 3, pt. 1 (October 1765): 33–36.

13. Ibid., p. 35.

14. The passage is sufficiently compact to warrent inclusion here:

". . . it seems to us that it will be seen that plantation colonies must not and cannot be regarded as producers of luxury goods; that if one should look upon them as such they would not be able to pretend as such to the feasibility of spreading the consumption and the outlets of the products of the main land, in as much as the producers of luxury goods of a State advantageously situated for the trade of its products never had this property. And finally that when they would be luxury producers, that would offer one more reason to admit the greatest competition possible in the supply of things which are necessary to them, and in the debit of their goods, since these producers are always to fear the competition of other similar producers and that they can support themselves and merit the preference in as much as they save on the expenses of their manufacture and on the debit expenses of their work" (DPDN, "Observations sur la Lettre précedente," *Journal de l'Agriculture* 5, pt. 2 [May 1766]: 116–17).

15. From DPDN in *Journal de l'Agriculture:*

The free coastal shipping of grains will be all the easier to establish since no law proscribes coastal shipping on the part of foreigners.

I should however comment that it would be perhaps fitting to grant this freedom by law. Independently of the fact that it befits the dignity of the Prince to express in no other way his will on important topics, it is certainly of public interest that the wills which influence trade be known and observed. [6, pt. 1 (July 1766): 204–5]

V.

Economic Writings during the Period
1767–72

A. His Book *De l'origine et des progrès d'une science nouvelle*

In the nineteen-month interlude between Du Pont's
editorship of the *Journal de l'Agriculture* and his editorship of
the *Ephémérides du Citoyen*, Du Pont's primary contribution to
economic literature was the book *De l'origine et des progrès d'une
science nouvelle*, which he wrote in 1767 and which appeared in
1768.[1] To put the work into perspective, it should be recalled
that by 1767 Quesnay had stated or had prompted statements
by others of the major ideas of physiocracy; in 1767 Mercier de
la Rivière published his book, *L'Ordre naturel et essentiel des
sociétés politiques*, which synthesized physiocratic theory but
dealt with it in abstractions not easily understood by, and
hardly appealing to, the general reader of the day.[2]

Du Pont's book had a two-fold purpose: to describe the
origin of physiocratic doctrine and to restate in popular language the theoretical synthesis of Quesnay's ideas constructed
by Mercier. In this eighty-four-page work Du Pont presented
the clearest explanation of the origins, philosophy,
economics, and politics of the physiocratic doctrine and the
nature of the society envisioned by the physiocrats in terms
that were easy to understand.

Because many of Du Pont's contributions to the *Ephémérides*
between 1768 and 1772 were to be restatements of ideas contained in this book, it is fitting to set forth these ideas in their

order of presentation in *De l'origine.* In the first quarter of the book Du Pont credited Montesquieu with having opened men's eyes to the need for a society founded on a constitution of law, but noted that it was lesser writers after Montesquieu who realized the importance of natural law on which society's constitution should be molded. He did not, incidentally, allude to John Locke, who had originated the idea of the social contract founded on natural law a half-century before Montesquieu. Du Pont summarized the founding of physiocratic doctrine by Quesnay, noted Gournay's independent arrival at nearly the same conclusions (pointing out, however, Gournay's rejection of the important doctrine of the net product and the single tax that followed from it) through his work in administration, and praised Mercier's recent *Ordre naturel et essentiel.* The remaining three-quarters of Du Pont's book is taken up with "une idée nette et rapide des principales vérités dont la chaîne, découverte par le Docteur QUESNAY, est si supérieurement et si clairement développé dans ce Livre sublime" by Mercier.[3] Du Pont begins with the assumption that

> there is a natural Society, previous to all convention between men, founded on their constitution, on their physical needs, on their evidently common interest.[4]

Following the philosophical reasoning of the eighteenth century, the argument traced man's establishment of societies in which social contracts bind men in mutually beneficial behavior. To the physiocrats, however, one particular aspect of the contracts was particularly significant: that of private property. Without the protection of goods through private property men would not be encouraged to plant or to improve the land. A landowner was thus encouraged by private-property rights. Moreover, he might legitimately contract with others who worked his land; the owner and the operator might sign an agreement called a *lease,* whereby the lessee operated the land for a fixed sum over a period of time. Either one or both the landlord and the operator (i.e., cultivator) might make improvements to the land and would receive accordingly a proportion of the resulting increased income. Next, Du Pont discussed the purely economic aspects of physiocratic doctrine, whereby cultivator and landlord received a payment that both covered their operating and fixed costs and provided them with net product. Then, before discussing the tax system, Du Pont reverted to an exposition of the political system, in which the head of state, whether hereditary or elective, was responsible for maintaining the executive and legislative functions of government, yet one in which the system of justice was upheld by magistrates divorced from the pressures and influences of the other arms of government. Government was to be frugal; its expenses were to be met by only one tax: a tax levied on the recipients of the net product. The exact assessment of the tax was to be decided by magistrates in accordance with physiocratic doctrine, just as all other matters of justice were to be decided by the magistrates.

In most physiocratic writing it is unclear whether the landlord or the cultivator was to pay the tax. The comments of Du Pont on page twenty-four of the Dubois edition make it clear that if the levels of fixed and annual costs, rents, and grain prices were such that all the net product was paid by the cultivator to the landlord in the form of rents, then it was the landlord who had received all the net product and he who was to pay the tax. In earlier works Du Pont had called for higher grain prices to allow gradual rises of rents as the older leases expired until high stable prices and rents had been attained at precisely the right levels for rents, and net product, to be equivalent for all farms; in this case the incentive for investment would have rested with the landlord, for the cultivator would not have been motivated to make investments when he had nothing with which to invest nor any evidence of obtaining a return therefrom. In this 1767 writing, based on Mercier's theoretical clarification, there is no inconsistency in the sharing of the net product between cultivator and landlord. As Du Pont put it,

> it is therefore evident that the tax must be levied directly on the net product available from the land wealth. For then it will not

upset the legal and necessary combinations of the cultivators to whom giving up a part of the net product to the Sovereign, or to the landowners does not matter.[5]

Thus, net product was viewed as a fund out of which came rent, the cultivator's (or operator's) profit, and taxes. Whether the cultivator paid the landlord a sum of rent out of which a portion was assessed for taxes from the landlord or whether the cultivator paid a lower rent and submitted the taxes directly to the government was a question of accounting to the physiocrats; in the long run, that is, after all leases had been adjusted, the net product would accrue totally to the landlord who alone would pay the tax. Du Pont performed a useful service in clarifying these mechanics, which were generally referred to by other physiocrats in vague and sometimes contradictory terms.

This last point plays up the importance of Du Pont's interpretive genius: Quesnay may have invented physiocracy, and Mercier may have systematized it; but Du Pont clarified its theory and interpreted it in a manner capable of being understood by the general literate public. But understanding does not necessarily carry with it acceptance of a theory, as Du Pont was to discover when he took over the editorship of the *Ephémérides du Citoyen* from Baudeau in the summer of 1768.

B. His Economic Thought in the *Ephémérides du Citoyen*

To examine Du Pont's thought in the *Ephémérides*, both in his contributions before he became editor and in his period as editor, mid-1768 to early 1772, it will be convenient to select seven themes that cover what Du Pont had to say: history of economic thought; economic theory; enlightened government; free trade in grains; transportation; monopoly; and slavery. The exposition of these themes will make evident the fact that particularly during the period 1769–71 Du Pont's interest turned sharply from the promulgation of physiocratic theory toward involvement in the details of government administrative reform suggested by physiocratic thought.

1. His History of Economic Thought in the Ephémérides

The first of these seven themes is the history of economic thought, which was an important topic in three different contributions by Du Pont to the *Ephémérides*. The first of these is one of the longer continuing articles in the *Ephémérides*. This article appeared in nearly every monthly issue of 1769 under the title "Notice Abrégée des différents Ecrits modernes qui ont concouru en France à former la Science de l'économie politique."[6] The theme occurs in another article, "Catalogue des Ecrits composés suivant les principes de la Science économique," in which Du Pont provided an annotated bibliography of physiocratic writings, presented chronologically from 1756.[7] A third and final source for this theme appears in extended footnotes by Du Pont to Beccaria's acceptance speech upon nomination to the first chair in political economy, established at Milan.[8] These three sources provide the bulk of Du Pont's comments, both in the *Ephémérides* and indeed in his earlier period as a whole, on the works of earlier and contemporary thinkers.

In the continuing article, "Notice Abrégée," there is no doubt that Du Pont viewed earlier French economic thinkers as having pointed out the need for a theory such as physiocracy, as in the writings of Montesquieu, and as having demonstrated through their inconsistent writings in the absence of such a general theory the need for one. In this article little mention was made of non-French writers. Of the eight installments of "Notice Abrégée" only the first one included comments on predecessors of Quesnay and Gournay; the remainder dealt with the development of these two men's thought and the subsequent writings of their disciples down to 1769. While many of the publications discussed were almost contemporary with Du Pont in 1769, the overall context emphasized the historical development of physiocratic economic theory, which was to Du Pont the only economic theory. In this view Du Pont was not necessarily narrow-minded, but rather struck by the fact that indeed, until the physiocracy, there was no body of theory that could answer so many questions and offer solutions to so many of the economic problems of his century.

As Du Pont saw it, Montesquieu (1689–1755) had first posed the need for such a theory in his *L'Esprit des Loix* (1748). Du Pont consequently saw 1748 as the date of the awakening in men of an awareness of the need for the study of political economy. Although Du Pont did not so state, it is clear from his earlier writings that he was aware of the economic problems of his country during the earlier part of the eighteenth century. But it was not so much these problems that called forth the beginning of theory to explain them, as it was the appearance on the scene of Montesquieu (and some years later, Quesnay), a genius equipped with superior tools for considering these problems:

> The period of upheaval which led the mind to apply itself to the study of Political Economy, dates back to Montesquieu. It was the inspiration of his genius, the charms of his style . . . which characterize the multitude of observations which he gathered in the Laws, which showed to our still so frivolous Nation that the study of men's interest grouped in a society could be preferable to research into abstract metaphysics, and even more evenly agreeable than the reading of small novels.[9]

Du Pont saw the origin of economic theory as a response not to a need to explain how town markets operate, why trade takes place, nor how specialization adds to wealth, but rather as a response to a need to explain how government should behave in encouraging men to behave in their economic activities in accordance with natural law. Montesquieu's *L'Esprit des Loix* was to be followed ten years later by Quesnay's specification that operation in accordance with natural law required recognition of the truth that all wealth issued from the net product of agriculture. But until Quesnay, the second genius, was to specify the source of economic wealth, others were to grope with economic problems unsuccessfully, because, in Du Pont's opinion, they did not hold the key to the theoretical door to be opened by Quesnay in 1758. For him, these writers between Montesquieu and Quesnay simply lacked the requisite genius to provide the necessary framework for dealing with such problems. Indeed, Europe "fut inondée d'un déluge d'Ecrits sur la Législation, sur l'Agriculture, sur le Commerce, sur les Manufactures, sur la Population, etc."[10] but these writers were hopelessly mired in their own arguments because they had no common theory in which to accommodate their diverse opinions.

Du Pont alluded specifically to one controversy, that between the followers of Jean François Melon and Dutot.[11] Melon had argued for the production of luxury goods as a stimulus to economic activity, while Dutot had cautioned against government encouragement of such industrial undertakings, which resembled the "mercantilist" policies of Colbert a century before. Du Pont pointed out that Melon had sought a tax on the wealth resultant from such nonagricultural production similar to that proposed by Vauban in his *Dîme Royale* of 1707. In Du Pont's view, this was a grievous error because Vauban and Melon had written prior to Quesnay's revelation that the net product of agriculture was the only source of wealth. The similarity between the one example chosen by Du Pont to illustrate this period of prephysiocratic argument, and Du Pont's own initial controversy with Roussel over the form of the national tax base, is a striking reminder that Du Pont's own initial motivations to enter the lists of public debate in 1763 with Roussel were part of the same general involvement that urged other men to write on these topics: the growing economic problems developing out of the social ills of the last century and the war taxes of the earlier part of the present one, an amalgam of heavy taxation and stagnant economic activity, combined with the intellectual insights of men such as Montesquieu (and later Quesnay and Turgot, in Du Pont's opinion).

Thus, one lesson to be learned from a study of Du Pont's writings on the history of economic thought is already suggested: the common origin of his thought and action in the general mélange of mid-eighteenth-century France, in response primarily to the socioeconomic situation and secondarily to the great thinkers' reactions to that situation and to each others' thoughts. Moreover, Du Pont clearly saw that some men were intellectual giants and others were not.

The remainder of Du Pont's comments on this period immediately preceding Quesnay's first economic publications in the *Encyclopédie* consists of two themes: the first, a theme that was stronger in Du Pont's earlier writings, namely, restatement of (physiocratic) economic theory, and the second, a theme that was to become more important in the years following the *Ephémérides*, that of the enlightened use of sovereign power. Both these themes are tied together in Du Pont's world view: political man solving social problems in accordance with natural law as revealed by physiocratic theory.

2. Du Pont on the Idea of Individual Liberty

Although Du Pont's views on enlightened government will be discussed more fully elsewhere, it is worthwhile noting that in reference to the period 1748–58 Du Pont saw that the discovery of the idea of liberty as a right of man was a significant step toward establishing the conditions both of an enlightened sovereignty that would respect such liberty and of an economic system in which free trade was an essential characteristic. Even though Jean Jacques Rousseau's *Le Contrat Social* appeared in 1762, Rousseau's name is not used by Du Pont in describing those who popularized the concept of liberty during this period. This absence may be accounted for, first, by the fact that Rousseau's work did not appear until four years after Quesnay's initial economic writing, and, second, because Rousseau's name had not yet become the rallying cry it was to be for men in search of authority for their political views in the 1780s and 1790s.[12]

As the following quotation from the first installment of Du Pont's "Notice Abrégée" reveals, in his view, until 1758, men felt that liberty was somehow right and good, but their minds were still ruled by traditional ways of thinking:

Some could see however as a whole that freedom was man's right, that it was the foundation of trade, and that it should be good for everything. But their noble and kind heart told them this even louder than did their mind. It was a truth guessed rather than known; and more strongly felt than it was calculated. As a matter of fact, those who campaigned against this freedom, and who wanted to weigh it down with a great deal of more or less plausible regulations, held the majority of the votes.[13]

Again, it was the thought of Quesnay, first published in the *Encyclopédie* but only widely disseminated when Du Pont published several of the master's works in the *Journal de l'Agriculture* and separately, that provided a vehicle to free men's captive minds.

3. Du Pont on the Development of Physiocratic Thought

From this point on, Du Pont devoted the "Notice Abrégée" to summaries of physiocratic works, beginning in 1758 and continuing down through and including articles published in the *Ephémérides* itself in 1769. His comments are concise and frank; he speaks of Mirabeau's works before and after the Marquis's conversion by Quesnay. His comments as of 1769 reveal no change whatever in his opinions on physiocracy from 1763 and no change from the comments he was to offer in his unfinished autobiography in 1793.

a. Importance of the Tableau Economique. One significant point of a positive nature does arise from his summary of physiocratic writings: the importance he attributed to the *tableau économique*, an importance, notwithstanding Du Pont's preaching, that was lost on subsequent generations, only to be rediscovered a century later:

The TABLEAU ECONOMIQUE is a mathematical formula which permits one to calculate rapidly and accurately the effects of various disturbances which might be caused by the distribution, circulation and reproduction of wealth, be it for good or for bad. However, as no public operation can be carried out by a government without influencing wealth, the Tableau Economique offers a very prompt and very clear means of estimating equitably the value of all these operations through the precise spread of profit or damage that they must cause humanity, the community and the various types of men of which it is formed. That is why the invention of this formula has come to be looked upon as the complement of the Science of Political Economy.[14]

b. Du Pont on Gournay. Another point of interest in this look backward at the development of physiocracy is Du Pont's opinion of Gournay (1712–59), Turgot's master. This opinion was set forth in 1769, six years after Du Pont met Turgot but five years before Du Pont was to become Turgot's assistant in the Finance Ministry. Consequently, the favorable opinion expressed by Du Pont concerning Gournay cannot be attributed to Du Pont's later adulation of the reformist finance minister. Significantly, Du Pont's opinion ran counter to those expressed in general studies of physiocracy, where Gournay is considered to have been either a divisive or an insignificant force in shaping Quesnay's thought. Du Pont, however, saw Gournay's influence on the movement in its emphasis on liberty and felt that Gournay had set an example of laissez-faire in his long service as public administrator:

> The name of MONSIEUR DE GOURNAY, so dear to the Citizens, cannot be recalled without rendering homage to the beauty, vigor and wisdom of the genius of this excellent man, who, in a magistracy, apparently dedicated solely to *regulating* trade, had dared to break the bonds of custom, who . . . led his Colleagues . . . to sum up successfully with the single word "*freedom*" all the operations, before him so complex, of the administration of which he was in charge.[15]

c. Du Pont on Du Pont. The only other fact worthy of mention in his review of physiocratic literature is that he did not revise his opinions expressed in his two pamphlets of 1763 nor in his *De l'exportation et de l'importation des Grains* of 1764. He modestly, although accurately, stated that the pamphlets of 1763

> have no other merit than to stutter out two true principles, and of having drawn to the Author . . . the benevolence . . . of two respectable men [Quesnay and Mirabeau].[16]

His summaries of his own writings from 1764 down to 1769 are notable only for their accuracy and for the absence of any effort to embellish or overstate their original arguments. The only exception to his self-imposed rule of noneditorialization came with his January 1765 "Lettre sur la différence . . . entre la grande et la petite culture," where he acknowledged the criticism of others by noting the all-too-hazy distinction in that work between large- and small-scale farming, as in the earlier work by Quesnay on the same subject.[17] Turgot himself criticized the distinction, based on whether ploughing was done with oxen or with horses, as a useless one.

d. Comments on Non-Physiocratic Writers. Toward the end of the final installment of the "Notice Abrégée", Du Pont noted that it had been reserved for Frenchmen to compose a theory of economic science, but that he was aware of several non-French writers who exhibited

> an infinity of scattered truths and wise Principles, which could have been infinitely profitable to humanity if prejudices, unfortunately dominating, had not prevented the People from lending to them all the attention which they should have aroused.[18]

Jean Jacques Burlamaqui (a Swiss ethical philospher whose publications on natural law appeared in the 1740s), Child, Culpeper, Deker [*sic*], Diego de Saavedra, Hirzel, Hübner, John Locke, Schmidt d'Avenstein, Wit, Wolf, and Zannon are lumped together and referred to only by their last names. However, Josiah Tucker received more attention, characterized by Du Pont as an "Apôtre de la paix et de la liberté universelle, chez une Nation jalouse et livrée au monopole de ses Marchands;"[19] Benjamin Franklin had, according to Du Pont, "adopté les Principes et la Doctrine de nos Economistes françois;"[20] and the Marquis César de Beccaria-Bonesana was described as a "partisan nécessaire de toute étude qui tend à établir parmi les hommes l'esprit de fraternité et de justice."[21] Whether or not Du Pont was personally acquainted with the writings of all the men he named is not clear from his comments, although he expressed his ignorance of several non-French writers mentioned by Beccaria in the article to be discussed later.

At the conclusion of this recitation of economic philosophers from the time of Montesquieu (1748) to the time of his writing (1769), Du Pont expressed his dismay that, in spite of the physiocrats' ample publications and his own journalistic broadcasting of their truths, the general public yet remained unconvinced and applied the appelation of "sect" to the physiocrats:

> We have heard People for whom it was apparently easier to find, against the Doctrine that we strive to spread, an injurious expression rather than a good reason, to accuse us, and the Philosophers who have discovered and developed this Doctrine, *of forming* a SECT. We know that this imputation is bitterly spread among the Public and that it serves as a pretext for frivolous minds, to do away with the study of truths which this *supposed sect* brings forth, and for men with private interests or a vanity to satisfy, to avoid answering to the facts that it states and the principles it reestablishes.[22]

Thus, in 1769 Du Pont clearly exhibited a frustration with his apparently fruitless crusade to convince the thinking public of the truth of economic science as revealed by the physiocrats and of the consequent sagacity of undertaking administrative reforms instituted in accordance with physiocratic principles. The quotation thus symbolizes a turning point in Du Pont's life—from expressing physiocratic theory to attempting to carry out administrative reform based on physiocratic theory.

A second of the three articles in which Du Pont discussed the works of earlier economic writers is "Catalogue des Ecrits Composés suivant les Principes de la Science Economique," which appeared in volume 2 of the 1768 *Ephémérides*, four months before Du Pont's assumption of the editorship.[23] It is simply a list of physiocratic articles, pamphlets, and books from 1756 to 1768 and adds nothing to the information provided in the "Notice Abrégée" except the evidence that Du Pont was interested in making the public aware of every physiocratic publication that had appeared down to that time.

The final source of Du Pont's comments on earlier economic writers is the acceptance speech of César Beccaria, which Du Pont commented on in running footnotes to the speech. In Beccaria's opinion:

> the English found in BACON the first seeds of these [economic] sciences which other great men of this outstanding Nation, have since then developed, and brought to fruition.[24]

Having thus already contradicted Du Pont, who saw the germ of the search for modern economic thought to have originated with Montesquieu, Beccaria went on to call Vauban the father of French political economy, which prompted from Du Pont a repetition in footnote form of his argument that although Vauban was a well-meaning man, he lacked the insights to be provided by Quesnay fifty years after the appearance of Vauban's *Dîme Royale*, and that Vauban proposed a solution to the nation's fiscal difficulties not in accordance with natural law as indicated by the physiocratic principle of the net product.[25] Beccaria went on to group "l'immortel Montesquieu" with Melon, Ustariz, Ulloa, Hume, and l'abbé Genovesi ("créateur de cette science en Italie"), all of whom Beccaria praised.[26]

Concerning this list Du Pont admitted that he was not acquainted with the works of Genovesi; thought that Melon, who advocated the preservation of barriers to interprovincial trade in grains, was unworthy of mention; and clarified his own position concerning Montesquieu. Although Du Pont gave Montesquieu credit for interesting Frenchmen in ordering their thought on political economy, Du Pont thought Montesquieu was wrong in failing to tie natural laws of a social nature to the physical laws of the sources of wealth discovered by Quesnay. In addition, he felt that Montesquieu failed to see that agricultural production was founded on the principle of property rights that Montesquieu himself had so firmly emphasized.[27]

In the same footnote Du Pont referred to "le Philosophe HUME" as an ingenious observer, a wise historian, and an

interesting writer, but a man whose thinking was marred by
failure to discern neither

> the natural principles of taxes, nor the advantages of complete
> freedom of Trade and of work, nor in the scope of the indelible
> *right* which men have to this freedom, when he published his
> revered writings.[28]

Du Pont did not fail to note as well Beccaria's omission of
Gournay, Quesnay, Mirabeau, Mercier de la Rivière, and
other physiocrats from his list of economic thinkers but gener-
ously attributed Beccaria's silence in respect to physiocracy to
the same lack of international communication that had kept
Du Pont in ignorance of the Italian economist Antonio
Genovesi.[29] As Schumpeter points out,[30] some of the works of
Child, Hume, and Josiah Tucker had been translated into
French by Gournay and Turgot, which may at least partly
account for both Du Pont's familiarity with, and his respect
for, Hume. Hume's presence at Quesnay's entresol soirees
during the 1760s may also have influenced Du Pont's attitude.

Thus, commenting on earlier economic writers in the three
articles cited, Du Pont sometimes expressed his opinions of
nonphysiocratic writers, but, when he went into any detail
about their thought, he was quick to assume that since they
did not have access to, or after 1758 did not accept, the insights of Quesnay into political economy, they were destined
to flounder in a sea of unanchored arguments over government
policy or moral philosophy. In short, Du Pont held that because physiocracy is correct, all nonphysiocratic assumptions,
arguments, and conclusions must be incorrect.

4. His Economic Theory in the Ephémérides

In turning to the second of the themes contained in Du
Pont's writings in the *Ephémérides*, that of economic theory,
one finds his more important comments in five articles: "Supplément à l'article des Critiques Raisonnées;"[31] "Analyse de
l'encyclopédie économique ou système général d'économie
rustique par la Société d'économie politique de Berne,"[32]

"Fragment d'un ouvrage intitulé: *Elements de philosophie économique* par l'auteur des *Ephémérides*;"[33] "Lettre de Mr H. à l'Auteur des *Ephémérides du Citoyen*, sur la marche naturelle des erreurs et des vérités;"[34] and his footnotes to the "Discours prononcé le neuf Janvier 1769, par M. le Marquis César Beccaria Bonesana à l'ouverture de la nouvelle Chaire d'Economie Politique, fondée par S. M. l'Impératrice Reine dans les Ecoles Palatines de Milan."[35]

   a. His Attack on Galiani's Dialogues. The first of these five articles, "Supplément," is a strongly negative review of *Dialogues*, by the Italian protectionist and political thinker, Ferdinando Galiani. Du Pont's characteristic of rapid reaction when angered is revealed in his rebuttal of what was to Du Pont the supreme challenge: a formal treatise that argued, as Du Pont saw it, point by point against almost every physiocratic tenet and policy position. Du Pont described Galiani's *Dialogues* as a dangerously important work because of the very fact that it attacked the concept of natural law as a foundation of society, the principles of free and unprotected trade, the encouragement of agriculture, and even the view that government policy should be based on principle. That Du Pont felt both affronted and endangered by the brash iconoclasm of the pragmatic protectionist is evident from the following quotation:

> If the Author is correct, all of the principles which have thus far been presented to our Readers, which are the fruit of the meditations of the most enlightened Citizens and Philosophers, which have influenced legislation, which have merited the vote of the most illustrious Companies and the most respectable Magistrates, are nonetheless false and pernicious.[36]

To meet Galiani's challenge to the legitimacy of physiocracy, Du Pont proceeded to repeat the essence of physiocracy in all its theoretical, commercial, and political grandeur in the remainder of the fifty-four page article. Du Pont's feeling of urgency in presenting a strong and speedy rebuttal to Galiani's work is underlined by his decision to print his review as a supplement to volume 11, rather than include it in the next monthly number, volume 12.

   b. His Clarifications of Ideas and Terms. An example of more contemplative and consequently more rational writing on economic theory appears in his generally favorable review of the Swiss *Encyclopédie économique ou système générale d'économie rustique*,[37] in which he offered clear and detailed definitions of the various kinds of investment (or "*avances*") in agriculture as used in physiocratic writings. These definitions are worthy of quotation for their own sake, both because Quesnay and other physiocrats were sometimes unclear in their uses of the three kinds of *avances* and because modern commentaries have not always clarified the distinctions among the various uses of the term.[38] The distinctions are critical for a clear understanding of physiocratic arguments for investment in agriculture, taxation of rents, and the wealth-producing cycle exemplified in the *tableau économique*. Although critics often limit their distinctions to two categories, original improvements, alternatively translated as fixed investments (*avances primitives*) and annual or variable investments (*avances annuelles*), Du Pont used the term *avances foncières* for initial improvements made to the land itself, reserving *avances primitives* for the capital that is combined with the land, as the following passage reveals:

> The *avances foncières* are those which remain inseparable from the *land,* and which make it ready for cultivation. There are some lands that never need to be renewed, and others that need only be maintained by keeping them up less regularly than other lands. Clearing trees in new lands, pulling up roots, draining swamps, structures necessary for working, roads, the initial clearing, all the fixed improvements are *avances foncières.*
>
> The *avances primitives* comprise all the movable wealth that one must have or acquire *originally,* in order to undertake any improvement whatsoever, and which it is necessary to undertake and renew without ceasing in the service of this same working of the land, so that it should not decline. The tools and machines of all types, the work animals and the cattle are *avances primitives.*
>
> The *avances annuelles* are those necessary to cover all the day

wages and the annual expenses and to allow the workmen to subsist.[39]

Du Pont defined and clarified other key physiocratic concepts, such as net product, the treatment of interest on advances, and the proper classification of food consumed by farm workers' families; his definitions also included commercial terms; and he defined macroeconomic concepts such as wealth as well. ("Toutes les choses qui ont *valeur vénale* sont des *richesses*."[40] He generally approved of the definitions in the *Encyclopédie économique*, adding his own definitions usually as refinements rather than corrections of the editors'. Consequently, this *Encyclopédie* would seem useful as a guide to the modern student's search for definitions of economic and commercial terms as understood and used by the physiocrats.

The lessons to be drawn concerning Du Pont, however, are that he was capable of precision of statement and used his expository skills to expand on vague points of theory whenever the opportunity arose. This opportunistic approach to theoretical exposition, however, resulted in no consistent coverage of all physiocratic theory. His explanations also reveal, if there was any doubt, that he continued to accept completely physiocratic doctrine as of 1771, after eight years of exposure to, and writing about, *la science économique*.

c. Early Theory of Population. In a stylistic affectation typical of eighteenth-century literature, Du Pont wrote a short article in the form of "Chapters IX and X" of a nonexistent treatise entitled *Elements de philosophie économique*.[41] Chapter 9, "L'Augmentation des richesses qui naissent du territoire, multiplie la population," is followed by a chapter that, typical of Du Pont's expository style, sought to foresee and refute all possible objections to his argument. This is the only work from Du Pont's pen that is devoted primarily to the theory of population, until he undertook to debate Malthus in his final work in 1817. Du Pont's "Fragment" in the *Ephémérides* etched deeply the role he saw for population in assuring a shift in production from inefficient to efficient growers, as population, output, and wealth increased.

Unlike most of his other writings, the "Fragment" is neither a refutation nor a defense of another writer's work, nor is it fodder for a debate over policy. It does, however, with the greatest of ease, clarify the reasons that led physiocrats to favor modernization of agriculture and liberalization of trade in grains, reasons that involve the question of population. His argument proceeds as follows: In general, as agricultural production increases, population increases. In particular, God has built into the function of the human species such a sweetness in the procreative process that populations tend to increase naturally. Their only limits are difficulties of agricultural production. An increasing population sustains the market value of agricultural products and (since wealth is defined as the sum of the market values of all goods) contributes to the growth of wealth. Thus, increasing wealth (invested, of course, in agriculture) augments agricultural production that in turn augments wealth once more. At the same time, this upward spiral provides the food that supports a growing population that in turn supports market prices of agricultural goods and consequently, in turn, the level of wealth. As this overall increase in wealth, food, and population continues, there occurs a net shift in wealth from backward to modernizing farm proprietors. When the point is reached at which all land is cultivated, cultivators who have applied themselves through investment in modernized agricultural methods have well earned the right to be the initial distributors of all agricultural production (and thus, under the system envisioned by the physiocrats, the reapers of the bulk of the profits therein). Cultivators who have not modernized cannot compete in the free commodity markets at the same prices as the efficient growers. These high-cost producers should not receive protection or support, for their commodities should not be permitted to impinge on the profits deservedly earned by those who have modernized.

Du Pont's argument did not deal with the mechanism by which eventual equilibrium in agricultural output would stabilize population; this gloomy mechanism would be specified twenty-five years later by Malthus. Not having pushed the argument as far as Malthus was to do, Du Pont did not go the one step further to consider the possibility that high-cost producers would be able to sell their produce and even set the market price in a world short of grain. But Du Pont's world was in reality eighteenth-century France, where the specter of underpopulation, not overpopulation, haunted the mind, and his theoretical world was one of free trade in grains both internally and internationally, where a grain shortage could always be met through increased efficiency and importation from newly opened areas. In short, he did not see the population problem as envisioned by Malthus because there was none to see, and he did not consider the consequences of grain shortages foreseen by Ricardo because he was not living in Ricardo's period of increasing population and corn laws.

Nevertheless, Du Pont's comments on the mechanics of the relation of population, food, and wealth go far beyond the more general comments on the subject offered by other physiocrats, including Quesnay.[42] They presage Du Pont's insightful analysis of Malthus's work, which is considered elsewhere in the present study.

d. Further Explanations and Defenses of Physiocratic Theory. The fourth source of Du Pont's views on economic theory in the *Ephémérides* is his "Lettre de Mr H., à l'Auteur des *Ephémérides du Citoyen,* sur la marche naturelle des erreurs et des vérités."[43] It is more typical of Du Pont's polemics against non-physiocratic economic thought. He opened the letter with a discussion of man's capacity for holding right and wrong ideas, concluding that a man's wrong ideas about economic behavior may come not from his dishonesty in misrepresenting economic principles but in his imperfect understanding of them. To cite an example, he pointed to those who see an increase in wealth accompanying an increase of urban industrial activity and who conclude therefrom that the wages of urban workers are the cause of the creation of a market for increased production and consequent wealth. Then he explained the true physiocratic doctrine, which showed that shop workers in fact produced nothing. Having presented an example of wrongheaded thinking, he went on to conclude that thinking men who studied the science of physiocracy could not but become physiocrats themselves. This fourth source was typical of his attempts to convince others that physiocracy was the one true social science, but the tone of his argument in this "Lettre" reveals feelings of fatigue and disillusionment with his seemingly futile task of convincing the public of the veracity of physiocracy.

   e. His Commentary on Beccaria. The first four sources of Du Pont's economic theory in the *Ephémérides* were writings contributed by himself. In contrast, the fifth and final source consists of extensive footnotes to Beccaria's acceptance speech, discussed already in relation to the history of economic thought. As in his other writings since the final, November 1766, issue of the *Journal de l'Agriculture*, Du Pont expressed once again in his notes to Beccaria's speech his belief in the existence of natural law:

> It is not so for the Sciences expressly made for man, and which deal only with relations at our reach, and which have been destined by Providence to serve as rules for our behavior in all our actions, such as the Moral and Political Sciences.[44]

He went on to repeat his conviction that it was indeed possible to discern these underlying principles of moral and political science, because their fundamental principles—"le *droit*, le *devoir*, la *Justice essentielle* et l'intérêt *réciproque*"—reveal themselves to those men who seek them, or, sometimes, to those who do not. Thus, by studying these principles, he felt that it was possible to discern the logic of the system and from that set of relationships to predict the outcomes of moral and political behavior.

   f. Du Pont's Theory of Interest. The second revelation in Du Pont's notes to Beccaria's speech is that of his own view of the rate of interest. When Beccaria spoke of the desirability of low interest rates, Du Pont replied that low interest rates were usually a sign of unhealthy industry caused by a country's poor agriculture. He clarified his argument by adding that low levels of interest rates were determined not by legislation, but by a scarcity of money issues.[45] Having thus stated a direct relationship between the rate of interest and inflationary money issues, which in modern terms would hold only if he had specified that he meant the money, rather than the real, rate, he offered the caveat that high general levels of interest in a nation did not necessarily attest to the country's poverty or wealth, but that the general level was determined by what modern thinkers would call "exogenous parameters": customs, a nation's leisure-work preference ratio, and the degree of sophistication of money markets. Thus, to Du Pont, given a country's financial and social institutions, its level of interest was sensitive to the rate of inflation created by money issues, but not to edicts on usury issued by royal administrators. Unlike his analysis of the values of other commodities, which are determined by the *valeur vénale,* or market prices through competition, Du Pont failed to state here that the interest rate on money was similarly determined, although he did use the phrase, "le taux de l'intérêt."[46] Rather, he included market factors in the exogenous parameter of the money market's sophistication. It is too tempting to fault Du Pont for failure to realize the value of concentrating on the prices of money in physiocracy, an economic theory that emphasized the allocation of investment into agriculture, because physiocracy conceived of agricultural investment to be generated primarily from internal flows of funds: the net product. In a system where internally generated funds were automatically ploughed back into the operations, the external market rate of interest should have been of no concern. A man not unfamiliar with practical finance, Du Pont realized that an external rate of interest that appeared higher to the agricultural entrepreneur than his expected internal rate of return, would be tempted to lend out his money, rather than invest it in agriculture, which had, in fact (though not in appearance), the higher rate. Consequently, the government was wise, in Du Pont's view, not to raise the apparent market rate through money issues.

Although Du Pont only indirectly suggested the preceding mechanism in his marginal comments on Beccaria's speech, it is fair to say that his comments fit perfectly into the general physiocratic scheme and reveal a complete grasp on his part of the doctrine's analytical uses.

g. *The Function of Money*. The third and last specific of economic theory discussed by Du Pont in these notes to Beccaria's speech is the definition and function of money. Put briefly, his comments reveal the following views on money: *L'argent* (the French noun both for money and for silver) is not an unalterable absolute value by which all wealth may be measured. On the one hand, *argent* as money provides an "intermediate gauge" of equivalency between goods bought and sold. On the other hand, *argent* as a metal with several uses has a *valeur usuelle* that differs from a normal good's *valeur vénale* by the fact of its preciousness. Thus, an increasing scarcity of money (or silver) increases both its own *valeur usuelle* and, since it is an index of market value, the *valeur vénale* of goods. Obviously, then, Du Pont's use of the term *valeur vénale* corresponds to the modern monetary term *money value* rather than *real value*. In these footnotes, however, Du Pont did not state such a distinction; his interest lay in stating that the use of money as a standard of equivalency among goods gives rise to delayed payment, hence to credit, and to standards of accounting, which in turn makes possible the functions of public finance.[47]

5. *Du Pont on the Economic Theorist versus the Economic Activist*

The preceding review of those comments by Du Pont that add to an understanding of his interpretation of economic theory call for some clarification of his view of the distinction between the economic theorist and the public administrator, a distinction that defines the boundary he is about to cross over at this juncture in his career. The nature of this distinction is indicated by a passage that occurs near the end of his review of the work *Rétablissement de l'impôt dans son ordre naturel*.[48] In the passage quoted here Du Pont hinted at frustration with his self-imposed limitation as editor of the *Ephémérides* not to overstep the bounds of theoretical speculation into the area of policy recommendations, where he felt he spoke without authority:

> Our obligations [as editor of the *Ephémérides*] impose upon us the Law of discussing *principles* and their consequences; but we do not make plans. It is perhaps, at this point that the Learned, who are but that, must stop, and that the particular task of the *Administrators* begins. When the latter are *learned* themselves, it will not be difficult for them to form a temporary but wise arrangement, as close as possible under their circumstances to what would be strictly required by the principles with which they are familiar. It will not be difficult either, as long as they be somewhat *courageous*, to overcome obstacles.[49]

But while Du Pont was devising a scheme for a modus operandi between savants and administrators, his own mind was turning increasingly to the means by which reform could be achieved by the French government.

6. *Du Pont on the Role of Government*

Because the eighteenth century was an age that sought to find mankind's moral guides in the ordered composition of the physical universe, eighteenth-century man's ideas on any one segment of man's behavior, such as economics, were not self-contained, and are only with difficulty disentangled from the web of human and universal ties. Du Pont, as an avid absorber and elaborator of the ideas of his century, was no exception. This interrelatedness is particularly evident in Du Pont's views of the necessary role of enlightened government in establishing the conditions for operation of a physiocratic economic system. His comments on the enlightened use of sovereignty are widespread throughout his writings in the *Ephémérides*. They reveal a stronger conviction in the same view of enlightened government demonstrated in the inquiry into that same topic in his writings in the *Journal de l'Agricul-*

ture. Du Pont's position on enlightened government is important for an understanding of his views on public policy as expressed, or implied, in the *Ephémérides*: in Du Pont's own analysis of the answers to questions involving economic behavior, he saw the junction of economic activity, public policy, and social behavior in accordance with natural law, to lie in the enlightened ruler. Without enlightened government the economy could not operate perfectly in harmony with the laws of nature. Accordingly, his views on government as expressed in the *Journal de l'Agriculture* and reaffirmed in the *Ephémérides du Citoyen* constitute a necessary background for an inquiry into his positions on policy issues, which are to be discussed below, beginning with his role in the debate over free trade in grains.

7. *Factors Influencing Du Pont's Laissez-Faire Position*

The physiocratic position of free trade in general emanated from two sources: the practical influence of the administrator Gournay and the realization by Quesnay that government's assurance of free trade in general would assure free trade in grains in particular, a necessary condition for the operation of physiocratic principles in the economy. Du Pont's respect for the importance of free trade was discussed in relation to his writings in the *Journal de l'Agriculture* during 1765–66. As editor of the *Ephémérides*, two years later, Du Pont was matured in his position, experienced in his explicative ability, and, consequently during this period, contributed some of the strongest and best organized arguments for liberalized grain trade to come from the physiocratic school.

Another force that shaped Du Pont's comments on free trade in this period, in addition to physiocratic economic theory, is seen on the political level. One of the few times the physiocrats were successful in having their policy proposals implemented by the government was with the liberalization of trade that occurred, domestically, with the edict of May 1763 and, internationally, with the edict of June 1764 permitting free exportation. The loosening of this trade, however, coincided with three successive poor harvests, which caused prices to rise sharply, precipitated sporadic shortages, and panicked the population. Du Pont's writings of the period 1768–72 on trade in grains constituted an attempt to defend the free-trade position in light of the general disenchantment with the apparent result of free trade of grain in general.

8. Du Pont on Free Trade in Grains

Of the several writings on the grain trade by Du Pont in the *Ephémérides*, the two most comprehensive were published separately as well: *Objections et réponses sur commerce des grains et des farines*[50] and *Observations sur les effets de la liberté du commerce des grains, et sur ceux des prohibitions.*[51] The first work, *Objections*, reviewed the justification for free trade in grain in physiocratic doctrine, described its actual liberalization in 1763 and 1764, catalogued the reasons for political opposition to it on the part of the common man as well as the grain trader, and discussed the three years of poor harvests. Du Pont characterized the coincidence of the edicts with the poor growing conditions as an "extraordinary" situation. He went on to chronicle the flaunting of free-trade laws at local levels by officials in response to the fears of the people, and their ultimate pardon by the national government, which made a dead letter of the edicts. After cataloging the possible objections anticipated by Du Pont on the part of doubters of free trade and his answers to them, he arrived at his final position on the controversy: that many wise and correct men still favored free trade, realizing that poor harvests—not free trade—brought about the grain shortages, and that their views would triumph in the end.

The other book, *Observations*, published the following year, attests to the negligible impact on the public of the first work. Apparently, with the mistaken belief that if one were to shout loudly enough he would eventually convince a disinterested public, Du Pont augmented his arguments of the previous publication with statistical series on grain prices from 1616 to 1741. In the separate publication in book form of *Observations*, he stated that the source of his statistics was tables published at the end of the work. There are, in fact, no such tables at the conclusion of, or anywhere else in, the book. A comparison with the text as it was printed in installment form in volume 6 of the 1770 *Ephémérides* reveals that he did not have space to include them in that monthly edition, but he did include them in volume 7. He used the statistics to point out that during the 125 years in question grain prices were in fact higher for over 60 individual years than they were during the recent period of free trade, in spite of poor harvests in that period. But, besides the fact that his tables are missing from their stated place in the serialized installments and absent altogether from the separate publication in book form, the reader's confidence is eroded by another use of the figures by Du Pont. He sought to prove that free trade during the period actually caused an increase in harvests over what they would have been under restrictions, in the following manner: He assumed that to achieve the net increase in grain production in 1770 over what it was the previous year, the total increase must have resulted either from breaking of new fields for planting or from improvements to existing fields. He then halved this figure, representing the increase for 1770 over 1769, and assumed that the half represented an amount of increase in grain production during 1769 over 1768 attributable to investments in existing or new fields. He halved that figure in turn and so on back to 1763. Then, he summed the totals for each year, which had been obtained by halving each year's increase, and arrived at a total of grain production for the period 1764–70, which he asserted he had thereby demonstrated as having originated from such agricultural investment. Thus, by asserting the premise that all agricultural investment comes from free trade, he "proved", to his own satisfaction at least, that free trade created a significant amount of output during this period that would not have occurred in the absence of free trade. All this conclusion is based on two single observations, grain output in 1769 and 1770, and on several assumptions that do not stand up to careful scrutiny: his premises are faulty in his assumption that any increase in capital investment was inevitably the result exclusively of the liberalization of trade, although free trade could have indeed been a contributing factor to any increase in capital investment. Also, the increases in grain production need not have been related to capital investments at all. Happily for his argument, the amount of increased grain production he arrived at exceeded the amount of grain exported from France during this period, enabling him to state that free trade gave France more grain (and more foreign exchange) than in its absence, even in this period of poor harvests. His statistics, however, are hardly such as to convince skeptics, especially in an age when statistics were not appreciated. Consequently, even those readers favorably disposed toward his position might well be convinced otherwise if they were to study the logic and seek the source of the computations supporting his assumptions in this work. All too often Du Pont used questionable statistics to bolster his arguments. However, he was hardly alone in this habit during his century.

Several shorter works that appeared only in the *Ephémérides* repeated the arguments of these two books.[52]

Thus, in the *Ephémérides* (including the two works published separately as well) Du Pont's arguments for free trade did not alter in concept from his earlier positions. However, they were applied differently: they were shrouded in murky historical comparisons and subjective figures in his effort to marshal every possible debating point against the forces threatening to revoke the free-grain-trade edicts. More positively, these writings reveal that Du Pont used physiocratic theory to argue logically for free-trade policies that, according to the theory, would improve agriculture and thus the economy. In this sense, there is little doubt that the sheer volume of Du Pont's applications of theory to policy questions, even at this early stage in his career, ranks him as one of the earliest forerunners of that race of intellectuals of sufficient strength of conviction to advocate positive economic policy recommendations whose only support was found in the theory on which they were based.

9. *Three Other Important Themes in His Contributions to the Ephémérides*

Of the three remaining themes of importance in Du Pont's *Ephémérides* writings, that is, of transport, monopoly, and slavery, the first two are important topics of policy debate for the physiocratic school, though they receive somewhat lesser emphasis in their arguments than does free trade in grain. Slavery itself was not an important topic to the physiocrats, although Du Pont anticipated its importance in his writings in the *Ephémérides*.

a. Transportation. The subject of transportation received more attention from Du Pont than from any other physiocrat. His writings on transportation during 1767–72 deal almost exclusively with roads and canals, hardly mentioning international shipping, and omitting the coasting trade altogether. During this period his major work on transportation was *De l'administration des chemins* (Paris, 1767), which appeared first as a separate publication and was subsequently serialized in the *Ephémérides*. Other noteworthy articles of his on transport in the *Ephémérides* include a running debate between Du Pont and "M. N***, ingénieur des Ponts et Chaussées," and his review of *Soirées Helvétiennes.*[53]

De l'administration des chemins is a well-laid-out argument in favor of altering public policy on building and maintaining roads and canals. The suggested changes would both eliminate unpopular and undependable methods used at the time and would allocate costs in accordance with physiocratic doctrine. The extension of physiocratic doctrine to an analysis of the transport system is due almost exclusively to Du Pont's writings on this subject, primarily found in this work. His suggestions include alternatives that would be more popular politically than the strictly physiocratic solutions he offered as a first preference. These "second best" solutions would still constitute an improvement over the existing system.

Under the *ancien régime* roads were built and maintained using labor conscripted through the infamous *corvée*. Under the system of the *corvée* rural laborers were forced to contribute a certain number of days, the exact number depending on local need, to work on the roads in their parishes. Work generally took place during the warm season and took men from their normal work in the fields. No pay was given. Because roads varied in their conditions from place to place, time spent in their upkeep varied as well. Consequently, these arbitrary work levies were unpopular. Moreover, they disrupted agricultural production, which made them antithetical to physiocratic ends. Although such labor was free to the state, other costs of road upkeep were met by user taxes, and, if these did not suffice, the difference was made up from the general revenues.

Du Pont's analysis of the expenses and benefits of the road system was clear-cut: roads benefited travelers and shipments of finished goods, to be sure; but their heaviest and most important uses were for the armies and for the shipment of agricultural products from farm to market and mill. The better the roads, the better the defense of the country; but, more important, the better the roads, the less expensive would be transport costs for primary producers. In accordance with physiocratic theory, net product, the exclusive source of wealth for the entire economy, was the difference between agricultural costs and the revenues obtained from selling the goods to middlemen, (e.g., grain merchants), to millers, or to the general public. Du Pont, as the only physiocrat to discuss transport in depth, felt that transport costs were a regrettable though necessary expense that ate directly into the amount of the net product over and above the costs of production. Thus, better roads meant that an agriculturalist might be able to sell directly in town markets otherwise beyond a day's round trip; or, if he sold to millers, they would put him within reach of a larger selection of mills, bringing millers and grain merchants under greater competitive pressure and thus increasing the amount of net product returned to the agriculturalist all the more. Du Pont interpreted the *corvée* system as both lowering the productivity of agricultural labor and retarding the efficiency of the transport system: men who worked under duress at a task without compensation generally produce poorer roads, which increase transport costs.

Consequently, Du Pont proposed that the *corvée* be replaced with military labor: soldiers' strength could be improved through such strenuous exercise, and they could be sent on maneuvers in the vicinity of the roads and works to be repaired, familiarizing them with a broader range of the country they might one day defend. Moreover, in peacetime soldiers constituted an obvious source of potential labor, unlike that of peasant laborers. Du Pont reasoned that in theory landlords should pay all remaining costs of the transport system, but that in reality such a proposal was sure to be politically objectionable. Accordingly, he argued that a provisionally acceptable alternative would consist of maintaining existing user taxes coupled with the proviso that all road construction and maintenance costs exceeding road tax revenues be assessed from landlords. His reasoning was that it was the landlords (or, as in the case discussed previously, the cultivators) who benefited from increased net product, and it was they who should pay at least the additional costs. As usual, Du Pont's work cataloged possible objections to his proposals and his rebuttals. Du Pont had at his disposal, however, the results obtained by Turgot, who, as intendant of the Generality of Limoges in the 1760s, had actually replaced the *corvée* within his jurisdiction by offering to reimburse parishes from the general taxes if they would move to raise funds within their individual parishes for replacing the *corvée*. Almost all agreed. He then covered the costs of such road expenses by assessing all parishes a proportionate increase in general taxes. The net result was that road costs were distributed evenly through a system agreed to voluntarily at the local parish level. Du Pont's detailed description of the administrative steps taken by Turgot attest to a growing favorable impression on Du Pont's part with the possibility of actually instituting reform rather than continuing to propagandize the theory of physiocracy.

His other writings in the *Ephémérides* on transport are detailed in their arguments, as with the Ingénieur des Ponts et Chaussées, as are his comments on Simon Nicholas Henri Linguet's *Canaux navigables* and the travelogue *Soirées Hel-*

vétiennes. Presenting the arguments in the works would add nothing to the interpretation of Du Pont's views on transport in general during the period. There are, however, some points worthy of special note.

When challenged on the expenses of the *corvée* by the engineer, who may have been a real figure or a fictional correspondent invented by Du Pont, he answered using quantitative data recalled casually from his own experiences:

> I have seen that in Countries that are very agricultural the amount of work yielded annually by a plough and its operator can assure the subsistence of about *seventy-six* persons; and a considerably higher number of animals, whose strength facilitates trade between us, and the transportation of things which are necessary; whose flesh and milk also help us to subsist; whose leather and wool are the composition of our clothing; whose fat gives us light; whose horns and bones even are used in a thousand useful ways.
>
> This very simple observation which should escape no one has led me to conceive of the importance of schedules for ploughmen, and the danger of distracting them from their work which is so profitable, better said yet, so indispensable to Society.
>
> Upon taking a closer look, I saw that the number of days under the system of the *corvée* varied a great deal in the various Provinces, because of the number of roads opened, also because of the need for repairs which are always greater on roads opened under the system of the *corvée*, on the premise that these roads have little or no *solidity*, as we *agreed* with Monsieur N.**** and his friend. These *corvées* usually spread over a period of 10 *days* up to 20 days for laborers, *who don't do one tenth of the work.* . . . The vehicles are used about the same number of days. It can be estimated at twelve days more or less. During these same twelve days, a ploughman, even poorly equipped, would have ploughed four acres *three* times. Without serving the *corvée*, he therefore could have been ahead in his farm by as much as twelve acres, or four acres done three times. But these four acres, yielding *six septiers* more or less, without counting the seed, would have yielded *twenty four septiers* of wheat which, at the rate of eighteen *livres* per septier, the ordinary price on the free market, would have been worth *four hundred thirty two livres*; which, spread over twelve days, represents an actual loss of *thirty-six livres* per day for the Ploughman, Owner, the Nation, and for the human species in general.[54]

From these and other casual figures Du Pont goes on to build a detailed table showing the losses for agriculture attributable to the *corvée*.

This example serves to underline the point that Du Pont applied data most sensibly to an accounting framework incorporating both the external and the internal costs of a project to be financed publicly, but his employment of social accounting methods is faulty both in its usefulness as a tool for correct prediction and as a means of convincing others, by data-gathering techniques that would have horrified modern-day statisticians.

b. Monopoly. Another point that arises in his comments throughout articles in the *Ephémérides* is one that may serve as a bridge between the themes of transport, concluded herein, and of monopoly, which follows. In his "Observations sur une Lettre de M. le Comte de *** à l'auteur des *Ephémérides* sur les canaux de navigation," Du Pont criticized the methods by which French canals were built and operated.[55] Several lines were deleted from this article by government censors in this, one of the last volumes before royal proscription of the publication. In the copy used for the present study, however, Du Pont has written in the censored lines, which reveal a strong attack on the sovereign for permitting private construction and operation of canals at what Du Pont considered extortionate toll rates imposed by government-sanctioned private monopolies. He proposed that the first and best method was to construct and operate canals with public funds; the second best method was to copy the Spanish method of building with public funds and operating them privately; he considered private entrepreneurship in public works to be a poor third alternative. All this analysis underlying his arrival at these points was based on his habit of attempting to measure both external and internal costs of operation, a habit imbued within him by the necessity of measuring the impact of the net product, which played an analytical role in his views on transport and other policy issues, including monopoly.

Perhaps Du Pont's best known work is his attack on the publicly sanctioned monopoly of the Compagnie des Indes. His incisive analysis contributed to the public's understanding of the amplitude of the graft going to its officers and the cost it incurred to the government and to the public, and may have contributed profoundly to the eventual control and limitation of private monopolies during the Revolution.

Du commerce et de la Compagnie des Indes (Paris, 1769) is a veritable tour de force. It attacks monopoly with a three-fold assault on the government-sanctioned Compagnie des Indes, which had until 1767 the exclusive rights to conduct French trade with Asia, Africa, and America. From one side Du Pont attacked the concept of monopoly as a diversion of resources away from better uses in the national economy; this attack was supported by strict physiocratic interpretation. From another side he told the story of the company's origins, its involvement in the financial schemes of John Law, and its ultimate refuge in the arms of the government whose insolvency it had nearly precipitated. His history emphasized its poor management and naive shareholders. Building on the strength of his physiocratic and historical assaults, Du Pont described the modifications made by the government in 1767 in limiting the monopoly power of the heavily indebted company, analyzed the modifications as hardly less inimical than the former arrangements, and pushed for the annihilation of the company and all monopolies, pointing to alternatives for the nation that could be agreed upon even by nonphysiocrats as salutary improvements.

His review of the history of the company's trade, administration, and finances appears to be well balanced and reveals a keen understanding on his part of the financial intrigue surrounding the company, the government, and the private underwriters of the company. But discussion of these details is not within the purpose of the present study.

Du Pont pushed the physiocratic analysis of the impact of the company's monopoly position on the economy to breathtakingly daring, though quite logical, conclusions by finding that it would cost the nation as a whole less in resources to purchase all goods, which were presently imported by the company, exclusively from other European countries that carried on such trade. Such an arrangement would enable the nation to employ investments presently required for the company, its colonies, and attendant wars (or which might be employed by other French traders if they were encouraged to enter the trade in competition with, or in place of, the monopoly) to be better employed in domestic capital formation and maintenance that would, under a physiocratic system, be equivalent to investment in agriculture in order to increase the *produit net* and thus the wealth of the nation. The level of sophistication reveals itself further in his observation that other European nations, having received French currency in exchange for goods they imported from the Indies, could use it only for purchases from France in turn, as the Hindoos, Africans, and American Redmen would have no use for French currency.

Finally, his recommendations included the sale by France of the company's trading posts to other nations, the proceeds to be used to retire debts of the company. The colonies operated by the company, the Isle de France and the Isle de Bourbon, were to be given the freedom to trade with France and other countries and thereby flourish. The French people would thus be relieved of the burden of paying for the company's excessive costs through high prices, and the net product would be able to increase through investment in agriculture instead of being diverted to the luxury spending of the wealthy monopolists.

The importance of this work lies in the point that although physiocratic doctrine was one of the vehicles that carried Du Pont to his analysis of monopoly and suggestions for alternative economic arrangements, acceptance of physiocracy was not a necessary condition to acceptance of the bulk of his analysis or of any of his policy recommendations by an observer raised, for instance, in the modern economic tradition. The modern observer can agree with every point through and including the release of investment for other uses than inefficient private monopoly. He parts company only on the question of whether that investment is necessarily likely to bring the highest social return when put into agriculture. A sophisticated financier might argue for efficient modern corporations to invest in the foreign trade; a socialist might insist on government channeling of funds into whatever sector of the economy was indicated by modern social accounting methods. But the physiocratic doctrine proved itself to be the first "economic science," and a functional one indeed, in its ability to suggest correct policy solutions, as in the case of Du Pont's analysis of the monopolistic Compagnie des Indes.[56]

c. Slavery. The final them culled from Du Pont's contributions to the *Ephémérides* and selected for exposure here is that of slavery. Although the question of slavery was not an important topic to physiocratic doctrine nor an important policy issued until the 1780s and 1790s, there appears in one of Du Pont's articles in the *Ephémérides* a moving appeal for the abolition of slavery. It consists of a rudimentary accounting of the costs of slavery as compared to the alternative costs of free labor; he concludes that free labor is more efficient and less expensive.

The fact that Du Pont's analysis of slavery is buried in the third installment of his review of a long narrative poem entitled "Saisons" has rendered it less than an obvious candidate for reverence by posterity. His analysis of the poem was serialized in the *Ephémérides* and also appeared separately. It is his review of the third part, entitled "Ziméo," that contains his dissertation on the economics of slavery.[57]

He stated that his calculations were inspired by a suggestion of Benjamin Franklin's in 1751.[58] Du Pont took issue with the assertion that the only costs of slaves were their purchase price and food and that these costs, prorated, were less than the costs of equivalent free labor.[59] Du Pont then detailed the expense of slave labor, as he saw it, and compared it with that of free labor. As in other cases, his statistics must be taken with some reservation because of their basis in hearsay and other unspecified sources.

Du Pont's economic argument for the abolition of slavery, published in 1771, contained the following approach. First he estimated the purchase price of a slave and his expected useful life span. Next he calculated from this a prorated yearly "rent." To this prorated annual cost, or depreciation, he added estimated annual costs for food, shelter, and clothing, and losses from runaways and from slave revolts. From this he concluded, after ten pages of explanation and calculation, that the total cost of a slave for one year was 420 French *livres*.[60] Du Pont went on to invite the reader to compare this amount with the annual earnings of a French agricultural laborer, concluding that French workers would willingly and happily work for less than the annual cost of slaves.[61]

Du Pont is to be commended for his acting under the inspiration of Franklin, physiocracy, and his moral imagination, to attempt to compare the costs of slave and free labor. However, it must be pointed out that his comparison is based on rather arbitrary estimates, for example, that the average life of a slave once delivered to the New World is ten years and that of a Negro overseer, fifteen. Moreover, his failure to mention the fact that the children of slaves become property of the slave holders casts further suspicion on the plausibility of his estimates. Further, in the section following the one summarized above, Du Pont jumps from his conclusion that free labor in France is cheaper than slave labor in the French Indies to the quite different, and unsupported, statement that white labor is superior to black slave labor in the sugar fields of the West Indies. His argument that a free man works harder than a slave might be acceptable, but his comment:

> the white European man, when he exercises his body, is one of the most lively and robust species that the heavens have placed on this earth. In this regard he comes before the negro, the asiatic Indian, and the natives of America, even in their own climate[62]

seems to be as unsupportable in this century as it was when he wrote it. His motive, however, was to build a base from which to argue for the replacement of black labor with white in the

Indies and removal of sugar cultivation from the Caribbean to West Africa where it grows naturally. Black Africans were then to be encouraged to cultivate and harvest the sugar native to their environment and to trade it to Europeans in return for goods. Under such a system sugar would grow more abundantly, Negroes would be free, and, moreover, they would be enjoying the fruits of their own physiocratic economy. The islands of the Indies would be planted with crops to which they are better suited than sugar and operated with free white labor.

Thus, Du Pont's analysis of slavery combines his own imaginative powers in creating plausible statistics to support an argument for the abolition of slavery that, although coinciding with Du Pont's own concept of moral justice, is based strictly on physiocratic principles. In short, Du Pont encouraged his reader to be convinced of the wrongness of slavery either by the persuasion of Du Pont's (imaginary) statistical example, by the force of his logical argument from physiocratic assumptions, or by Du Pont's romantic appeal to the reader's sense of moral propriety.

C. Summary and Conclusions Concerning His Writings, 1768–72

Perhaps one of the most annoying traits in Du Pont's writings during the period 1768–72 was his habit of inventing, or of manhandling already collected, statistics to prove his points. Particularly in his use of historical series on grain production, Du Pont seems more to be proving, on the basis of physiocratic theory, the correctness of his (at best) plausible assumptions concerning the relation between grain production and free trade, than to be proving the correctness of physiocratic theory on the basis of data. Indeed, in interpreting Du Pont's writings, it should be recalled that the direction of his logic flows from the assumption of the correctness of physiocratic theory to its policy conclusions. Appeals by him to existing or historical conditions, including statistical series, only serve as secondary confirmation of the correctness of his policy conclusions.

Therefore, the modern "positive economist" can only disagree with Du Pont's use of the deductive method. If the modern economist were to judge physiocratic theory by the "correctness" of its policy recommendations, he would have to mark it very highly for its predictive accuracy, as employed by Du Pont, in an eighteenth-century agrarian state. He can find fault with Du Pont's correctly employing the tool of logic he has chosen to use, only in the rarest of cases.

Admittedly, Du Pont was no theoretical genius, or if he was, his genius lay dormant beneath his veneration for Quesnay's own genius. Indeed, no physiocrat besides Quesnay, with the partial exception of Mercier de la Rivière, can be credited with adaptation of physiocratic theory sufficiently to render it an engine of analysis until years later.

Du Pont's talents for logical thinking and clarity of expression do stand out in his works from this period. Equally evident, however, is his growing frustration with his inability to change men's minds or the economy through his expository talents.

But the most outstanding facet of his writings in this five-year period is his aggressive application of physiocratic theory to solid policy issues of the day, notably free trade in grains, transportation, monopoly, and slavery. In these policy writings, which include some of his best books and articles, it appears that Du Pont wrote from strong personal conviction as well as from physiocratic premises. Although Quesnay had encouraged Du Pont's earlier studies of the grain trade, his works on this subject in 1768–72, as well as his writings on roads and canals, his piercing attack on monopoly, and his castigation of slavery, all leave the impression that Du Pont would have held very similar views had he never heard of physiocracy. Whether Du Pont would have had the opportunity to express his views if he had never heard of physiocracy is a different question and one in the realm of speculation. Put differently, his strongest policy arguments, although supported by and in agreement with physiocratic theory, are not in fact dependent on that theory. Physiocracy was the vehicle that led Du Pont to state his positions on economic policy issues, but it would also be, in subsequent·years, a hindrance in government circles to his successful implementation of that policy.

All in all, Du Pont's writings of this period are most outstanding for his use of physiocracy to analyze problems and suggest policy solutions to improve efficiency and equity in the economy. If Mercier de la Rivière is the theoretician who best refined Quesnay's ideas in the abstract, then Du Pont de Nemours must be credited as the one physiocrat who went furthest in applying physiocracy to the problems of his economy during this period.

Notes to Chapter V

1. DPDN, *De l'origine et des progrès d'une science nouvelle*, ed. A. Dubois (Paris: Geuthner, 1910).

2. For the lack of acceptance of Mercier's book see Dubois's "Notice," in ibid., pp. v–ix.

3. Ibid., p. 10.

4. Ibid., p. 11.

5. Ibid., p. 24.

6. *Ephémérides* 1 (1769): xi–li; 2 (1769): iii–xlviii; 3 (1769): iii–xix; 4 (1769): iii–xxiv; 5 (1769): iii–lvii; 6 (1769): 5–52; 8 (1769): 5–38; and 9 (1769): 5–78. Beginning with vol. 4, Schelle wrongly refers to the fourth installment as the "troisième partie" and so on, having missed the installment in either vols. 2 or 3.

7. *Ephémérides* 2 (1768): 191–202.

8. DPDN, footnotes to Beccaria's "Discours d'ouverture de la chaire d'économie politique de Milan," *Ephémérides* 6 (1769): 53–152.

9. *Ephémérides* 1 (1769): xi–xii.

10. Ibid., pp. xii–xiii.

11. Jean François Melon and [Charles de Ferrare?] Dutot were both in the administration of John Law. Melon's *Essai politique sur le commerce* (1734), which advocated government policies to stimulate business, was answered by Dutot's *Réflexions politiques sur les finances et le commerce* (1738), which clearly demonstrated the effect of increased government spending on the general level of prices.

12. Cf. Joan McDonald's *Rousseau and the French Revolution, 1762–1791*, University of London Historical Studies, no. 17 (London: The Athlone Press of the University of London, 1965).

13. *Ephémérides* 1 (1769): xiv.

14. Ibid., pp. xli–xlii.

15. Ibid., pp. vii–viii. Du Pont's italics.
16. Ibid., 2 (1769): xxvii.
17. Ibid., 3 (1769): xxiv.
18. Ibid., 9 (1769): 67.
19. Ibid., pp. 67–68.
20. Ibid.
21. Ibid.
22. Ibid., pp. 69–70.
23. Ibid., 2 (1768): 191–202.
24. Ibid., 6 (1769): 104.
25. Ibid., p. 141, n22.
26. Ibid., pp. 141–44.
27. "The immortal MONTESQUIEU will always be entitled to men's gratitude for having powerfully roused them to turn to the economic Studies. Their administration . . . will always be indebted to him. But he wanted to establish Governments on moral affections, on virtue, on moderation, on honor, on fear. He was completely unaware that the fundamental Laws of the social Order were physical Laws, and drawn from nature and the needs of man. . . . He misunderstood the Laws of the reproduction of provisions and that of the freedom of exchange, so directly dependent upon that of *property*. He thoroughly researched whether there were Nations to whom trade was disadvantageous: And he decided in favor of the affirmative" (ibid., pp. 143–44, n23).
28. Ibid., p. 146, n23.
29. Ibid., pp. 146–49, n23.
30. Joseph Schumpeter, *History of Economic Analysis* (New York: Oxford University Press, 1954), p. 245.
31. *Ephémérides* 11 (1769): 193–247. Referred to by Schelle as "Analyse des 'Dialogues' de Galiani."
32. Ibid., 9 (1771): 59–114.
33. Ibid., 7 (1771): 50–70.
34. Ibid., 2 (1770): 5–15.
35. Ibid., 6 (1769): 57–152.
36. Ibid., Supplement to 11 (1769), p. 194.
37. Edited and published by the Société d'économie politique de Berne, n.d.
38. Ronald L. Meek, in his "Preface to the Translations" of his very useful work (*The Economics of Physiocracy: Essays and Translations* [Cambridge, Mass.: Harvard University Press, 1963]), helpfully says of *avances annuelles* and *avances primitives:*

> These I have translated as "annual advances" and "original advances." There is of course a strong temptation to translate them as "working capital" and "fixed capital," which are perhaps the nearest modern equivalents, but the parallel is not quite as exact as such a translation would imply. [P. 41]

Meek also notes that "the 'original advances' comprise all the expenses incurred by the agricultural entrepreneurs prior to their receipt of the returns from the first harvest. They thus consist mainly, but not exclusively, of expenditure on fixed capital" (ibid., p. 274, n5).
39. *Ephémérides* 9 (1771): 78–79. Du Pont's italics.
40. Ibid., p. 98. Du Pont's italics.
41. DPDN, "Fragment d'un ouvrage intitulé: *Elements de philosophie économique* par l'auteur des *Ephémérides,*" *Ephémérides* 7 (1771); 50–70.
42. Cf. selections from Quesnay's writings translated in Meek, *Economics of Physiocracy*, particularly the extracts from "Corn" (pp. 72–87) and "Men" (pp. 88–101).
43. *Ephémérides* 2 (1770): 6–15.

44. DPDN, footnotes to Beccaria's "Discours d'ouverture de la chaire d'économie politique de Milan," *Ephémérides* 6 (1769): 65–66, n5.

45. Ibid., p. 69, n6.

46. Ibid., p. 70, n6.

47. Ibid., p. 91, n8.

48. DPDN, "Analyse du *Rétablissement de l'impôt dans son ordre naturel*," *Ephémérides* 8 (1769): 136–63.

49. Ibid., pp. 162–63. Du Pont's italics.

50. DPDN, *Objections et réponses sur commerce des grains et des farines* (Amsterdam[?] and found in Paris, 1769).

51. DPDN, *Observations sur les effets de la liberté du commerce des grains, et sur ceux des prohibitions* (Basel[?] and found in Paris, 1770).

52. DPDN (all articles in *Ephémérides*), "Lettre de M. H. à l'auteur des *Ephémérides*: Sage arrêt du Parlement de Paris," 8 (1768): 193–97; "Histoire abrégée des grains, depuis cent ans jusqu'à nos jours," 1 (1769):37–69; Analyse des "Dialogues de Galiani," *Supplement* to 9 (1769), pp. 193–247; "Grande et coûteuse charité, très dangereuse parce qu'elle est mal entendu en un point," 4 (1770): 186–201; "Comparaison entre le prix de l'argent et celui des denrées dans le siècle dernier et dans le commencement de celui-ci," 7 (1770): 43–76; "Observations sur l'état des défrichements publié du volume précédent," 8 (1770): 41–52; and "Observations sur l'effet du dérangement des saisons depuis cinq années," 1 (1771): 68–88.

53. Other articles containing comments by Du Pont, all in *Ephémérides*, on transportation are "Analyse de 'Canaux Navigables' par Linguet," serialized; "Des divers moyens que l'on peut employer dans l'état actuel de l'Europe, pour procurer la construction et l'entretien des grands canaux de navigation," 10 (1771): 43–61; and "Observations sur une 'Lettre de M. le comte de *** à l'auteur des *Ephémérides* sur les canaux de navigation," 11 (1771): 44–73.

54. DPDN, "Réponse à la lettre de M. H., ingénieur des Ponts et Chaussées, sur l'ouvrage de M. Du Pont qui a pour titre: *De l'administration des chemins*," *Ephémérides* 8 (1769): 99–101. Du Pont's italics.

55. *Ephémérides* 11 (1771): 44–73.

56. The only other work by Du Pont in the *Ephémérides* on monopoly is his "Révolution dans le commerce de l'Inde," 7 (1769): 276–82.

57. *Ephémérides* 6 (1771): 163–246.

58. Ibid., p. 178.

59. Ibid., p. 224.

60. Specifically, 630 *liv.*, *argent des Isles* or 420 *liv.*, *argent de France*.

61. For the entire text discussed here see *Ephémérides* 6 (1771):225–36

62. Ibid., p. 237.

VI.

Economic Writings during the Period 1773–1807

In the broad mid-period of Du Pont's economic writings, between 1773 and 1807, Du Pont largely neglected his economic theory, but he did apply his economic thought to policy problems and even camouflaged the physiocratic nature of that theory to make his policy recommendations palatable to the various administrations he served.

The primary purpose of this section is to document the fact that Du Pont contributed little new to his economic thought during this period. The secondary purpose is to assess the degree to which Du Pont applied his physiocratic economic theory to the policy problems he dealt with. To this purpose it will be useful to note the contents of those writings by Du Pont that are at least partially of economic substance. The majority of Du Pont's political and administrative writings of this period reflect his activities in various administrative and legislative positions before and during the Revolution and inevitably touch upon or go deeply into questions of an economic nature at the policy level.

A. Du Pont's Writings, 1773–83

During the two years (1773 and 1774) following the proscription of the *Ephémérides*, Du Pont continued to write reports on social, cultural, and economic matters that he sent to the Grand Duke (i.e., Margrave) Carl Friedrich of Baden and to the grand duke's son. This correspondence, much of which was published in Germany in 1892,[1] is an extension of Du Pont's ideas and attitudes as expressed in the *Ephémérides*.

The grand duke himself was involved in modernizing his extensive land holdings in the physiocratic image and was at the same time the political head of the independent Principality of Baden. Du Pont was asked to instruct the young prince, who one day would inherit the grand duke's lands and responsibilities. Consequently, Du Pont's advice to the grand duke and to his son contained a strong dose of economic policy recommendations clearly tied to physiocratic economic thought. This continuing correspondence is interesting for the light it sheds on Du Pont's *Table raisonnée des principes de l'économie politique*, his work on economic curves, his *Mémoire sur les municipalités*, prepared during 1775 and 1776 in Turgot's administration, and other topics down through 1783. These subjects will be treated chronologically.

Although Du Pont prided himself on being a disciple of Quesnay and a proponent of laissez-faire economics, his perception of himself did not keep him from recommending a strong role for government in those areas of social responsibility that would not be carried out efficiently by a freely operating market economy. His views on government's proper responsibilities and duties toward beggars, toward debtors, and toward the poor in general were outlined in essays he prepared in 1773.

1. Beggars, Debtors, and the Poor

In a letter to the grand duke's son[2] Du Pont expressed his opinion of a new law concerning the imprisonment of persons for nonpayment of just debts. Du Pont reviewed the historical necessity throughout Europe for imprisoning debtors: as commercial activities grew during the Middle Ages, Frenchmen were likely to avoid paying their debts in the absence of strongly enforced laws to the contrary. Du Pont agreed that the government had a necessary and proper role to play in enforcing laws that upheld the institutional framework of free trade, including the institution of credit. He recognized a necessary balance between government's enforcement of commercial laws on the one hand and a freedom from government intrusion into areas of individual liberty and private property rights on the other. Thus, he warned the margrave's son against laws such as one under consideration at the time in France to permit law officers to drag debtors even from their conjugal bed. Too strong a law would offer temptation to unscrupulous officials to blackmail persons by means of false bills of credit. Du Pont suggested that a more just law would imprison only fraudulent debtors. As for other debtors, because they borrowed property for a certain time and at a certain price, their own property should be attached if they are unable to return what they borrowed. Even a fraudulent debtor cannot repay his debt if he is kept from working. Therefore, Du Pont concluded, he should be released from prison on probation to work off his debt.

In another letter[3] Du Pont commented on the government's method of coping with the armies of beggars in France during the period. Although, Du Pont wrote, poverty was hardly a vice, he observed that the government treated beggars like criminals when they failed to pay the taxes that travelers, penniless or otherwise, were required to pay in their journeys. The government farmed out to companies the right to corral such beggars into workhouses where, Du Pont noted, living conditions ranged from bad to horrible. In Lyons, Du Pont wrote, beggars were used like slave labor in spinning mills. In Paris they at least worked at making useful objects for their own care. It would be better, he suggested, for the beggars to be formed into armies to work in the countryside on public works and roads.

Du Pont reasoned from the position that society needed to have carried out as many public works as possible for the least expense.[4] Therefore, beggars should be conscripted into the regular army, which would itself be utilized to improve works, which in turn would increase the net product of agriculture and pave the way for the replacement of all those taxes that were the cause of poverty with a single tax on the net product. Then, ultimately, there would be no more beggars.[5]

As for the poor in general, Du Pont was moved by the burning of that infamous poor house, the Hôtel de Dieu, in Paris to comment[6] that although government has a responsibility as a last-resort source of aid to the poor, the actual administrations that dealt with them were filled with incompetent and lazy persons. Yet, incompetence on the part of administrators was one thing to Du Pont; incompetence in the preparation of laws and programs to care for the poor was another. He outlined several suggestions for the rebuilding of the Hôtel de Dieu and the restructuring of the system of care for the poor.[7]

2. Government's Welfare Responsibilities

From Du Pont's comments in these letters on beggars, the poor in general, and debtors, it is clear that Du Pont believed in careful balance between, on the one hand, government's responsibilities in those areas where the free market failed to fulfill social needs (that is, in public works, aid to the poor, and maintenance of economic institutions that supported free markets) and, on the other hand, government's responsibility not to interfere with orderly market operations or the political institutions of liberty and private property that make such institutions possible. It is also clear that in his concept of political economy Du Pont did not differentiate between government activity and economic activity, but rather saw them as two necessary counterparts of one system. This system was best exemplified by the next work of his to be investigated.

3. Table Raisonnée des Principes de l'Economie Politique

The culmination of Du Pont's counseling activities for the ruling family of Baden was his preparation, at the grand duke's request, of a *Table raisonnée des principes de l'économie politique*,[8] which is in stature to Du Pont's system of thought what the *tableau économique* is to Quesnay's sytem. This remarkable table expresses Du Pont's view of the interrelationships of the political, social, legal, and economic facts of mankind's existence in nature. The 7,000-word document is the culmination of Du Pont's economic thought as developed in defense of physiocracy between 1763 and 1772 and in his efforts to convey to the margrave and the prince a unified theory to be used as a guide to enlightened governance.

It is in the form of a chart, four by four and one-half feet in size, and printed in type varying from one and one-half inches in height to extremely fine print. It is reminiscent of a detailed corporate organization and structure chart. It is, indeed, an organizational chart of the social system of physiocracy. The importance of the *Table raisonnée* as the keystone of Du Pont's economic system is without question. It systemizes his scattered arguments of the preceding decade, forms a system that Du Pont uses in his policy analyses of the coming decades, and is the point of reference for his final sallies into classical economics against Malthus and Say as late as 1817.[9] Moreover, its importance is heightened by the fact that Du Pont's thoughts over the forty-three remaining years of his life can be usefully interpreted in light of the *Table*. Accordingly, it is useful to describe the contents of the document at this point.[10]

The strength of this chart is also its weakness. Its topological arrangement illustrates the links Du Pont saw among social, political, and economic functions. These links expressed the ways in which institutions support, or are supported by, each other. But there is little indication as to how the links achieve what they are stated to achieve.

At the basis of the principles of political economy shown in this *Table* are man's needs, rights, and duties, which collectively give rise to society. To this typically eighteenth-century explanation of the origin and purpose of society, Du Pont tied four historical stages of economic development, culminating in agricultural capitalism.[11] From agricultural capitalism the chart descends to the functions of proprietors, agricultural capitalists, nonagricultural capitalists, and workers, who invest, produce, transform, and distribute the products of nature in accordance with the physiocratic concepts laid down by Quesnay. Du Pont gave the functions of government more emphasis than had Quesnay. The tax on the net product was divided between landed investments of the state and other state functions. Landed investments included improvements in transport systems, facilities for trading agricultural products, and research in improved agricultural technology, in short, anything that would lower the cost—and thereby raise the net return and thus the national tax base—of agricultural production. Other government functions included the protection of liberty (including that of trade), education, maintenance of free speech and thought, the establishment of a system of national accounts, and the provision of other unspecified public services that might or might not be supported through user payments.

The skeletal nature of this chart reveals a logically complete social constitution. Each part is justified by its orderly relation to all the other parts. Each part of the functions of government is sufficiently general to permit categorization by Du Pont of any function that he might determine to be useful to the overall constitution. Thus, his policy views of beggars, debtors, and the poor fell within the government's functions of maintaining order and servces that are not provided in the free market.

Although his *Table raisonnée* is hardly an economic model in the modern, functional sense of the word, it served Du Pont as an engine of analysis and a source of confidence in his investigations of economic conditions, his comments on economic and political policy, and his stand on the proper scope of economic science for the rest of his life. Therefore, it is most important for an understanding of his thought and writings.

4. Du Pont on Mathematical Economics

In 1774 Du Pont described in a letter[12] to the grand duke's son, Carl Ludwig, his lecture on economic curves, which he had presented at one of Mirabeau's Tuesday meetings earlier that year. This letter is the only description extant of Du Pont's work on economic curves.

Du Pont noted that regular laws seem to control price changes and that, if this is true, one should be able to describe the effects of price changes initiated in one part of the economy on all other prices and quantities of whatever was bought or sold in the economy. Du Pont stated that he had communicated his opinions on the usefulness of mathematics for defining economic laws to Daniel Bernoulli who, he hoped, would encourage further research in advanced mathematics by those more capable than Du Pont in pure mathematics. He held that the usefulness of mathematical analysis was in clarifying the effects of economic laws for the use of benevolent governments. But he saw the pursuit of the mathematical formulation of these laws to fall within the scope of mathematics rather than political economy.[13]

The example Du Pont used to illustrate the usefulness of mathematical curves in economic analysis was that of the effect of a surcharge on the price of an item in an economy initially in a state of equilibrium before the surcharge. He related the initial effect of a tax, for instance, on flour upon bakers' costs. It would initially increase the price of bread by the amount of the tax. But the mechanics of supply and demand would reduce both the price and the quantity of bread sold from this initially high offering price after the tax. Portions of the tax would be temporarily absorbed by the baker, the miller, and others, but as far as their costs including the tax would exceed their revenues, they would ultimately pass along the tax to the original producer of the grain who was the only one with any net product. As a result, the agriculturalist would have less net product to expend on purchases from merchants. Du Pont pursued the analysis to note that as the price of bread rose because of the tax, consumers would be forced to spend more of their budgets on this product. But since the tax created no new wealth, they had a smaller amount of their unchanged wealth to spend on other products. Additionally, the agriculturalists' reduction in spending would affect the sales of merchants. Du Pont applied the multiplier effect, which Quesnay had illustrated in his circular flow, to the increases and decreases in prices and quantities of goods to point out the magnified effect of a tax imposition on allocation of production and wealth in the economy as a whole.

Du Pont constructed two curves on one diagram. The lower extremity of the first curve is the net selling price (after tax) when excise taxes are imposed at various levels of manufacture. The upper extremity of the curve is the natural selling price for the good in the absence of any excise tax. This natural selling price is the price that would have prevailed if excise taxes had not been imposed and is the level to which the net price will return when taxes are removed. The curve rises at a declining rate over nine periods from the lower to the upper extremity. The periods represent stages of manufacture and also of time. If, for instance, a 10 percent excise tax had been levied at every stage of manufacture, and was then removed at once, the net price would rise marginally less in each subsequent period of manufacture and time. The declining marginal price level over the periods reflects a declining number of marginal periods of manufacture in the economy as a whole. That is, some goods involve only one period of manufacture, others two, and so on, with very few requiring nine periods.

The second curve on the diagram is a mirror image of the first. It measures the utility gained by the sellers from the removal of the excise tax. This utility rises (from right to left) in the same quantity (and at the same rate) as does the increase in net price over the periods on the first curve. Du Pont was careful not to state the level of the tax. Consequently, the difference between the natural price and the price with excise taxes was not stated. As noted elsewhere, Du Pont was aware of the fact that removal of a tax would not necessarily increase the net price by an amount equal to the tax, but he lacked the tools to measure the elasticities involved. Although Du Pont clearly showed the curves to be increasing at decreasing rates, he did not diagram the marginal changes, nor did his correspondence with Bernoulli result in an anticipation of marginal analysis in economic theory.

If Du Pont's letter to Carl Ludwig had not been preserved, it would have been difficult to fathom the exact view Du Pont held of a physiocratic economy in equilibrium under free trade with no tax but that on the surplus of nature. It is clear from this example not only that any tax was to Du Pont a distortion of the market allocative system of an economy, but also that Du Pont had a definite grasp of the mechanics by which such distortions were magnified in particular markets and in the economy as a whole. Yet, the influence of Du Pont's lecture on economic curves upon the development of mathematical analysis in economics is unknown. There is no record of any response to Du Pont's suggestions by Bernoulli, and the work itself lay forgotten until Knies reproduced the text of the letter (though not the curve itself) in 1892. Du Pont was never to resort to mathematical (as opposed to arithmetical) examples again, but there is no doubt from this work that he was fully aware of the potential usefulness of mathematics for discerning the natural laws that he felt underlay economic phenomena.

5. *His Writings in Turgot's Administration, 1775–76*

Du Pont was private secretary to Turgot during the latter's administration as minister of finance in 1775 and 1776. The extant correspondence between the two men leaves little doubt that the formulation of policy proposals which Turgot pressed upon the young Louis XVI and his Court was a joint product of the two men's minds. Which man originated the plans, and who composed particular sections of proposals, is nearly impossible to ascertain. It seems that Du Pont generally sought to efface his own role in the development of proposals presented by Turgot. However, Du Pont uncharacteristically set the record straight in reference to one piece of proposed legislation that he considered to be an important step in overall reform of the financial administrative machinery of pre-Revolutionary France.

The title of the proposal, presented in September of 1775, is "Mémoire sur les municipalités."[14] The outline of the proposed reforms in financial administration at the local level does not involve economic matters beyond notes on various economies to be achieved in particular administrative reorganizations. It certainly indicates nothing about economic theory in general. Thus, on the surface, as the document was presented to the king, it is a straightforward proposal for administrative reform and nothing more.

To Du Pont, however, the proposal was the leading edge of general reform that would have proceeded under Turgot's administrative genius to an eventual streamlining of government fiscal functions throughout the Realm. It is doubtful that Turgot, who did not share the physiocrats' belief that wealth came exclusively from agriculture, would have used the reformed administrative machinery to institute a single tax on the net product. Nevertheless, Du Pont recorded the fact that he himself had written the "Mémoire" as part of what he foresaw as an overall reorganization of government that would make possible a country-wide administration of the physiocratic tax. In a letter[15] to the grand duke of Baden Du Pont described the way in which the planned system of municipal courts would determine levels of tax on the net product according to the needs both of the national and of their own local levels of government.

The reforms contained in the "Mémoire," as in other products of Turgot's administration, are administrative improvements that would be desirable no matter what tax structure was ultimately selected for the country. What Du Pont's comments about the "Mémoire" reveal is that he personally saw in the reforms, which he was helping Turgot to devise, a means to the eventual implementation of a physiocratic system of taxation. The fact that Du Pont and Turgot could be of one mind on the broad range of reforms simply reflects the fact that the reforms would have been useful for the institution of any national tax system.

It is clear from Du Pont's comments on reform that his

physiocratic ideology was a stimulus to his own role in planning the actual reforms. It is also evident from the absence of physiocratic terminology in the proposals prepared by Du Pont for the Turgot administration that Du Pont was learning the knack of phrasing reform proposals so that they would not reflect the physiocratic principles underlying his own ideas.

Du Pont's ability to assume a pragmatic attitude toward policy matters served him well in the reform debates and proposals he was involved in just before and during the Revolution. The many policy writings to come from Du Pont's pen over this period fall naturally into three periods: (1) pre-Revolutionary writings, 1784–88; (2) policy proposals and debates during the Revolution, 1789–92; and (3) writings of the period 1793–1807, a period of hiding, imprisonment, and relatively low activity for Du Pont on economic topics. They will be surveyed in that order.

B. Economic Writings during the Pre-Revolutionary Period, 1784–88

Du Pont's economic writings of this period are the outcome primarily of his activities in two government posts, first as a member of the Administration de l'Agriculture in the Ministry of Finance between 1785 and 1788, and second as a member of the French delegation to the Anglo-French Commercial Treaty negotiations, concluded in 1786.

In his first work in the Administration de l'Agriculture, "Instruction sur la culture du lin,"[16] Du Pont reported on the mechanics of flax growing and its conversion to linen. He suggested that the government establish regional depots for the storage and sale of flax.

In his "Aperçu de la valeur des récoltes du royaume,"[17] Du Pont presented estimates for the value of the production of various agricultural commodities. He pointed out clearly the interrelationships among the various categories of agricultural production and the ways in which a decline in market value can affect market prices and costs of other categories.[18] Du

Pont admitted that the figures he used to illustrate these inter-relationships were far from exact, but he argued that their inexactness was a strong reason for demanding that local agricultural officials be more specific in reporting crop data to the government.

Du Pont went more deeply into policy recommendations in his "Idées sur le Département de l'Agriculture et sur les avantages qui peuvent résulter de la bonne administration de ce département."[19] In this report he argued that agriculture should be viewed as a very large industry. After presenting data attesting to the large production that came from this industry, he concluded that there was no more important kind of administration, or management, anywhere in the economy than that of agriculture. Obstacles to improved management in this most important industry included ignorance of, and lack of experience with, improved methods of production, marketing, and storage. He recommended that the societies of agriculture in Paris and in the provinces, whose membership consisted of those individuals interested in the improvement of agriculture, undertake specific programs to educate the agricultural community.

Du Pont saw poverty as a second obstacle to improved output in agriculture. Poverty was continued by social institutions inherited from the Middle Ages, including restrictions on trade, controlled prices, and the practice of seigniorage. To alter such institutions he recommended that the local societies become advisory bodies to the government. They would then be free to call for the lifting of taxes and other burdens to agriculture. He also recommended that the government undertake extraordinary, or one-time, projects, such as improvements in transportation, to strengthen the agricultural sector. Finally, Du Pont went on to argue that because of the position of agriculture as the largest industrial sector in the nation, the government would do well to learn that it could improve its own perilous financial condition by taxing agriculture less, not more. Agriculture, he asserted, would reward the state twenty-fold for any investment by the government in it. In subsequent reports[20] he followed up certain points in his argument in "Idées sur le Département de l'Agriculture." He concentrated on the idea that taxation of agriculture (particularly the *dîme*) should be analyzed primarily as an agricultural question rather than a financial one. He saw the *dîme* as restricting wealth at its source and therefore a tax that diminished the very base of taxable wealth.

In all his reports as a member of the Administration de l'Agriculture Du Pont restrained himself from urging physiocratic terms and justifications upon his fellow members. The physiocratic assumption that agriculture was the source of all wealth was transmuted by him to the more acceptable assumption that agriculture was the largest industry in the nation and thus a very important source of wealth. The physiocratic argument that any obstacles to free production and trade of agricultural goods necessarily diminished the base of all wealth was similarly transformed into the argument that ignorance, poverty, and heavy taxation restricted the growth of this important industry. Finally, the physiocratic conclusion that unrestricted and enlightened agricultural production would maximize a nation's wealth in a free economy was likewise altered to the conclusion that an agricultural industry freed of taxation and aided by public investment in works useful to agriculture would result in much greater national wealth and thus a larger tax base throughout the nation as a whole. Du Pont did not attempt to suggest the implementation of a single tax on the net product of agriculture. Indeed, it would have been difficult to camouflage so physiocratic an argument in any form. He had learned from his experience in Turgot's administration that such a tax was anathema to a large segment of government supporters.

There is one report by Du Pont from this series that sheds light on a minor theme running through Du Pont's writings from his earlier physiocratic tracts to his last critiques of Say and Malthus. In his June 1786 "Comparaison de l'état de l'agriculture en Angleterre avec celui de la France, d'après le mémoire de M. de Lazowski,"[21] Du Pont argued that another member of the Administration de l'Agriculture had overestimated the levels of agricultural production in England. In a footnote to Du Pont's argument the editors of the collected reports of the Administration, Pigeonneau and de Foville, writing in 1882, pointed out that Lazowski's estimates were too low, not too high, and that Du Pont's own argument rested on a misunderstanding of the size of the English acre.[22] The significant point is that Du Pont felt compelled to argue that English agriculture was much less productive than French agriculture, because within Du Pont's own system of thought a nation that emphasized industry over agriculture and imported many of its foodstuffs necessarily had to have a low agricultural output. Although Du Pont's figures may have been inaccurate, they convinced him and gave him renewed confidence in the correctness of his own physiocratic assumptions, which continued with him for the next thirty years.

In the same year, 1786, Du Pont turned his attention away from the Administration de l'Agriculture to the question of the government's responsibility to the destitute ill. Having been asked some years earlier to give his recommendations for the buiding of a new charity hospital, he published *Idées sur les secours à donner aux pauvres malades dans une grande ville.*[23] The method he employed to present his specific recommendations began with a statement of his assumptions concerning ethics, political science, and management, all of which he held were sciences susceptible to correct application through knowledge of the natural laws that regulated them:

> Ethics, Politics, Administration itself are also Sciences, whose principles, as those of other Sciences, must be looked for in nature; and which, like the other Sciences, present a great deal of problems, and it is hoped that most of the latter will become susceptible to rigorous solutions by calculations, and that the others will allow a degree of approximation sufficient to clarify, in practice, the intentions of a paternalistic Government.[24]

He then argued that whenever a poor person became ill and had no family to care for him, his neighbors should help. If there are no neighbors able to help, the destitute ill turn to their local government, and if it lacks the means to help, these persons appeal to higher levels of government. But the further they must turn for aid, the more they are humiliated. Therefore, Du Pont said, the state should provide a functioning system of public assistance so that these impoverished ill need not beg for help from their neighbors or from the government. In contrast to modern arguments, then, Du Pont held that the self-respect of the individual is enhanced, not demeaned, by the existence of government institutions prepared to assure the welfare of persons not protected by the shelter of the family. Du Pont cautioned that to minimize the expenses of the state, families should be made to care for their own wherever possible. Moreover, able-bodied poor who are unemployed should be put to work by the state. The more the poor are made to work, Du Pont reasoned, the less they will cost society, and the more their own moral fiber will be improved. Ultimately, Du Pont said, the state should admonish the poor that "God helps him who helps himself."[25]

Thus, Du Pont felt that the state should encourage the family and neighborhood to care for its own, but the state should be fully prepared with functioning programs to provide for those poor and sick who have no other recourse. In Du Pont's France this latter group constituted not an occasional exception, but an army of poor.

Du Pont's service to the French delegation that negotiated the Anglo-French Commercial Treaty during 1785–86 led him to defend the Treaty against those French merchants who felt that they were hurt by it.[26]

The arguments used by Du Pont to defend the Treaty are straightforward free-trade arguments that do not depend on physiocratic principles for their strength. To each objection put forward by the merchants concerning free entry of British goods into Normandy, he countered with an argument that inevitably concludes with an increase of wealth for France through free trade. For instance, the free importation of British low-grade wool into France would encourage the development by France of her own superior intermediate- and high-grade wool. He argued that the free importation of British goods into Normandy only legalized the lively contraband carried on by generations of local Frenchmen. And he dismissed complaints about depressions in various industries as downturns that would have occurred with or without the Treaty, for the products involved fell out of fashion. In his zealousness to defend the free-trade agreement Du Pont sometimes reached for examples that are more typically physiocratic than pragmatic, as in the case of the free importation of sophisticated British weaving machinery. Du Pont contended that such imports would force French manufacturers to turn to the production of simpler machines that peasants could operate in poor weather and during the winter:

> The most advantageous Factories will always be those where the work is done by peasants during winter days and those when bad weather causes a suspension of country work. All the materials which can be made in this manner, need only come to the big Workshops for their preparation, and several of them can be used without being prepared.[27]

The thrust of his arguments, however, was for free international trade. It was stated for the most part in a manner from which it would have been impossible for a reader to discern whether or not Du Pont had arrived at the free-trade position through physiocratic doctrine or through a logical extension of Gournay's practical laissez-faire. Du Pont concluded his defense of the Treaty with a glowing vision of future plenty and happiness for all:

> The experience of all times shows that one after the other Nations take Manufactures away from one another. . . .
> This is the goal which we must one day attain. We could never have reached it if we had not decided to start upon the only road leading there. Our mistake in not opening it earlier makes it necessary for us to proceed cautiously. Several branches of our industry, which were not stimulated by competition, remained at a level of inferiority such that it was necessary to maintain import taxes on English merchandise which were proportional to the cost of contraband. This wise and prudent measure was taken by the

Government. We could no doubt subsequently gradually decrease the taxes, in consideration of the fact that the equality of intelligence and of means would make foreign competition less fearsome for our Artisans. We can even foresee a distant but happy future in which there is neither any reason nor pretext for levying taxes on trade.

Therefore each Nation, enjoying with a profit all its means to buy in Foreign Lands, that is to say also to sell to them, will give the others all facilities and all possible opportunities to sell advantageously in her own land, that is to say to buy from there.[28]

It was only the character of the examples he used to illustrate the advantages of free trade that gave away Du Pont's physiocratic background. The examples revealed consistently a faith on his part in agriculture and closely related crafts as able to create greater additions to the country's wealth and to transform more efficiently the output of nature than concentration in heavy industry, which he would gladly leave to other countries, if they were insufficiently enlightened on the true sources of wealth so as to concentrate in industrial manufacture.

In support of his arguments Du Pont attached several appendixes to the work, including ones documenting his faith in the international (monetary) exchange market, which automatically adjusted exchange rates between France and Britain so as to reflect correctly the strength of each nation's trading position. He was satisfied that a floating exchange rate, free of government controls, facilitated trade and was far superior to barter or exchange rates set through arbitrary pegging of a nation's currency in terms of gold.

In one of the appendixes, "Note septième sur les erreurs commerciales de l'Angleterre,"[29] Du Pont once again revealed the opinions that underlie many of his ideas on political economy where a physiocratic economy is contrasted with an industrial state, best exemplified in Du Pont's eyes by Britain. In particular, he noted that:

in general we in Paris think that whatever comes from England is good, even prejudices. And if any Philosopher were to dare to say that, with the possible exception of five or six men of genius, such as *Smith, Price* and *Tucker*, the English people and Law-makers have no clear nor precise ideas about the rights of men, of the freedom which must be assured citizens, and of the commercial interests of their Nation, he would be considered as having set forth the most untenable paradox.[30]

Du Pont cited several examples of irrational British government control, such as the ruling that buttons must be different in color from the coats on which they were sewn, necessitating a hasty change of buttons by foreigners arriving in British ports. He cited other restrictions to liberty from the *Wealth of Nations* and concluded that Frenchmen had no reason to stand in awe of the British, a race that had managed to encumber its commerce and individual liberty with senseless restrictions. Because the French were more rational, he reasoned, they stood to benefit more from a free-trade treaty with Britain than did the British.[31]

This spirited defense of the Anglo-French Commercial Treaty of 1786 was the last work on economics to come from Du Pont's pen before he became involved in the Estates General and the French Revolution.

C. Economic Writings during the Revolutionary Period, 1789–93

Du Pont's writings during the Revolutionary period reflect his participation in the Revolutionary assemblies and his membership on the Finance Committee of the National Assembly. The revolutionary environment, one of constant change, was not a time for contemplative treatises. It was a time for pamphlets and reports: unofficial, semiofficial, and official. Such an environment was a hothouse for Du Pont's writing and debating skills. Consequently, his writings of this period form the longest list to come from his pen since the decline of the physiocratic school. From the beginning in June 1789 through the end of that year, he published eight reports or pamphlets totaling 468 pages. During 1790 he authored twelve works on economic policy, amounting to 467 pages. In 1791 the figures fell to two works and 22 pages, partly because his attention was turning from economic policy to defense of personal liberty as the Revolution became radicalized and partly because it has been impossible to determine the authorship of many committee reports on which Du Pont collaborated, since reasons of collective security led increasingly to joint signatures on reports. By 1792 Du Pont found himself to be a conservative and quite out of place in the Revolution. His rearguard action for individual liberty occasionally produced works touching on economic topics, but only two of his writings, totaling 29 pages, dealt with economic topics. By 1793 he had withdrawn from the field in Paris and retreated to the safety of the countryside until his arrest and imprisonment in July of the following year. His writings, now limited to personal correspondence and memoires for his children, contained very little economics. It is, then, the years 1789 and 1790 that contain the bulk of his economic writings during the Revolution.

1. On Public Finance

The most frequent topic to appear in his writings is that of public finance. In these writings he demonstrated an unwavering faith in a staunchly nonexpansionary monetary policy, in the face of popular demand for such expansion to support the operations of a government intent on reorganizing 500 years of social stagnation in one glorious burst of activity.

His very first report[32] advised the government to reverse its decision to raise funds through loans carrying an interest rate lower than the going market rate for equivalent loans. These loans to the government offered no advantage to the lender to compensate for his loss of interest, which he could have had elsewhere. Du Pont further cautioned that if the government wanted to renegotiate loans at a lower interest rate, it must determine whether the lenders are willing to do so. Coercion by government, he argued, was anathema to a free market in loanable funds. In the free market there is a certain level of interest that will attract lenders. But the riskier the loan, the higher that level of interest will be. Moreover, he said:

> One must in this connection know the human heart, and take advantage of the various speculations that a reasonable head of family may be willing to enter into for himself and for his children.[33]

In the same vein, the government should abstain from manipulation of the market in order to avoid corrupting national customs and habits, which would lead to a diminution of useful and productive works. Therefore, Du Pont advised that long-term government loans be avoided, because their fixed interest rates might retard adjustments in market interest rates as a country became more productive. He did not discuss the possibility that a free market might trade government paper (or in modern terms, bonds) in a market whose yield would constitute an effective rate of interest on the loans. Such a market would adjust the prices of government loans in accordance with market trends. But Du Pont viewed the best loan as one that would offer the head of a family a steady return equivalent to what he would expect elsewhere in the capital market at the same risk. Not only is such a government strategy right, but, he felt, it is the surest way for the government to successfully float its loans. He acknowledged that one constraint did limit the total amount of interest the government could pay: the taxes collected would always have to cover the interest payments owed by the government in any period, even during the Revolution, if the government was to maintain its good credit.

Later in 1789, in a book-length work,[34] Du Pont sought to prove to the government that the *dîme*, or tax on gross agricultural output, actually lowered the level of operating capital annually ploughed back into agricultural investment to such an extent that the growth of wealth in the economy's largest sector, and consequently national economic growth generally, was retarded. He called for replacement of the *dîme* by a tax on the net profit of agriculture. Du Pont presented long lists of figures in an effort to demonstrate that taxes on the net profit of certain agricultural commodities would actually have raised more revenue than the *dîme*'s proportional tax on gross revenue.

For instance, Du Pont felt that the wine industry had been particularly burdened by high taxes for so long a period that the industry had become starved for capital to maintain and improve its capital investments. As a result, costs were increasing and profit margins decreasing, with total output shrinking as highest-cost producers were forced to close down. He felt that his recommended change in the tax structure would both increase the profit margin and restore profitability to the high-cost producers who had closed down. Most importantly, the tax change would attract capital into the industry, reducing long-run costs and raising long-run net revenues across the board. Further, he felt that the wine industry faced an elastic demand curve and that if its output was once again increased it could increase its markets both domestically and internationally. Taxation of the resulting increased net revenue, he argued, would actually provide more funds to the government than a *dîme*, which was strangling this most basic industry. Du Pont also called for regional agricultural schools to improve techniques and thus lower costs and improve profit rates in agriculture.

The major difference between Du Pont's recommendation to the National Assembly and the physiocratic economics upon which it is obviously based is in its scope: Du Pont was not calling for a shelving of the total national tax structure in favor of a single tax on agriculture. Instead, he was calling for a partial implementation of the general theory, by removing a tax that had in fact depressed much of French agriculture during the century and was a symbol of oppression in the popular view. His argument that its replacement by a tax on net revenue would revive that sector was similarly appealing in its logic. His argument that it would actually increase the government's revenue in the long run through increasing agricultural production was not merely a call for tax relief to reestablish full employment. Indeed, revival of agricultural industries would have restored purchasing power to the peasants, who constituted the majority of the economy's consumers. But the force of Du Pont's argument went beyond restoration of full employment to the goal of economic growth. Increased profits would encourage capital investment that would then lower costs, permit lower prices, and expand markets domestically and internationally. Such growth would take place only if a tax on net revenue replaced the *dîme*. The resulting prosperity, economic growth, and increasing profitability in agriculture would inevitably provide more tax revenue than the *dîme* whose base was shrinking.

Throughout the year Du Pont appealed to the example of the efficient and profitable farms operated by the Church to support his argument for abolition of the *dîme*. He maintained that the Church's untaxed wealth from agriculture should not be viewed as improper, but should be taken as an example of the prosperity that the nation's agriculture as a whole would enjoy if it were freed of the burden of the *dîme*.[35]

It was not so much his physiocratic doctrine as his general grasp of macroeconomics that led Du Pont to take a strong stand against the Revolutionary government's growing resort to the issuance of paper money. In March of 1790 he prepared a report[36] for the Committee on Finance, which warned against the Assembly's resort to financing revolution through the use of paper money. As an alternative to printing money Du Pont recommended that the government reduce a proportion of its increases in spending on new programs and that it temporarily retain, though at a reduced rate, the taxes on salt, bouillon, and furs, which it was about to abolish. If any deficit remained in the government's budget after these actions, it was to be made up by a surcharge on all other remaining taxes. The following month he restated his case, citing the dangers of inflation, but by then the paper money, or *assignats*, had already been printed.[37]

As the Assembly increasingly abandoned all traditional forms of taxation and voted new spending programs with abandon, Du Pont continued to call for the maintenance of some forms of taxation. In April 1790[38] he told the Assembly that although he was philosophically committed to a system of simplified taxes, his experience in the administration had shown him that too rapid a change in this area was unwise. Because so many traditional taxes had already been abandoned, he called for the retention of the tax on tobacco until the government's tax structure could be stabilized. He reasoned that at least a portion of the burden of such a tax would fall on the tobacco producer, who was generally not French. Although his analysis omitted any investigation of the market for tobacco in France and estimates of the extent to which the consumer bore the burden of the tax on tobacco, it was a fact, he argued, that the abolition of this existing tax would provide a windfall to the foreign producer to whatever extent the foreigner bore its burden.

As political opinion turned increasingly toward more indirect taxes, Du Pont retreated from his support of a tax on the net revenue of the wine industry. He noted in October 1790[39] that if only indirect taxes were politically possible, then a tax on wine would be preferable to taxes on wheat and other food. The tax would be borne by vintners and would have the same general effect, he now argued, as a tax on their net revenue. But because wine was not a necessity as compared to wheat and other food, a tax on wine (and liquor) would not oppress the poor as much as taxes on all food. He also suggested that the elasticity of demand for wine was less than for other agricultural products. Therefore, he felt, if all agricultural producers were taxed, and all their products rose in price, consumers would reduce their purchases of other products to buy wine. As a result, other agricultural producers would be hurt more than the vintners, unless the tax was limited only to the vintners.

Du Pont advised on taxes in several other reports. In one he called for the abolition of taxes on manufactured goods.[40] His argument rested squarely on physiocratic foundations. In another he supported the maintenance of certain import duties.[41] Here his argument was strictly pragmatic: to maintain a source of steady income, these duties, borne particularly by the foreigner, should be retained until the government could successfully restructure its tax system. Elsewhere he argued against the raising of taxes through a national lottery.[42] He felt that it was not the government's role to raise taxes by corrupting the workers' morals and sturdy work habits by offering them games of chance and hopes of unearned wealth.

As his efforts to influence changes in the tax system continued, Du Pont became alarmed at the extent of the government's reliance on paper money. In September of 1790 he published two pamphlets on that subject.[43] During 1790 the government had been issuing interest-bearing *assignats*, or paper notes, to cover its current expenses. Toward the end of that year the Assembly proposed to expand greatly the issue of *assignats*. The new issues were to be used to redeem government bonds, to cover operating costs not met by taxes, and to enable expansion of government programs. Unlike earlier issues, however, these *assignats* would not bear interest. Instead they were to be backed by public lands confiscated from royal families and the Church. The Assembly proposed to redeem its new issue of *assignats* for land at some future date. In effect, the *assignats* would circulate as money, backed by confiscated land instead of metal.

Du Pont agreed that the government had to pay its debts and that additional taxation was not the proper means to such payment. Indeed, he observed that a reduced level of taxation was needed to encourage economic growth through the free market. His objections to the *assignats* rested on the following reasons: the business community's confidence would be lost if interest-bearing *assignats* were replaced with non-interest-bearing *assignats*. Also, the requirement that the government's creditors *must* accept these *assignats* as payment was not in the spirit of the new Constitution, which upheld man's freedom of choice. More important yet was the fact that even the interest-bearing *assignats* had lost 6 percent of their value against silver in the few months they had circulated. He warned that the proponents of the new *assignats* actually planned to issue far more *assignats* than they announced. As the supply of *assignats* increased rapidly, prices would rise to the extent that the money supply exceeded the quantities of goods and activities (i.e., services) in the economy. With rising prices silver and gold would be hoarded and would flow abroad in exchange for cheaper foreign goods or for speculative purposes. As the value of *assignats* declined relatively to silver, the small proprietor would suffer as he was forced to exchange *assignats* at a discount for fractional denominations of silver money to make small payments for wages and other resource costs.

Moreover, Du Pont argued, when the *assignats* finally were redeemed, severe deflation would follow the severe inflation. Further, he indicated, the transfer of land upon redemption would be only to holders of *assignats*. Consequently, the government would receive a lower price for the land than if it had been gradually auctioned off to the highest bidders in a free market. Day laborers and others who received low wages could hardly share in the distribution of the national lands. For all these reasons Du Pont thought the plan for massive issuance of *assignats* without interest to be ill advised.

He proposed an alternative that called for the issuance of interest-bearing *assignats* backed by land, but only in amounts just sufficient to cover the nation's operating expenses that exceeded ordinary tax revenues. The national debt was to be redeemed in either gold or silver or in new national bonds that bore sufficient interest to make them competitive with outstanding *assignats*. He acknowledged that some degree of inflation was likely to accompany the modest issuance of *assignats* he proposd, but he accepted this mild inflation as a necessary but temporary cost to pay until a revised national tax structure and natural economic growth should have reestablished fiscal solvency. The *assignats* would gradually be redeemed by sales of land over a decade, but all citizens could bid for the land, and payment could be in either *assignats*, national bonds, or hard currency.

Du Pont's exposition of these arguments demonstrates a clear understanding by him of inflation, real prices, money prices, and the recent experience that he cited with paper currency in the United States. The fact that Du Pont was willing to accept a moderate issuance of *assignats* and government bonds with some inflation when the only alternative was increased taxation with further unemployment of all resources reflects a pragmatic grasp on his part of the trade-off conditions underlying the modern Phillips curve.[44]

Significantly, Du Pont did not attempt to relate his arguments to physiocratic theory. He was, in fact, in the position of analyzing the economic situation with an understanding of the economy gained from years of physiocratic analysis, and of making policy recommendations that would not have differed significantly from those of a Smithite. He was perhaps the first policymaker to have risen to such a position not from experience in commerce, trade, or finance, but, basically, from years of application of intellectual abstractions to economic conditions. In a period of violent change it was Du Pont's firm grounding in physiocratic thought that gave him confidence in his policy recommendations. So long as the economy remained basically agricultural, his physiocratic solutions, tempered with pragmatic realism, appear reasonably correct in retrospect.

2. On Grain Trade

Du Pont's recommendations concerning grain shortages during the Revolution constitute another example of his ability to combine theory and pragmatism. He authored two reports on this subject during the period.[45]

One was a recommendation for emergency controls over grains during the shortages to prevent exportation and prohibit their speculative movement to provinces where grain prices were high because of shortages. The government itself was to transport grain to such areas and sell it at fair prices. His reasoning for government intervention was to provide grain where an orderly market had fallen victim to speculative pressures and to assure that speculators did not withhold their supplies from the market to push famine-level prices higher yet. Du Pont also included recommendations for long-range programs to prevent such local shortages in the future.

His other work on this subject was a compendium of data and arguments from earlier publications, meant to demonstrate that over the preceding hundred years grain prices and output had been stabler whenever free exportation and importation of grain had been permitted. Both articles on this subject are from the earlier, calmer period of the Revolution. Consequently, they are broader and more obviously physiocratic in their recommendations than are his later Revolutionary writings.

3. On Banks

One other writing from the Revolutionary period is worthy of note: his *Discours sur la Caisse d'escompte.*[46] In this work Du Pont disagreed with the position of Mirabeau (the younger) that the prime virtue of the Bank of England was its secrecy and that France should emulate the British bank's secrecy by establishing a state bank whose policy would likewise be set in confidence. Du Pont defined a bank as

> an establishment created in order to furnish solvent debtors who cannot, however, pay at that very moment, the APPEARANCE of a present means of payment, and to sell them these FICTI-TIOUS means cheaply.[47]

Thus, he saw banks as, foremost, passive institutions, established to provide merchant liquidity rather than investment funds. But he noted that a bank fulfills its highest function when its notes are used to direct capital to those investments that pay the highest returns.[48] Investors will have the greatest confidence in a bank, therefore, when it can assure them of its solvency. Secrecy, he argued, was not the way to attract deposits. Therefore, a bank should always back its notes with a high proportion of sound capital investments, and it should publicize its portfolio.

These comments are valuable as a rare expression of Du Pont's opinions on banking. Although his views on secrecy hardly reflect those of an experienced banker, they do reflect a view of the function of banking in consonance with a perfectly functioning capital market. His stand in favor of complete information in capital markets may be interpreted as an extension of his belief that enlightened entrepreneurs would invest in agriculture, which under a single tax on net revenue would pay them the highest return available.

4. Other Economic Writings

The foregoing writings reflect a succession of political debates over economic institutions in Revolutionary France. It was only when the Constituent Assembly was dissolved in 1791 and Du Pont established his own press shop that he found time for broader reflection. During this period he wrote one pamphlet, which expressed his overall view of the relationship between government expenditures and the economy.[49] This work finds the justification for public expenditures to lie within the typical historical development of society as outlined in his *Table raisonnée* of 1773: Men come together principally to achieve common economic ends at lower costs than each could do in isolation. As society, the economy, and government develop, it becomes necessary to economize on public finances. He described the criterion by which the ideal society would evaluate its public expenditures: the way to minimize costs and maximize benefits is to select public administrators who have proven their abilities to economize in private business. These administrators should be paid high salaries, at least as high as equivalent managers in the private economy. By this means he felt that the economizing energies of the free market system could be channeled into public finance.

This writing is the closest Du Pont came to commenting on economic topics for the remainder of the period through 1807. He was more involved with political writings, which eventually forced him to flee Paris for his personal safety. Following his imprisonment in 1794 and his subsequent reinstatement, Du Pont expended little energy on economic writings. The intellectual climate had changed, and most of his acquaintances had either been executed or had fled the country. His *Philosophie de l'univers*, published in 1796, contains a broad collection of essays and reflections on art, zoology, anatomy, and other topics, but nothing on economics.[50]

Similarly, Du Pont's period in the United States between 1799 and 1802 provides no evidence, even in correspondence, of his economic thought. If his failing commercial ventures left him any time for contemplation of economic theory and policy, it was unwise to put those ideas into correspondence that had to cross the ocean during the Napoleonic period. Even his brief period, after returning to France, as a director of the *Banque Territoriale* during 1803 and 1804 produced no writings or correspondence that comment on his economic thought.

It was not until he set himself the task of expanding his earlier work on Turgot's life and administration into his *Oeuvres de Turgot* that his mind returned to the world of economic theory, a world that was for him, by 1807, largely one of reminiscence.

Notes to Chapter VI

1. Carl Knies, ed., *Carl Friedrichs von Baden Brieflicher Verkehr mit Mirabeau und Du Pont*, 2 vols. (Heidelberg: Carl Winter, 1892).
2. DPDN to Carl Ludwig von Baden, January 15, 1773, in ibid., 2:25–31.
3. DPDN to Carl Ludwig von Baden, n.d. [1773], in Knies, ed., *Carl Friedrichs von Baden*, 2:99–107.
4. ". . . society needs to carry out as many public works as possible at the lowest possible cost" (ibid., p. 102).
5. ". . . we must not make any beggars, and . . . that is the best means of ensuring that we are not overloaded with them; . . . we must, in order to avoid making any, do away with all indirect and arbitrary taxes, and only base public revenue on a proportional share of the net product of agriculture, paid by the land . . . (ibid., p. 105).
6. DPDN to Carl Ludwig von Baden, n.d. [1773], Knies, ed., *Carl Friedrichs von Baden*, 2:32–34.
7. Thirteen years later he would be asked to submit his recommendations for the actual rebuilding of the poorhouse; his comments at that time are interpreted elsewhere in the present study.

8. DPDN, *Table raisonnée des principes de l'économie politique* (Karlsruhe: Maklot, 1775).

9. In Du Pont's 1815 letter to Say, published in his final book, he stated that he was transmitting a copy of the *Table* to Say. Du Pont distributed copies to others as well. Du Pont's son, Victor, reported having seen a copy of it framed and hanging over the mantle when he visited Benjamin Franklin in 1788.

10. This monumental organizational chart of moral, political, and economic society, given its fine print, constitutes in itself the equivalent of a thirty or forty page booklet. It has remained unpublished in full size over 200 years now, and the publishers of the present book decided not to reproduce it as a pull-out appendix to this work for reasons of bulkiness and publication cost. (It was at one time reproduced as a quarter-size photostat by the Karlsruhe State Museum, but most of the contents are illegible in such a reduced form.) I know of no English translation; certainly none has been published. Indeed, the full-scale publication and translation of the *Table raisonnée* remains an unattained landmark in the history of economics. The original copy may be seen in the Eleutherian Mills Historical Library, Greenville, Delaware.

11. The first stage, "La Recherche des Productions Vegetales Spontanées" (the gathering of foodstuffs that grow wild); the second stage, "La Chasse et la Pêche" (hunting and fishing); the third, "La Vie Pastorale" (nomadic herdsmen); and the fourth, "Un Commencement de Cultivation" (agriculture).

12. "Des Courbes politques," related in DPDN to Carl Ludwig von Baden, n.d. [1774], in Knies, ed., *Carl Friedrichs von Baden*, 2:289–300. Knies's reproduction of the letter omitted Du Pont's diagrams of the curves. For an English translation of the letter, including a reproduction of the curves, see DPDN, *On Economic Curves: A Letter Reproduced in English Translation with the Original Diagram*, ed. Henry W. Spiegel (Baltimore, Md.: The Johns Hopkins University Press, 1955).

13. The long-run nature of Du Pont's opinion is affirmed by his rather brusque reply to a letter from A. N. Isnard requesting Du Pont's support for Isnard's work in mathematical economics. This coolness was balanced by the fact that Du Pont retained, and brought to America, a copy of Isnard's *Traité des Richesses* (1781), which is in EMHL and was listed in "Catalogue of Books Listed according to Size" (1799[?]), p. 9. For an analysis of this neglected work see William Jaffé, "A. N. Isnard, Progenitor of the Walrasian General Equilibrium Model," *History of Political Economy* 1, no. 1 (1969): 19–43.

14. DPDN, "Mémoire sur les municipalités," in Knies, ed., *Carl Friedrichs von Baden*, 1:244–83. Also reprinted in various collections of works by Turgot where authorship is sometimes attributed to Turgot. Cf. DPDN, ed., *Oeuvres de Turgot*, 9 vols. (Paris: Belin, 1811 [vol. 1]; Delance, 1808–10 [vols. 2–9]); Eugène Daire, ed., *Oeuvres de Turgot* (Paris: Guillaumin, 1833); and another collection by the same title edited by Gustave Schelle.

15. DPDN to Carl Friedrichs von Baden, February 12, 1778, in Knies, ed., *Carl Friedrichs von Baden*, 1:192–99.

16. Appeared December 9, 1785. Reprinted in Henri Pigeonneau and Alfred de Foville, eds., *L'administration de l'Agriculture au contrôle général des finances (1785 à 1787): Procès-verbaux et rapports* (Paris: Librairie Guillaumin et Cie., 1882), pp. 95 ff.

17. In ibid., pp. 140–48.

18. Du Pont's primary example in "Aperçu" involved wheat:

This production of wheat is linked to the production of straw, spring grain, hay, poultry and cattle, which feed particularly on spring grain and hay. This point includes the production of cows, calves, butter, cheese, which are made in farms, lambs, wool, poultry, eggs and vegetables raised or harvested on the farms. It is considered an axiom by cultivators, that it is on these different objects that a good menagerie pays its rent and that the grains serve to pay the costs of cultivation, the tithes, and taxes.

The value of this sown earth and of the products of the poultry yard are generally and barely estimated to be half the value of the wheat. [P. 142]

19. In ibid., pp. 148–54.

20. "Mémoire sur la différence qui existe et qui doit exister entre l'Assemblée d'Administration de l'Agriculture et la Sociètè d'Agriculture de Paris," in ibid., pp. 199 – 202; "La question des dîmes ecclésiastiques," in ibid., p. 26; "La question des dîmes," in ibid., pp. 32 – 34; "Mémoire sur les dîmes," in ibid., pp. 223 – 31.

21. In ibid., pp. 255–64.

22. Ibid.

23. DPDN, *Idées sur les secours à donner aux pauvres malades dans une grande ville* (Paris, 1786).

24. Ibid., pp. 6–7.

25. "Aide-toi, le Ciel t'aidera," in ibid., p. 16.

26. DPDN, *Lettre à la Chambre du Commerce de Normandie; Sur le Mémoire qu'elle a publié relativement au Traité de Commerce avec Angleterre* (Rouen [?] and found in Paris: Moutard, 1788).

27. Ibid.

28. Ibid., pp. 80, 85–86.

29. Ibid., pp. 248–66.

30. Ibid., p. 248. Du Pont's italics.

31. Du Pont concluded:

We must praise the English; for they have character and genius. We owe them some gratitude; for they have helped to enlighten us, although involuntarily. We should cherish them, if they grant us benevolence equally; for they can still be very useful to us by their speeches, their enlightenment, by those of their examples which are good, by their very competition. We must help them when help will be mutual; for when our two Nations live in harmony, they will uphold peace in the world, and will determine its destiny. But if they should forget or ignore their own interest through the passion to harm us a little, and the folly to harm themselves a lot: may they be free to do so. We should not fear them in any way. The violent remedy which they would apply to us, even more costly for them than for us, would consolidate and perfect our constitution, the true basis for our future prosperity. [Ibid., p. 266]

32. DPDN, *De la manière la plus favorable d'effectuer les emprunts, qui seront nécessaires, tant afin de pourvoir aux besoins du moment, que pour opérer le remboursement des dettes de l'Etat, dont les intérêts sont trop onéreux . . .* (Paris: Baudouin, 1789).

33. Ibid., pp. 8–9.

34. DPDN, *Discours prononcé à l'Assemblée nationale sur l'état et les ressources de nos finances (avec pièces justificatives)* (Versailles: Baudouin, September 4, 1789).

35. Ibid. See also idem, *Discours sur les biens ecclésiastiques* (Paris: Baudouin, October 24, 1789); and idem, *Principes et opinion de M. du Pont* [*sic*] *. . . sur le disposition que doit faire l'Assemblée Nationale de Biens Ecclésiastiques en générale, et de ceux des Ordres Religieux en particulier* (Paris: Baudouin, December 17, 1789).

36. DPDN, *Rapport fait au nom du Comité des Finances sur les moyens de remplacer la gabelle et de rétablir le niveau entre les recettes et les dépenses ordinaires de l'année 1790* (Paris[?], March 11, 1790). See also idem, *Rapport fait au nom du Comité des Finances à l'Assemblée Nationale . . . sur la répartition de la contribution, en remplacement des grandes gabelles, des gabelles locales et des droits de marque de cuirs, des marques des fers, de fabrications sur les amidons, de fabrication et de transport, dans l'intérieur du royaume, sur les huiles et savons* (Paris: Baudouin, August 14, 1790); idem, *Troisième rapport fait au nom du Comité des finances . . . sur le remplacement de la Gabelle et des droits sur les Cuirs, les Fers, les Huiles, les Savons et les Amidons* (Paris: Baudouin, October 8, 1790).

37. DPDN, *Opinion . . . sur les assignats* (Paris: Baudouin, April 15, 1790).

38. DPDN, *Opinion . . . sur le revenu public produit par la vente du tabac* (Paris: Baudouin, April 23, 1790).

39. DPDN, *Rapport fait au nom du Comité de l'Imposition . . . sur les impositions indirectes en générale et sur les droits, à raison de la consommation des vins, et des boissons en particuliers* (Paris: Baudouin, October 29, 1790). And see idem, *Examen et parallèle des différents projets de droits sur les boissons . . .* (Paris[?], n.d. [1790]); idem. *Réplique de M. Du Pont à M. Didelot au sujet des droits d'Aides sur les boissons . . .* (Paris: Imprimerie Nationale, [December 25, 1790] 1791).

40. DPDN, *Rapport sur les taxes, vulgairement nommées droits à l'entrée des productions et des marchandises dans les villes, fait au nom du Comité de l'Imposition* (Paris[?], 1790), "Annexe" attached.

41. DPDN, *De quelques améliorations dans la perception de l'impôt et de l'usage utile qu'on peut faire des employés réformés* (Paris: Imprimerie Nationale, January 6, 1791).

42. DPDN, *De la lotterie* (Paris: Imprimerie Nationale, March 1791).

43. DPDN, *Effet des assignats sur le prix du pain* (Paris[?], September 10, 1790), reproduced in Eugène Daire, *Physiocrats*, 2 vols. (Paris: Guillaumin, 1846). DPDN, *Opinion . . . sur le projet de créer pour 1,900 millions d'assignats monnoie sans intérêt* (Paris[?], September 25, 1790), published in English as *Du Pont de Nemours on the Dangers of Inflation: 1790*, trans. Edmond E. Lincoln (Boston: Baker Library, Harvard Graduate School of Business Administration, 1950).

44. A. W. Phillips, "The Relationship between Unemployment and the Rate of Change in Money Wage Rates in the United Kingdom, 1862–1957," *Economica*, November 1958, pp. 283–99.

45. DPDN, "Rapport fait à l'Assemblée Nationale au nom du Comité des Subsistances, par M. du Pont [*sic*], Député de Bailliage de Nemours, le 4 Juillet 1789," *Procès-Verbal des Séances de l'Assemblée Nationale de France, Tenues en l'année 1789 et suivantes; Précédé du Récit des Séances des Députés des Communes, depuis 5 Mai jusqu'au 12 Juin suivant; du Procès-Verbal des Conférences pour la verification des Pouvoirs; et de Procès-Verbal des Séances des Députés des Communes, depuis le 12 jusqu'au 17 Juin 1789* (Paris: Imprimerie Nationale, 1791), 1: 180–210. Also: idem, *Analyse Historique de la Législation des Grains, depuis 1692, à la quelle on a donné la forme du Rapport à l'Assemblée Nationale* (Paris: Petit, 1789).

46. DPDN, *Discours sur la Caisse d'escompte; imprimé sur l'ordre de l'Assemblée sous ce titre: Discours prononcé à l'Assemblée Nationale par M. Du Pont sur les banques en général, sur la caisse d'escompte en particulier, et sur le projet du premier ministre des finances, relativement à cette dernière* (Paris: Baudouin, November 14, 1789).

47. Ibid., p. 4.

48. A Bank reaches its peak of perfection when its bank notes find many more profitable uses than that of being brought back to its cashiers so that the latter will not be presented with more than they can pay. [Ibid., p. 5]

49. DPDN, *De la véritable et la fausse économie dans les dépenses publiques d'une nation* (Paris: Imprimerie Du Pont, 1792).

50. DPDN, *Philosophie de l'univers* (Paris: Imprimerie Du Pont, 1796).

VII

Du Pont's Last Economic Writings, 1808-17

Du Pont's economic thought during the last decade of his life is to be found mainly in two works, his nine-volume *Oeuvres de Turgot,* published between 1808 and 1811, and his *Examen* of the works of Malthus and J. B. Say, published in 1817.

A. *Oeuvres de Turgot*

Between 1808 and 1811 Du Pont edited the *Oeuvres de Turgot*[1] and published them in nine volumes. This was the first collection of Turgot's works and the only edition to appear until the publication of Daire's *Oeuvres de Turgot* in 1833.[2] The first volumes of Du Pont's edition had appeared in 1782 (in Paris) and 1788 (in Philadelphia) under the title *Mémoires sur la vie et les ouvrages de M. Turgot.* The first two volumes are straightforward descriptions of Turgot's career and contain nothing of Du Pont's own economic thought. In the remaining seven volumes Du Pont's introductions and notes take up approximately forty pages, and only a small portion of that material sheds light on his own economic ideas as of 1808–11. Therefore, with one exception, the few comments to be found in this work that are useful to an interpretation of Du Pont's thought will be discussed as the particular points arise in the reconstruction of his economic system as revealed

159

primarily in his final work on Malthus and Say. The exception concerns Du Pont's discussions of the schools of Gournay and Quesnay and Turgot's place in relation to them.

B. Du Pont as Historian of Economic Thought

Insofar as Du Pont may be called an historian of economic thought, the appellation is best limited to his descriptions of the French economic circles with which he was associated as a young man. Previous sections of this work reviewed the highly defensive position Du Pont took concerning economic ideas that were antagonistic to the physiocratic position in pre-Revolutionary France. His perceptions of the schools of Gournay and Quesnay, as well as of Turgot's own thought, were not so strongly colored with the hues of battle as his comments on their detractors. Consequently, Du Pont's comments on all these men are worthy of investigation as he recorded them, a half-century after the initial propagation of their ideas.

In his seventh decade the aging physiocrat viewed the ideas of Gournay and Quesnay as reciprocal parts of what blended into one overall view, through the years, of economic activity. It was Gournay who provided the insights into public administration and market distribution that together provided the concept of laissez-faire.[3] It was Quesnay who declared society's foundation to rest on natural law and who discerned the uniqueness of the net product.[4] Du Pont saw that over the half-century since their views had first been revealed, an amalgamation of their insights had led to that higher state of economic science achieved by their followers, in Du Pont's view, over the intervening years between their propagation and his writing in 1808–11.

Among Gournay's own disciples Du Pont placed Morellet, Trudaine (the elder), Price, Josiah Tucker, Hume, Beccaria, and others.[5] Within Quesnay's school he included Mirabeau (the elder), Abeille, Roubaud, Le Trosne, Saint-Péravy, Vauvilliers, the margrave of Baden, Emperor Leopold, and himself. Two others within Quesnay's school he considered as forming a distinct branch, maintaining the desirability of an absolute monarch: Mercier de la Rivière and Baudeau, along with a ruler influenced by them, the Emperor Joseph II.[6] Between these two schools he placed other writers whom he saw as influenced both by Gournay's and by Quesnay's thought: Turgot, Smith, Garnier (Smith's early translator into French), Lord Lansdowne, Say, and Sismonde.[7]

Although most modern writers correctly respect Turgot's wish never to be categorized as a physiocrat, they generally recognize that Turgot agreed with their doctrine of the exclusive productivity of nature. In a footnote in *Oeuvres* Du Pont further clarifies the point, noting that whereas Gournay held that a worker actually adds to the sum total of wealth by fabricating material into goods, Turgot agreed with Quesnay that the value of the worker's energy transferred into seemingly new wealth in the products of his handiwork is equally derived from the value of the food he consumes and that the worker's tools similarly added, over their lifetime, value to the goods only to the extent that the tools embodied value from natural resources.[8]

Du Pont's notes to Turgot's writings are filled with similarly fascinating details, and would form a worthy study in themselves, particularly as they constitute the starting point for subsequent interpretations of Turgot's thought, from Daire[9] and Oncken[10] down even to the current work of Ronald Meek.[11] Nevertheless, these details involve more the thought of Turgot than of Du Pont and are better left for subsequent study in another work.

C. His Final Contribution to Economic Thought

Du Pont's final contribution to economic thought consists of a 159-page book published in French in Philadelphia in 1817. As its full title, *Examen du livre de M. Malthus sur le principe de population; auquel on a joint la traduction de quatre chapitres de ce livre supprimés dans l'édition française; et une lettre à M. Say sur son Traité d'économie politique,* indicates, this work consists of three sections. The first section is an expanded version of a critique of the 1806 French edition of Malthus's second edition of his *Principle of Population.* The original version of Du Pont's critique consisted of a book review written in 1810 and published in 1811 in an obscure provincial journal.

The second part of Du Pont's 1817 *Examen* is a translation into French of four chapters of Malthus's *Principle of Population,* which were omitted from the edition published in France under Napoleon. It is not important to this study.

The final part of the *Examen,* however, reprints a long letter written by Du Pont to Say in April of 1815 concerning the second edition of the latter's *Traité d'économie politique,* published in 1814. It contains an extended explanation of Du Pont's differences with Say. In a broader sense, too, it encapsulates many of the differences between the physiocrats and the pre-Ricardian classical economists (or, as Du Pont called them, the Smithites). This letter is the major piece of correspondence in a series of eight letters exchanged between Du Pont and Say between 1814 and 1816.

Consequently, this final publication not only permits an interpretation of Du Pont's opinions of Malthus's population theory and Say's general economic thought, but opens a window to Du Pont's own view of the nature of economic thought and the final state of his own economic theory fifty years after his adoption of the physiocratic creed. Accordingly, Du Pont's final economic thought will be distilled from his examinations of Malthus and Say, and his views on the two men's positions will themselves be interpreted. His economic thought and his critiques of Malthus and Say, as revealed in this work, will be augmented with information from his correspondence with Say during this final period of his life.

1. Du Pont's Economic System as of 1817

a. Basis in Natural Law. At the heart of Du Pont's economic system were natural laws. Natural laws were at the base of social institutions, human behavior, and the economy. He attributed the discovery of these natural laws that govern the economy to Quesnay's insights sixty years earlier into the cause, existence, and effect of the net product. The precise operations of natural laws were for men to discover through the use of reason. Thus, natural law remained at the foundation of Du Pont's view of the economy, even as it had been the main support to Quesnay's physiocracy.

Examples in his last writing of the operation of these laws in the economy include the fact that wealth was produced only by nature in the fruits of the land and water. Another operation of natural law was the mechanism that dictated that population, once it had expanded to the maximum size supportable by existing food supplies, could expand at a rate no higher than that at which the food supply itself expanded. The operation of all natural laws in the economy was, in Du Pont's view, like these two: their operation exerted forces in the universe that were basically good for mankind. Mankind could either suffer by failing to act in accordance with these laws or could adjust its behavior in accordance with their operation to the ultimate and maximum benefit of humanity.

b. Institutional Framework. Du Pont held to the view that men had come together in society to secure and expand their rights. They had established government for the passage and enforcement of laws. These laws might be legislated either wisely, in accordance with the operation of basic natural law, or unwisely, in ignorance of the operation of natural law. It was a function of government to assure the maintenance of property rights. Property rights, in Du Pont's system, made three things possible: social stability, savings, and harvests or returns on investments (that is, collection of the basic production of nature, which included the net product). Government was to undertake a laissez-faire policy in the economy with but three exceptions. First, government provided those goods and services whose social return exceeded the private return that would accrue to individual investors. Second, government guarded against monopoly, which distorted the functions of resource allocation normally carried out by private markets. The third exception was that government, and society in general, should spread an understanding of the uniqueness of basic production in providing wealth. Because the social return from the creation of wealth (the net product) could not be distinguished by comparing the profit rate in agriculture (and in mining and fishing) with the profit rates in industrial and commercial activities, investors would have to be educated to the greater social benefits of basic production in comparison to the creation of luxury goods.

In Du Pont's view of the economy there were two main social classes that were distinguished from one another by their economic functions. There was a working class, willing to labor for low wages. The actual level of these wages might vary, depending on the general wealth of the economy. But the poorest of these workers always bordered on poverty. The labor of this working class supported another class that fulfilled three functions. This second class provided employment for the working class. It provided tools and machinery (i.e., physical capital) for the use of the working class. And, finally, it provided the means of feeding the working class until its work was completed and payment was received by the employer for the product in the market place—in short, it provided a wages fund, although Du Pont did not use that term. Du Pont referred to this second class broadly as the capitalist class, and its payment was generally the price of capital. In specific cases he distinguished between the entrepreneur, or *salariant* (literally, the "payer of wages"), who borrowed capital, hired labor for his enterprise, and received a profit on his venture, and the owner of physical or money capital, that is, the capitalist proper, who lent capital for a price called rent or interest. Although Du Pont was not explicit on this point, it may be inferred that the roles of capitalist and entrepreneur could overlap and that the work undertaken could be either primary production, industry, or commerce. A distinction was made between rich and poor businessmen. The small businessman's existence was at the mercy of the business cycle, because he had a low level of capital at his disposal. Nevertheless, he was part of the capitalist class rather than the working class, because he used capital and received profit rather than a wage.

The working class received wages whether it was employed in primary production, industry, or commerce. Mobility between classes was possible. Movement of workers occurred whenever a worker, through superior work and frugality of savings, amassed sufficient savings to become a lender of capital. The process of acquiring such saving habits was slow; consequently, such a move was accordingly slow. The reverse direction in class mobility was also possible and could be relatively abrupt in periods of business downturns.

Education played a significant role for both classes. Education of the capitalist class sharpened the reasoning ability of men who controlled investment, and it permitted them to discern from the study of natural laws the proper place to invest for the greatest benefit of society. Education also encouraged those minds that could grasp complex ideas to concentrate on the useful arts and sciences, thereby providing a constant impetus to technological advance. These great minds were drawn from the children of both classes. The purpose of the government's assurance of a broad, basic education for the working class was to encourage strong morality (with its attendant sturdy work habits and honesty) and reason (enabling the working class to see where its best interests lay, as regards, for instance, the inverse relationship between family size and standard of living).

The government was to provide welfare or work programs for the impoverished, their children, the aged poor, the unemployed, and other unfortunates. Work programs were not, however, to be so attractive as to encourage the temporarily unemployed not to seek other employment.

c. Value. Value was not accorded careful treatment in Du Pont's final work. In contradiction to Say's definition of economics as the study of wealth, Du Pont described wealth as a measure of the utility derived from conformance with natural law. Wealth, in Du Pont's view, consisted not only of goods that are traded, but of such nonmarketed entities as a woman's smile. A nation's stock of wealth was therefore much broader than what is measured in the market. But Du Pont's final work failed to state the relationship between wealth (*richesse*) and value (*valeur*). In contrast to Du Pont's writings of the 1760s, rich in definitions and use of the terms *market value* (*valeur vénale*) and *original value* (*valeur originale*), the term *value* rarely appeared in his final work. Rather, Du Pont spoke of *price* (*prix*), as in his discussing the prices of labor, capital, or goods, all of which were set by market forces, or might be artificially set by government decree (which, however, was undesirable). Because Du Pont included almost no discussion of money or inflation, the distinction between real and money prices was not mentioned, although it is clear from his private correspondence of this period that Du Pont had not forgotten this distinction.

Wealth itself was seen as a stock, whose level increased or decreased according as original production exceeded or fell short of consumption of original production in any one time period. There was no rigorous analysis of the relation between price and wealth. Indeed, since Du Pont's definition of wealth included goods that bear no price (e.g., a woman's smile), one suspects that he placed little confidence in prices as accurate measures of wealth.[12] Price, then, was an inadequate measure of wealth. If wealth itself was a measure of the success with which man conformed to natural law (primarily through his maximization of the net product of nature), it follows that if Du Pont were to have explicitly and rigorously pursued this line of reasoning, market price could not adequately indicate the maximization of wealth from the net product, because it did not accurately measure wealth. And although such a conclusion was not so reasoned in his work, its absence can be interpreted merely as a gap in his argument, for throughout his work runs the theme of inconsistency between social return and private return. Before Du Pont is too harshly faulted for such a gap in his argument, it must be remembered that his presentation was not written as a formal explication of his views but rather in the form of two critiques of others' views.

Time and again Du Pont called for the necessity of government investment where the benefit to society from a certain activity exceeded the interest rate, or return to capital, from such an investment. An apparent flaw in his logic, however, was his position, on the one hand, that primary production exclusively created all wealth, but that men must be enlightened to see its potentiality because the market return on investment of capital in agriculture did not reflect it, and his failure, on the other hand, to include government entrepreneurship (or some other form of economic incentive such as tax relief) in this particular and most important case of social benefit.

Thus, wealth was the sum of everything that gave mankind pleasure. Such wealth, which is insufficiently measured by market prices that often failed to reflect a higher social value, nevertheless derived from the net product. The term *value* (*valeur*) was no longer employed in his final work.

From this synopsis of his faulty concept of value comes a basic insight into the shortcoming of Du Pont's economic thought. Throughout all his writings from 1763 to 1817, Du Pont never quite resolved the conflict in his system between two basically contradictory dicta, both of which had been imbedded in his thinking at an early age. Quesnay had absorbed from Gournay the rule of thumb that government should not intervene in the economy. The doctor transformed this pragmatic guideline into an economic law of laissez-faire that he passed on to his eager disciple Du Pont. The general usefulness of this concept, and Du Pont's aversion to critical analysis of a body of thought that was to him almost a religion, led him to intone the dictum of laissez-faire as a basic pattern of the behavior of government.

In his earliest writings Du Pont had held the view that government should play a role in the economy in those cases where the internal rate of return to private enterprise was less than the benefit to society. His best works during the height of physiocracy dealt with this problem, and it continued to be the topic of his best economic contributions through the Revolution. The irony is that the conflict of this basic feeling with the laissez-faire position instilled into Quesnay's physiocracy had not been resolved in Du Pont by the time of his last writings fifty years later. Du Pont still failed to see, or at least to admit to himself, the inconsistency of a position that called for government entrepreneurship in all minor cases where net social return exceeded private market return, but no government entrepreneurship in the one major case where social return exceeded private return: that of agriculture.

Because agriculture (and mining and fishing) constituted such a large proportion of economic activity and, in his view, supported all other activity, the physiocratic law of laissez-faire applied to it automatically. Government activity was not even considered. Indeed, in such an important sector the advocacy of government would have undermined the physiocratic concept of laissez-faire and its related institutions of the market system, private property, and a single tax on net product. All of these institutions were at the base of a system that, after all, was a useful tool for analysis of economic problems and therefore, in Du Pont's eyes, evidently correct.

Consequently, his final position was one wherein government, or society in general, was to call on wise men to become enlightened and to see the superior benefit of such investment. Such a position is an invocation to man's will to behave in accordance with moral principle. Only by the inclusion of morality within the scope of economics could Du Pont's economic system overcome the ultimate conflict between laissez-faire and maximization of a physiocratic source of wealth that was not reflected in the market system.

d. Production. In Du Pont's system the term *production* was reserved for those goods which come directly from nature, for what would be called today *primary production.* Du Pont's *production*, therefore, included goods derived directly from agriculture, mining, and fishing. All other kinds of activity that would be called production by Smith and his followers, as well as by twentieth-century economists, were to Du Pont the reworking, or transforming, of goods produced by nature. He in fact used the word *transformation* to describe such activities.

Thus, Du Pont's *production* and *transformation* are together equivalent to the classical category of production. In Du Pont's system labor and capital were combined with nature's resources *in situ* to create goods. These goods contained net product, which was the source of all wealth. If society were enlightened as to the exclusive nature of this net product, the natural market price of such goods would be equal to the labor and capital costs of its production plus the net product. In effect, then, Du Pont's position on the exclusive source of wealth had not changed from the physiocratic stance he had maintained in his earlier writing.

The word *transformation* is a new term in Du Pont's writings; yet it represents an older idea, namely, the concept of "sterile" production associated with sterile classes. Labor, capital, and primary goods were reworked, or refashioned, into different goods. These reworked goods might in turn be combined as intermediate products with labor and capital to make yet another, more highly fashioned, category of goods, called luxury goods. Such luxury goods were those goods that had been refashioned to the greatest extent. But, unlike *production, transformation* of goods entailed no creation of net product. In fact, it entailed a diminution of the stock of society's wealth. While laborers reworked the goods, they had to eat and consume other basic necessities. Any reworking, then, involved a loss of wealth, at the same time as a good that was refashioned might provide a new use. Because Du Pont accepted the basic proposition that wealth was created only in primary production, he found it unnecessary to investigate the possibility of whether the combination of resources in his *transformation* process might in fact provide a reworked good whose value was higher than the cost of the resources that went into it. Du Pont's view was that, if its price was indeed higher, it was an excessively high price that overstated the social benefit to be derived from such a good. To his mind the ultimate irony was to be found in a luxury good whose market price, at the time of its fashioning, was very high and whose high labor content consumed a high quantity of primary output, but whose market price would fall nearly to zero when the fickle fashion whims of the wealthy changed.

Du Pont held that the higher the capital-labor ratio in the *transformation* process, the less wealth was lost to society in its transformation. He observed that machines did not eat and therefore did not use up wealth. He did not inquire into the rates of depreciation on machinery. From Du Pont's comments it is abundantly clear that he was thinking about social costs and social benefits in all *transformation* activities. The loss to society of food consumed by workers was not accurately reflected in the wages paid them, for his system allows for workers to consume less than the total of their wages. Nor were the payments made to capital a reflection of a loss of wealth to society. Over and above wage and interest payments the entrepreneur might hope to make a profit that was not, however, an increase in society's wealth. Beyond this, nothing can be said, for Du Pont did not inquire into the cost accounting within the *transformation* process.

Within this framework Du Pont called for the encouragement of both primary production and the works of every kind that combine the wealth created in primary production.

In reference to his comments on the market price of the labor resource in both agricultural production and the reworking of goods, Du Pont held that the price of labor was determined by the market forces of demand by producers and of supply by laborers. Workers would refuse to supply labor at prices below the subsistence level. And although most workers were satisfied with a low wage, some would be motivated to work harder by a higher wage. There was no distinction offered between different skill wage levels. Consequently, the supply schedule of labor was infinitely elastic for general labor. The supply of workers offering something more than unskilled labor is best interpreted as a different set of infinitely elastic supply curves, one for each difference in quality or productivity, because Du Pont did not indicate an awareness of either an increasing or a decreasing marginal physical productivity of labor.

The nature of the demand curve for labor was not spelled out. It was presumably governed by market conditions in the firm's product market. Such a derived demand curve would have a negative slope if for no other reason than the fact that the demand schedule for products in his system sloped downward. The demand for luxury goods, for instance, was a function of fashion: their price was assumed to be high and they were bought by an exclusive circle of fashion followers. A decrease in price would elicit hardly any more demand. The demand for food was also less than unitarily elastic: as food prices increased, people would have to spend all, if necessary, of their subsistence incomes on this necessity. If the prices for food were to rise so high as to cause the total revenue to exceed total disposable income, workers would demand higher wages.

Du Pont envisioned an important role for that range of goods between luxuries and necessities. After the economy had grown, workers' disposable income after purchase of basic necessities would constitute a stable source of demand for these items of simple pleasure that would have become an accepted part of the standard of living. For these goods demand would perhaps be elastic, encouraging their increased production at lower prices as technology improved. In any event, their demand schedules would be downward sloping. Consequently, the demand curve for labor, a derived demand from these, would be downward sloping too. Production of goods for broad-based markets, however, was to await a time when increased agricultural production would have floated wage levels above the subsistence level.[13]

Du Pont indicated that interest is the price of capital and that the interest rate on capital allocates it among alternative production and transformation activities. He further noted that profits can be allocated by the capitalist class either into luxury consumption goods or into (1) agricultural, (2) industrial, or (3) commercial ventures. It is sensible to infer from his general statements, such as this, an analogy between the interpretation given to the market forces he interpolated as gov-

erning the markets for labor and the market forces he saw as
governing capital markets, although his comments on capital
markets are not so numerous as those on labor.

One reason for his paucity of comments concerning the
interest rate as the allocative mechanism in the capital market
may be related to the contradiction he felt existed between
social and private return, which was analyzed in the preceding
section on value. The most that can be said is that it appears
that Du Pont held that interest rates do, in fact, guide investment into activities that give the highest private return, but
that he felt this return to be a misallocation of investment as
compared with the social rate of return on investments. However, at no place in the *Examen* did he spell out this distinction. Therefore, the clarity of the distinction between private
rates of return of capital investments and social rates of return
in his own mind is open to question. From scattered bits of
advice such as "Do not encourage investment where there is
high social cost in spite of high private rates of return," it is
obvious that he held some notion of this concept. Nevertheless, his ideal society would achieve allocation in accordance
with such social rates of return only to the extent that government undertook the projects, as in transportation, or to the
extent that men were enlightened as to the existence of
higher social benefit, as that in agricultural production.
Whether or not their concern for investment in these areas of
higher social return would actually raise the interest price paid
for such capital investment, or whether that investment was
taken at a private loss is an incorrect formulation of the problem. Another outcome of the problem, in keeping with Du
Pont's faith in the existence of net product, is that once men
invest in primary production, they will in fact realize a higher
return, in a physiocratic society, because of the net product
provided by nature. This higher return will then encourage a
bidding up of the interest price for such capital investment.
Essentially, then, the lower rates of interest in agriculture as
compared to other ventures will be converted into a higher
rate once capitalists become sufficiently enlightened to dis-

cover the higher return from net product. Thus, his capital market is characterized by the imperfection of incomplete information and an unfavorable tax structure and will remain so until some future time when investors discover the potentially high rate of private return in the net product and the single tax is instituted.

e. Distribution. The theory of income distribution contained in Du Pont's final economic writing may be phrased in terms of wages, interest, profit, and rent. In Du Pont's system the factors of production (when speaking of agriculture) and the factors of transformation (when speaking of nonagricultural production and commerce) consist of, first, either natural resources or intermediate goods that themselves came originally from the resources of nature; second, labor; third, capital; and fourth, the entrepreneur, whether in agriculture, industry, or commerce.

Natural resources and intermediate goods are paid their market prices. If the business activity is primary production, the entrepreneur pays rent for the land (and its improvements when they are provided by the landlord); he pays wages to agricultural laborers; and he repays capital loans together with interest. Such loans may cover the costs both of capital goods and payments to labor during the growing season. Thus, these funds permit capital improvements and provide a wages fund. Whatever remains in excess of these costs is the agricultural entrepreneur's profit. This profit, or net product, comes from the bountifulness of nature. But his profit does not necessarily include all of the net product produced by nature in this harvest. Because buyers and sellers are unaware of the existence of the net product, it is not perfectly reflected in the prices for primary products in the market. The precise functioning of markets that brings about a price below that level which would include both the agricultural entrepreneur's costs and the total net product contained in the harvest will be spelled out below. For the moment it is appropriate to note that the agricultural entrepreneur's profit is simply that part of the net product remaining to him after his total costs are deducted from total revenue he receives upon marketing his harvests. Du Pont made no distinction between normal and economic profit in his comments on income distribution.

The entrepreneur in all activities other than primary production pays wages to his labor force, pays the costs of resources and intermediate goods at their market prices, pays rent for fixed capital, pays interest to lenders of money capital, and has a residue of profit for himself.

Du Pont did not explicitly distinguish between the terms *rent* and *interest* as payments to capital. It appears from the context that he used the term *rent* when considering a fixed resource. Most generally, he used the terms *interest*, the more specific *market price of capital*, or even the *cost of capital* to indicate the payment to this resource. The distinction between money and real capital appears clear to him, though he did not dwell on the details of capital markets in his system. If the businessman has used his own capital, its return is part of his profit.

Because no wealth is created in Du Pont's *transformation*, or nonagricultural production, Du Pont was less sanguine and less specific concerning the nature of the nonagricultural businessman's profit. There is no doubt that it exists in his system, for he spoke of its diminution or total disappearance in business cycles and under tax burdens. Du Pont concluded, in fact, that the lowering of the profit rate in business downturns or when tax rates rise has the effect of undermining the willingness of the entrepreneur to undertake business ventures at all. Thus, some implicit mechanism of risk-bearing underlies Du Pont's concept of nonagricultural profit (as distinct from the net product of agriculture), but whether Du Pont had any conscious grasp of the entrepreneur's profit as compensation for risk-bearing is not revealed in these final writings. The problem of the source of this profit was not a simple one for Du Pont to explain. If such business activities leave the businessman a profit after payments are made to labor, capital, and natural resources, then either this profit is simply the payment for his own labor, compensating him for the wealth he had to consume in the pursuit of his entrepreneurial activities, or else it is a residual caused when resource, labor, and capital markets underestimated in their market prices the true values of some of those resources.

If the former were the case, then the businessman must make only as much more profit than a laborer draws in wages in proportion as he consumes more wealth than the laborer in providing his entrepreneurial services. This conclusion follows logically from the conditions of market prices for resources as correct reflections of their true value and the accounting equality between the value of all resources (natural resources, intermediate goods, labor, capital, and entrepreneurial expenses) that went into the activity, on the one hand, and the total revenue of that activity, on the other. For in the case of such nonagricultural production, there is, in Du Pont's system, simply no net product or net increase of wealth to society from such an operation. This first possible conclusion is contradicted, however, by Du Pont's statement that businessmen (excepting the poorest of that class who, he admitted, are as lowly compensated for their activities as are laborers) are also members of the capitalist class and quite apparently have economic profits to spend on luxury goods, to invest, or to save. Therefore, if Du Pont's logic is correct, he must hold that some or all of the resource markets understate the true value of their resources.

However, nowhere does he offer any comments to suggest that the resource of labor is paid less than that which is sufficient for its maintenance, that is, less than a subsistence wage. Indeed, one contention with Malthus was that laborers would refuse to work for less remuneration than was needed for consumption by all at a subsistence level. In short, workers' wages are but a payment equal to the stock of food and other resources they consume in order to work. In fact, if the markets for food do not cover the net product embodied in their production, it is the middleman, not the worker, who benefits from such an undervaluation, for the worker consumes the total amount of the food he purchases, regardless of its market value, with generally nothing left over to himself from his subsistence wage.

The interest payment to capital is not so neatly justified. Real capital consists of tools, machines, structures, and other resources that are not labor and are not primary resources or intermediate goods. But an investigation of the source of these capital goods reveals that they, too, are brought about by means of a *transformation* activity. Consequently, the interest payment to the owner of capital may be nothing more than the capitalized market cost of that capital good, based on its cost of production, whose resource markets may or may not have reflected the correct value of the resources going into the *transformation* of that capital good. Ultimately, then, the question of whether interest payments themselves represent payment for some value over and above that embodied in the capital reduces to the same question as whether the businessman's profit consists of wealth whose value is not reflected in the market prices of the resources going into his activities.

The answer to this riddle is seen to be in the second alternative conclusion, that the resource markets do not, in fact, reflect the true social wealth of the resources involved, and, ultimately, do not give to the agricultural producer a remuneration covering the total of the net product contained in his production. In such a view, capital has embedded in it some quantity of social wealth not reflected in its market price. Similarly, natural resources that the businessman buys on the open market, or that are transformed into intermediate goods that he then purchases for his own operation, all contain some net product carried forward from the original agricultural source of these products but not reflected in their market values. This net product for which the agricultural entrepreneur received no compensation accrues to the nonagricultural entrepreneur as his economic profit.

Exactly how could it come about that the market prices of primary resources do not reflect the net product, if indeed there is such a net wealth embodied in them? Quite simply, from the assumption in Du Pont's system that only agricultural production offers a net increase in wealth, it follows that if the accounts of nonagricultural activities appear to show a net profit, the markets must underestimate the net value of primary products at their source and overestimate them in subsequent activities. This, of course, was Du Pont's contention. Thus, once his assumption as to the exclusive productivity of agriculture is accepted, his theory of distribution is found to be logically complete.

Other effects follow from the acceptance of this assumption. Through his insistence upon the fact of the creation of wealth only in primary production, Du Pont interpreted the market forces underlying all prices as incorrect reflections of wealth. Agricultural prices understate the value of the net product. Other prices, such as those of primary goods refashioned time and again, in each reworking reflect incrementally a larger proportion of the total value of the net product that is embodied in them, quite falsely reflecting, to Du Pont's mind, an addition to wealth in each reworking. In extreme cases, highly worked, that is, luxury, goods may actually have a market value that far exceeds their total embodied wealth, because the wealth consumed by the labor involved in fashioning these luxury goods was assumed by Du Pont to greatly exceed the ordinary value of the resources embodied in them.

f. Consumption. In Du Pont's view of the economy wages are labor payments set by market forces determined ultimately by the level of subsistence and the demand for labor. The characteristics of the demand and supply conditions governing the level of wages have already been discussed. As indicated in the interpretation of Du Pont's class system, in the absence of economic growth, wages are spent totally on consumption with the exception of the case of workers who combine more industrious (i.e., productive) labor with frugal habits to receive higher wages, a portion of which they save.

Likewise, the capitalist class (including entrepreneurs) receives interest, rent, or profits. Du Pont argued that in a static society their income from these sources is divided between consumption on luxury goods, on the one hand, and investment on the other. He ignored the possibility of their spending some income on simple primary products. No doubt his experience led him to conclude that the quantity of simple products they buy is an insignificant proportion of their total income. Even their food would be elaborately prepared. His comments on the proportions of their allocation of income between consumption goods and investment are vague. Indeed, Du Pont says that the proportion will differ among societies according to custom. He did offer suggestions concerning the desirability of changes in their consumption-investment ratios, which will be discussed below in the interpretation of his theory of economic growth.

If the preceding descriptions of Du Pont's prescriptions of production, distribution, and consumption were viewed graphically, it would be clear that Du Pont's perceptions of these markets were of a primitively microeconomic nature. His demand curves would be downward sloping in individual markets, and his supply curves would be totally elastic, reflecting a lack of indication on Du Pont's part of increasing marginal costs. Although Du Pont indicated that a higher price for grain would elicit a greater amount of supply of the grain, he did not indicate that higher marginal cost would be associated with that increased production. Thus, it is impossible to complete his models in diagrams familiar to students of neoclassical supply and demand equilibrium models. Accordingly, it is equally impossible to speculate as to the types of industry, or total, demand and supply elasticities that would obtain in primary production, consumption good, capital, or other resource markets.

The inability to construct such diagrams reflects the limits of Du Pont's achievements in expressing the relationships between his perceptions of individual markets and the generalizations he drew from them concerning the economy as a whole. Whether or not he assumed certain relationships to exist between demand and supply in the particular markets he discussed in the *Examen,* on the one hand, and the general conclusions he drew concerning aggregates at the macroeconomic level, on the other, is simply not ascertainable from these comments in this last work.

However, lest he be unjustly accused of presenting an incomplete picture of his model, let it be recalled that the present interpretation is based on those of his comments found not in an expository work but rather in a work of criticism of the ideas of Malthus and Say. The fact remains, nevertheless, that these gaps in interpretations of Du Pont's system inevitably leave many of the necessary links between levels of production, distribution, and consumption in the various sectors of his economy open to the question of whether Du Pont had a clear idea of exactly how agricultural production would generate change in the economy. But these considerations are better explored through an orderly interpretation of his system of economic growth.

g. The Role of Money. There is a curious lack of emphasis on money in Du Pont's final book. However, it is obvious from the contents of the work that he was fully aware of the veil of money and the mechanics through which prices reflect underlying demand and supply conditions. Evidence of such an awareness on Du Pont's part comes from numerous comments within the *Examen.*[14] He discussed, for instance, disruptions in resource allocation from artificially low food prices.[15] He assumed that his readers were knowledgeable concerning the distinction between money capital and physical capital.[16] Furthermore, he discussed the effect of taxation of interest on the ultimate lending rate for capital investment.[17] He commented that workers might save part of their incomes to lend entrepreneurs for investment in physical capital.[18] But he did not discuss inflation.

Because neither monetary theory, banking institutions, nor government support of a monetary system was mentioned in his final work, it follows that the problems and uses of monetary policy were not specifically related to the operations of his system. An absence of explicit considerations of monetary theory in Du Pont's system may be interpreted as much a strength as a weakness. Abstraction from monetary complications permits his distributive, productive, and growth mechanisms to be analyzed all the more incisively.

None of these comments are meant to suggest that Du Pont was unaware of the significance of monetary policy on the day-to-day operations of the economy. His work on inflation in the National Assembly and his term as a director of the Banque Territoriale leave no doubt of his awareness of monetary principles and problems, including inflation. It is fair to assume that between his earlier writings and his later critiques of Malthus and Say he did not lose his awareness of the importance of money to an economy, but rather found no need, in the questions he was raising in these last writings, to set forth his views on monetary aspects of a system whose underlying operations take place through a price system that presupposes the existence of a self-regulating monetary system.

h. Taxation. Stated briefly, just as Du Pont continued to accept in his final work the essentiality of agricultural production, so he kept to the conclusion that follows from this basically physiocratic position that any political redistribution of wealth, that is, any government economic activity not based on user cost, should be financed exclusively by a tax on the essential net product of agriculture.

Du Pont analyzed existing tax systems, noting that any increase in taxes on wages would be shifted totally onto employers in the form of higher wages by the amount of the tax. Such a shift would occur because workers, already employed at a subsistence level of wages, would be unwilling, indeed unable, to work for lower net wages after taxes. Similarly, in Du Pont's view, an increase in tax on the return to capital was shifted totally onto the borrower in the form of higher interest rates. There is no underlying justification, corresponding to the minimum subsistence wage necessary to labor, to account for a total shift of a tax on interest onto the borrower. In modern terminology, the supply of funds would have to be infinitely elastic at the going rate of interest on capital investment for a tax so levied to be shifted totally onto the borrower. Such a supply curve is in accordance only with the perceptions of the individual borrower in a purely competitive market for capital, and reaffirms the weaknesses noted earlier concerning Du Pont's insufficient analysis of his supply functions. Thus, Du Pont's analysis of the supply of capital in this manner suffers from the fallacy of composition of the supply schedule when moving from the perception of the individual borrower to the market condition of the country as a whole.

His perception of the demand schedule for capital, however, was keen enough: he clearly saw that a rise in the effective rate of interest caused by the imposition of a tax would lead to a diminution of the quantity of capital actually borrowed. Ultimately, then, he saw the businessman, who transforms resources, employs labor, and borrows capital, as the exclusive bearer of the tax burden under existing systems, with depressing effects on the business cycle and on the macroeconomic magnitudes of output, income, and growth.

As a remedy for such a depressant system, Du Pont suggested the physiocrats' single tax on land. However, he prefaced his remarks on the single tax with a historical analysis of three "national tax structures" founded on land: (1) the land tax of pharaonic Egypt, which was based on the land area of property at the time of sale or inheritance; (2) the tax on gross agricultural revenue, which obtained in the kingdoms of Israel and Judea as well as under the *ancien régime* of France in the form of the infamous *dîme;* and (3) a national tax structure based on the net revenues of agriculture. Du Pont found the Hebraic system to be superior to the Egyptian one: the latter led to extensive government ownership of land whose tax payments were defaulted upon the owners' death. He found that a combination of mismanagement of such lands by the government and the shrinking tax base of remaining privately owned lands led to the downfall of the Egyptian tax system. The Hebraic system, also employed in medieval and Renaissance France, discriminated in its levy on gross revenue against capital investment in agriculture and discriminated in favor of better land whose sale price was dependent, nevertheless, upon its net revenue or net product, and which also discouraged capital improvement in agriculture. The third system, which Du Pont advocated, reflected the fact that a land's value is determined by its net revenue. This system would involve the levy of a neutrally proportional (i.e., neither regressive nor progressive) tax on net revenue. Such a tax would not discourage capital investment in agriculture nor cause increases in any agricultural costs, because the tax would fall only on profits.

Although it could be argued that such capital improvements would lower net revenue, Du Pont was firm in his faith that capital improvements, if not positively discouraged by a tax system, would, through technological progress, be seen to increase the net revenue, or net product, through decreased costs, thereby increasing both the agricultural entrepreneur's profit and tax revenues. The actual level of the tax on net product would vary in Du Pont's system among government jurisdictions according to the needs of the society for social goods and services. The tax would take nothing from wages or the interest payments on capital and thus would not fall on businessmen, who, after all, have no net product resulting from their operations under Du Pont's system to absorb the tax painlessly. Consequently, the tax would distort the efficient allocation of products and income neither in free markets nor in private contracts.

Du Pont was so confident of the efficacy of his tax system that he outlined a program for the gradual reduction of the levels of existing taxes and their replacement over a long period (to permit adjustments in prices and contracts made under conditions of the old tax burdens) by the single tax on net product. As Du Pont's perception of national economies was colored by the predominantly agricultural natures of eighteenth-century France and early nineteenth-century America, he did not question whether the tax would provide a sufficient base for all social expenses, which was, in another time, an objection to Henry George's single tax on land. Indeed, in Du Pont's view, the question could never arise, for *all* wealth came from production of agricultural goods. Consequently, the extreme limit of a 100 percent tax on net product would in itself be a tax on all newly created wealth in society. Put bluntly, there was no other source of wealth to be taxed. Although Du Pont certainly never advocated such a high tax, he acknowledged that as an economy matured and a greater proportion of social goods became required, the proportion of the tax would be raised accordingly. He was confident that the profit rate in agriculture, after taxes, would always compare favorably with the profit rate in general, particularly since, in his system, the high return to agriculture through technological improvements and high profit would contrast with a lower profit in business whose markets would at last come to reflect recognition of a lack of net product in their trading activities.

i. Economic Growth. Just as the tax system suggested by Du Pont brings about the maximum in efficient production and distribution, in his economic system, through a recognition of the exclusively bounteous nature of agriculture, so, too, his tax system rightly encourages technological improvement in agriculture, which maximizes the growth of the economy. Du Pont's economic system is preeminently one of economic growth. The source of this growth is a combination of technological innovation, primarily in the agricultural sector, and a resultant increase in production, capital accumulation, and population. The mechanics through which technology and increasing productive factors raise the level of wealth at a stable rate may be analyzed by first noting the conditions of his system before growth and tracing the mechanics of growth that result from these conditions.

Du Pont likened the wealth of a nation to the area of a circle whose circumference constitutes poverty. The size of the population dwelling within this area is circumscribed by the circle, with a marginal class of poor always bordering on the outer ring of poverty. As society's wealth increases, the area of the circle increases, permitting an expansion of population. Thus, even with economic growth there will always be a marginal class of poor, but the most impoverished poor become a smaller proportion of the population just as the ratio of the circumference of a circle to the area it circumscribes diminishes as the area grows.

This image illustrates but does not explain the mechanism of growth in Du Pont's system. That mechanism depends on the changing habits of two classes of income earners (namely, wage earners and earners of interest, profits, and rent), both in their spending and in their saving.

Du Pont advised that to combat poverty one should neither discourage nor encourage population growth, but rather encourage investment in agriculture (as, for instance, by restructuring the tax system and educating men to the bounteousness of nature). Educated men will invent ways to improve the techniques and output of agriculture. Du Pont's faith in the inevitability of technological progress was emphasized in his final work:

> The greater number of men there are, the greater number there will be of intellectuals, of wealthy people, of ingenious and able people, of scientists, artists, philosophers whose intelligence, talents, qualities, can multiply the provision and make the distribution thereof more useful, more equitable, can improve the mores, make life easier, more pleasurable or decrease the hardships of life for everyone.[19]

In his system population will grow at a natural rate, and although the poorest will always border poverty, if the economic growth is slow and steady, customs will change among the workers on two fronts. On the one hand, they will come to realize that large families are an alternative choice to the enjoyment of consumption goods and will consequently adopt habits that limit family size and stabilize population at a rate consistent with growth of agricultural production. On the other hand, as the condition of the working class gradually improves, workers will come to appreciate the little pleasures of simple consumption goods and will create a steady market for such goods, a permanent demand for such products.[20] This stable, broad-based demand for goods constitutes a high proportion of total demand in society and contrasts in its stability with the highly cyclical demand that results from an economy based on the *transformation* of resources into fleetingly fashionable luxury goods for a wealthy class and for export.

Interest, which, generally speaking, is the income of the wealthy class,[21] is allocated between consumption of luxury goods and reinvestment. In Du Pont's growing economy the wealthy class comes to demand the same simple pleasures (e.g., perhaps central heating) of those goods demanded by the workers in place of the frivolous luxury goods it formerly demanded. Its growing capital returns are invested primarily in agriculture, thus continuing the spiral of increased production, and secondarily into those stable industries providing simple consumption goods. To the extent that profits are reinvested into primary production, the faster the economy will grow. To the extent that profits are reinvested into industry and commerce, the distribution of wealth will be improved through higher wages in all sectors. Thus, a stable growth rate requires some ideal proportion (or changing proportion—Du Pont does not specify which) between investment in agriculture and investment in business and commerce, as well as an unspecified but ideal proportion, or change in proportion, between both consumption and total investment. The first ratio assures both an increase in wealth, which comes only from agriculture, and an increase in distribution, both of goods and income through business and commerce, and the second ratio assures the maintenance of demand for goods as well as reinvestment of savings in whatever proportion is needed to keep the economy at a steady, constant, and fully employed rate of growth.

Although Du Pont admitted that he was uncertain as to what proportions were needed at different levels of growth, he expressed confidence that market prices would clearly dictate the desired proportions, once market prices had been adjusted in general to recognize and compensate the true origin of new wealth in the agricultural sector. His system contains a recognition of the fact that demand for food will not grow as fast as overall wealth and permits an absorption of rising wealth through an increasing penchant on the part of workers to spend their rising wages on new, but simple—that is, not highly reworked—consumption goods.

Because, in Du Pont's view, capital goods, unlike workers, do not consume wealth as they transform wealth, he saw a higher capital-labor ratio also as permitting the economy to grow at a rate higher than the natural rate of population growth itself. Essential to this overall stable growth in resources, output, and technology is a sufficiently long period of time over which habits of demand for consumption goods and attitudes toward family size can adjust themselves to permit a decrease in the ratio of food to consumption goods within the constantly growing total of wealth.

j. International Trade. Just as in his view of the growing economy, dependence of industry upon demand for luxury goods on the part of the wealthy and the foreign markets was seen as a prime cause of instability and an obstacle to a growing, broad-based market for consumption goods, it followed that production for export should be deemphasized. Du Pont advised that surplus agricultural commodities and simple consumption goods be exported for what can be bought more cheaply abroad. He counseled against an economy's becoming, as Britain was, dependent on foreign markets and foreign sources of food for the domestic labor force. Such markets and sources are at the mercy of the vagaries of sea disasters, foreign politics, wars, and foreign business cycles.

k. An Example of Disequilibrium. Although Du Pont was no more explicit in the mechanisms he envisioned than their description in the preceding interpretations of production, distribution, consumption, and growth in his economic system, he illustrated their operations in his economic system by demonstrating how they would fail to function properly if a government were to encourage the production of luxury goods rather than agricultural products.

Du Pont viewed a national policy of encouraging investment in the transformation of resources into luxury goods for rich men, both at home and particularly abroad, as he perceived to be the case with Britain, to be a policy fraught with the following deleterious effects for the country's population.

Craftsmen and businessmen in these industries earn high wages and profits until fashion, and thus demand, shifts away from the industries in which they are engaged. The inventories, capital investments, and labor skills are locked into worthless industries. Each shift in demand, or a war, can set off a business downturn, disrupting the entire economy. In some cases an economy that has population concentrated heavily in these industries will also have a low concentration of her population in agriculture. Such countries are dependent on the importation of food, which ceases if exports fall (for who, he asks, would want to sell that country food if they could not buy from the country in return?), or if war occurs. Thus, an economy based on luxury-good industries, especially for export, is very sensitive to shifts in fashion, with resulting business cycles, permanent unemployment of people with outmoded skills, and even food shortages.

Moreover, in such an economy some workers and businessmen become temporarily well off: being newly comfortable, if not rich, they do not save frugally but tend to spend their income as soon as it comes in, or at the other extreme, hoard it for their heirs, but in neither case do normal saving habits have time to develop before another business cycle throws them, too, out of work. The resultant lower rates of overall saving impede capital accumulation and therefore impede growth of the economic system. Capital accumulation itself is necessary both for capital investment and provision of a wages fund. Thus, the descriptions pointed out by Du Pont would cause both cyclical drags on economic growth and a lower overall rate of growth from constantly lower saving propensities. Finally, such an economy would have an overall shortage of primary production, whose net product is the only source of all wealth.

Du Pont expressed no amazement that such an economy should fail to reward its population with a higher standard of living, as he saw the situation in Britain at the close of the Napoleonic Wars. Britain's apparently unstable growth, achieved seemingly at the expense of a working class battling with starvation, contrasted sharply in Du Pont's mind with his own vision of a steadily growing economy based on physiocratic principles.

It was with the certainty of this vision that Du Pont took up his argument with Malthus over the causes and cures of the working class's poverty. It was with this same vision that Du Pont called upon Say to return to the physiocratic tradition of a broader scope of economic science, a tradition that Du Pont saw as the cradle of classical economic thought.

2. Du Pont's Criticism of Malthus

In Du Pont's initial comments in his *Examen* of Malthus's *Principle of Population*, Du Pont characterized Malthus's main thesis to be the assertion that whenever population has exceeded food supply, misery has resulted. According to Du Pont, Malthus had distorted the meaning of this idea that had originated with the physiocrats. The physiocratic dictum that the amount of food is the measure of the population was, to Du Pont, a fact that Malthus saw starkly silhouetted against the populationist policies of European nations at the turn of the century. In these nations, in Du Pont's view, governments saw population as a measure of the power and wealth of their countries. Consequently, these governments pursued policies of encouraging population growth in the steadfast conviction that their labor would ultimately increase each nation's wealth. According to Du Pont, Malthus realized that the number of grown men living in comfort is the true measure of a state's power and wealth, rather than a measure based on the number of infants born. Du Pont emphasized that Malthus realized the fact that more children simply add to the burden of poverty.

However, Du Pont lamented what he interpreted as the

fatal error in Malthus's logic that led the parson astray. This error was the fact that, as Du Pont put it, Malthus thought that population grows geometrically, while the food supply grows only arithmetically and may even decline. Du Pont conceded that on these assumptions Malthus was correct in concluding that the increase in food production can never keep up with the rate of increase in population. But, Du Pont argued, Malthus's two assumptions are contradictory: Malthus actually demonstrated that population cannot possibly exceed the level of food supply and that the geometric increase in population could hardly proceed without a corresponding increase in the food supply. Thus, Du Pont triumphantly concluded, Malthus and all other population theorists would be forced to admit that it is a natural (not political, economic, civil, or rhetorical) law that the food supply is indeed the measure of population. In effect, Du Pont misunderstood Malthus's assumption: Malthus said that population tended to increase geometrically and would do so if not constrained by food limitations. Nevertheless, it is tempting to think that Du Pont delighted in pointing out that Malthus could not be empirically certain of a geometric progression as underlying population expansion if there in fact had never been such expansion.

Thus, the major difference between Du Pont and Malthus on the question of the governance of population by food supply is one of perspective: Malthus saw misery resulting from a food supply that does not grow sufficiently to keep alive all the children born. Du Pont was pleased that the natural laws that permit an orderly operation of the universe require that, for better or for worse from man's point of view, population can never grow larger than that food supply which is necessary to sustain it.

Du Pont proceeded to describe the dismal physical deprivation that results in brutal limitations of population by means of death rates that increase to compensate for any rise in the birth rates over the growth in the food supply. Du Pont attempted to argue that Malthus's entire thesis of the cruel means of population limitation inherent in a state of limited food supply should be subsumed within a physiocratic argument. Du Pont went on to assess, and suggest alternatives to, Malthus's solution to the population problem in moral constraint for the masses. Specifically, Du Pont argued that since Malthus was using an essentially physiocratic argument to explain the limitations of population within the supply of food, although Malthus was not aware of the fact that he was thus a physiocrat, all those conclusions that would follow from the physiocratic proposition he unknowingly accepted are pertinent to the population question and are, in fact, the conclusions at which Malthus should have arrived, had he thought correctly, instead of this palliative of moral restraint.

The first of these physiocratically correct conclusions, based on the natural law that food supply determines the population, is, according to Du Pont, the necessity of upholding the institution of private property that in turn underpins social stability, accumulation of savings, collection of harvests, avoidance of food shortages, and ultimately the misery foreseen by Malthus. In a society founded on the natural right to private property it follows that there is inevitably a class of poor people, frustrated in their attempts to raise families.[22] Du Pont's own image of the effect of poverty on society, as contrasted to Malthus's geometric and arithmetic rates of increase, consists of an iron band of poverty surrounding an area representing society. The population lives within this iron circle, but the poorer people, those with less property, or those who are indirectly affected for worse by the system incorporating private property, occupy the outer regions of the circle close up against the circumference of poverty. The iron band is a representation of the limitation of food; an increase in food production will, given this image, increase the circumference of the circle and thus provide a greater area for population. Implicit in, but not explained by, this image is Du Pont's opinion that the poorer class on the margin will not be as worse off as Malthus's starving poor. Du Pont's reasons for so thinking become clearer only after reviewing his entire critique of the Malthusian world.

Du Pont commented on Malthus's observation that the extension and improvement of agriculture could never bring the rate of growth of the food supply up to that of the population. This is the point at which Du Pont ceased in his effort to put Malthus's thought into a physiocratic framework, for he acknowledged that Malthus's rejection of the possibility of agricultural plenty as a salvation for mankind is the opposite of the physiocratic position. Rather, Du Pont went on to argue that Malthus was misguided in his pessimistic opinion concerning man's inability to increase food production sufficiently to cover the requirements of population. Du Pont argued to the contrary that by extending and improving agriculture, the circumference of the circle of poverty will be increased, permitting a larger population.

The arguments behind Du Pont's alternative view of the population-subsistence struggle involve Du Pont's updated, but still basically physiocratic, view of an economic system as outlined in the preceding section. Under this system even the poor benefit from the simple pleasures that accompany a steadily growing economy, as consumer goods become common and establish a stable and permanent demand for the productive, transformative, and commercial forces of the nation. Although Du Pont saw that all members of the population would become wealthier as the economy prospered, he did not go so far as to foresee an equal distribution of income. His class system provided that only one major group would own significant private property and would invest wisely the returns to its capital. If anyone were to question the sagacity of his division of wealth upon the foundation of private property, Du Pont was prepared to counter the arguments by quoting, as he did in his critique of Malthus, the authority of Jesus who said, "The poor will always be with us," as satisfactory evidence of the continued existence of a poorer class even in Du Pont's physiocratic system.[23]

To support his argument against Malthus that the rate of growth in the food supply does not necessarily decline, Du Pont appealed to the idea of technological growth, which he argued is a positive function of population growth.[24] Such technological improvements will be sufficient to overcome the suffering of a growing population, given that certain other conditions obtain, as explained below.

An explanation of Du Pont's own views concerning the natural rate of population growth when food supply is not a constraining factor properly awaits an interpretation of his opinions concerning Malthus's own solutions to the problem of population growth. It is only with knowledge of his views of Malthus and his own alternatives that one can understand how Du Pont could confidently argue for nations not to follow Malthus's advice to restrict the population (but also not, of course, to encourage its growth, either government action being an operation contrary to natural law), but rather to emphasize the increase of the food supply, which in the physiocratic framework is an operation in accordance with natural law.

Du Pont expressed the opinion that only a proportion of men would practice the moral constraint suggested by Malthus in his second and subsequent editions, and, moreover, that the greater part of those who would use such constraint would be educated men already aware of the population problem, whose own families were already safely above the poverty line, and who could, unlike those at the subsistence level, enjoy alternative pleasures to those of the marital bed.

As an illustrative argument, though hardly as a logically conclusive rebuttal of Malthus's position, Du Pont noted that even if one nation in one period of history were somehow able to achieve a society in which wages were above the subsistence level because of successfully limited population through the operation of moral constraint, that country would be subject to invasion from other nations covetous of its apparent wealth, and foreign workers would invade the country, offering their labor at lower wages, with the final outcome being a reduction of wages in that country. Such a fall in the standard of living would represent a greater emotional shock to the citizens of that country than if they had been at the subsistence level all along; consequently, their work habits and moral standards would decay. Du Pont's hypothetical case is colorful, but if it were possible for one country to achieve such a status in a given epoch, then it must be possible for the world as a whole to achieve such a condition. Du Pont's main argument is thus not strengthened significantly by his example, but the fact remains that no such moral constraint can possibly succeed in limiting population, in his view.

Du Pont lacked Malthus's hope in the possible success of education of the masses in moral constraint, for, although Du Pont was not a pessimist concerning the possibilities of mass education as a means to enlightening all men, such attempts in the field of moral constraint would fail because they contradicted the logical operation of basic laws of nature: any interruption of man's natural gift for procreation, which is evidently good, as judged by its ability to continue the race and to give great pleasure to mankind both in the procreative act and in the bosom of the family, can only lead to an unnatural imbalance in the operation of the system of natural law. But because the opposite of discouragement of population growth, that is, its encouragement, is also alien to the operation of natural law that allows but does not force births to occur beyond a certain natural level, as regulated by fertility, such encouragement would also be an unnatural intervention into the natural operation of society. In short, Du Pont argued for a laissez-faire population policy as the only way to avoid interference with the laws of nature.

However, his conception of laissez-faire in regard to the numbers of mankind did not extend to the numbers of other living things. There is no parallel in his physiocratic thought between the increase in the numbers of mankind and increase in the numbers of other living things that sustain human life. Du Pont began from the assumption that it is in accordance with nature for man to strive to maximize the efficient growth of food and other primary products created from nature. Consequently, agricultural production is not left to take a course of its own in an otherwise laissez-faire world. Given that man becomes enlightened, he will see that it is in accordance with natural law to maximize efficiently such production, admittedly through the laissez-faire operation of the economy in general.

This is not to say that in Du Pont's view of food production such an attitude toward agriculture that will maximize food supply is sufficient in itself to assure that food supply will always be, in fact, sufficient for the population growing at a natural rate. His argument is more circuitous: given the physiocratic proposition that the food supply is always the measure of population, if, then, population is permitted to grow at a natural rate (and by "natural" is here meant not one that is necessarily limited by the ravages of starvation—for the relationship is less direct and less brutal), and given that truly enlightened investment will be made under laissez-faire government policy, then, according to Du Pont, a technologically induced growth rate in the food supply will keep the food supply growing at a sufficiently high rate as to remind the poorer classes who are on the outer rim of his circle of poverty that they are flirting with poverty, though they are not staring starvation in the face.

The growth of population and food supply would be sufficiently steady and slow, in Du Pont's alternative to Malthus's economy, to permit even these lower classes to conclude that they face the choice of more children or more consumer goods. Given Du Pont's faith in the common people's long-run preference for consumer goods of a simple but basic nature, and given a time horizon of a long period in which business depressions and other shortages of food and goods are rare, the people will come to see where their interests lie, and a decline in the birth rate will occur naturally. In sum, Du Pont thought, or perhaps hoped, that given the free operation of natural law, man, who is a creature of nature himself, has built-in mechanisms that will lead him subconsciously or physiologically to lower the net rate of births over deaths sufficiently to avoid the necessity of starvation. This scenario will unfold in consonance with historically rising standards of living. All this is not to suggest that, although Du

Pont used the term *fécondité*, or fertility of man, he had a grasp of modern demographic principles and of the use of the term in its modern biological sense. As an amateur zoologist, Du Pont's observation of differences among species is the more likely source of such perceptions on his part concerning a long-term reduction in the sizes of populations.

Du Pont further justified the encouragement of agricultural production with the argument that it is men's basic needs that keep them from idleness. Idleness would bring about little food production. Therefore, if man did not actively cultivate nature, there would be only a sparse population living in poverty. Because slothfulness is evil, the natural order has forced upon man certain needs that he cannot fulfill without labor. Consequently, man's working with nature, whether in raising crops, herding animals, mining, or fishing, or any industrial activity that reshapes the products of nature, or enables their transportation and trade is good activity. Therefore, to Du Pont, any social institution that aids in the efficient production, distribution, and preservation of the wealth of the earth is in itself desirable. On this basis he justified his two-class system of laborers working for low (though not necessarily subsistence) wages and an enlightened upper class wisely investing its capital. Du Pont believed that he saw the outlines of his own vision of society operating in his observation of the fact that in spite of the social disruptions of revolutions and wars, the average worker in Europe in 1815 enjoyed a higher standard of living than his counterpart in 1715. It is most unlikely, however, that Du Pont had been in a position to observe conditions in early nineteenth-century Britain, which he never visited. These conditions, caused by industrialization, had only begun to become common on the Continent when Du Pont left for America in 1815.

Du Pont referred to yet another example in which he saw the mechanisms of his ideal in operation: the efforts of Presidents Jefferson and Madison to improve the lot of the Cherokee Indians, not by encouraging them to practice moral constraint, but by providing them with potatoes and other crops, the tools with which to raise them, and the education sufficient to know how to grow such food. With these agricultural aids and with the smallpox vaccine, the presidents sought to lower the Indians' death rate rather than their birth rate. Du Pont acknowledged that the lowest of the Cherokees would not be much better off economically under their new system, but argued that even the lot of the lowest would be somewhat improved. He did not point out that land was readily accessible to the Cherokees, nor for that matter did he ever consider the likely effects of limited land supplies on food output. His confidence in technology was too deep for an analysis of the behavior of food costs as arable land became scarce.

Thus, Du Pont's alternative to Malthus's control of population size through moral constraint was the argument that population, always limited by the level of food supplies, and always within it, is therefore not a bad thing in itself. A population always includes a margin of poor people whose burdens can, however, be lightened through the increased wealth of a growing economy.

Whereas Malthus saw the duty of government as the education of working people in the virtues of moral constraint and a movement away from populationist policies, Du Pont saw government's duty to lie in putting no obstacle before the normal operation of reproduction of the species, nor toward free trade and investment, which, if men are knowledgeable as to true conditions of wealth and their own true best interests under the rule of nature, will be invested where the return is greatest to society as a whole. Thus, government would encourage in its general policies conditions favorable to production involving a high proportion of new or unworked agricultural goods, rather than roundabout production (his *transformation*), which requires much labor and therefore uses up much wealth in the process of refashioning products.

Other points of contention between Malthus and Du Pont arise from their distinctive views of the economy. Du Pont railed against Malthus's arguments for making those parents who cannot possibly support their children nevertheless responsible for their children's well-being. Du Pont revealed that he thought that welfare, organized privately where private concern exists, or by the government in the absence of private charitable interests, should aid the poor, the old, and the helpless, including the children of the poor, as well as the unemployed. The unemployed should be provided work that is not too appealing, however, lest they prefer the workhouse to employment in the free market.

At one point Malthus condemned the custom of building cottages for peasants near large estates that had occasional need of their labor. This system encouraged many poor people to continue to live at a subsistence level, but nevertheless be close enough to the land to be personally assured food no matter what the size of their families, while factory workers enjoyed no such advantage. Such an arrangement was seen by Malthus as an impediment in the way of efforts to restrain population growth. What Malthus saw as an obstacle was turned by Du Pont into a veritable paragon of the ideal modern agricultural estate. Workers residing in cottages, he argued, would put to good use their garden plots for nourishing and intensively cultivating garden vegetables and would raise fowl in their yards. The husband, between chores on the estate proper, would employ himself at some craft such as weaving the wool shorn from the sheep on the estate, and the wife would be employed in crafts also closely associated with agriculture. The result would be that when the efficiently run large estate did not require the workers' labor, they would zealously make use of their own cottage and parcel of soil, much as the collectivized peasant of the present century who is said to attend his personal plot with greater vigor than the collective lands to which he is attached. Du Pont's large estate, unlike the collective, however, is either operated, or both owned and operated, by an enlightened capitalist who knows how to maximize the net product to his own and to society's benefit. Nor did Du Pont neglect to mention in this example that the worker's children will tend to develop good work habits and a healthy attitude toward life and will enjoy the benefits of clean air and life in the countryside. Both children and parents will benefit from the paternalistic interest of the estate operator in their welfare.

Just as Du Pont turned a brief comment by Malthus concerning cottagers into a rebuttal and essay of several pages in favor of that which Malthus condemned, so, judging by the debating techniques observed in Du Pont's early writings such as in the *Ephémérides*, one could expect that if Du Pont's physical strength in these last years had been greater, he might have transformed every sentence of Malthus's *Principle of Population* into a lengthy rebuttal or, where he agreed, affirmation of Malthus's arguments. In a sense, then, Du Pont's own waning physical capacity for work forced him to be more concise and to the point in these last writings than in his earlier writings, where his physical strength and the need to fill monthly issues with articles from his own hand in the absence of contributions from others, had motivated him to be anything but concise and to the point.

Du Pont capped his critique of Malthus's *Principle* by presenting his own view of the operation of the economy and by illustrating that the poverty Malthus thought is due to the inevitable tendency of food supply to grow at a lower rate than population is in fact due to government policies that interrupt natural law either by emphasizing population growth (as Malthus would agree) or by emphasizing roundabout production. Du Pont saw this roundabout production as the cause of misery and food shortages in England. Consequently, he saw the solution to the problem of misery to lie in an enlightened laissez-faire government policy that would promote only stable and therefore gentle changes in growth rates of food supply and of population, allowing the latter to adjust to the former in an orderly manner, while the former was nevertheless strongly encouraged by markets reflecting enlightened awareness of net product.

Du Pont complimented Malthus on his general idea of mass education, although Du Pont did not agree that the usefulness of such mass education lay in its training of the working class to practice moral constraint. In his view, infants were born good but were corrupted by the harsh conditions of their surroundings. Education would assure the maximum development of hearts and minds and would pinpoint those members of society who were geniuses likely to make discoveries and inventions to the ultimate physical benefit of mankind. Du Pont felt that such general education would lead married couples to be able to see the results of their having large families on their living standards and that they would act in accordance with what they saw to be correct and best for themselves and for humanity. Thus, Du Pont agreed with Malthus that general education would ameliorate poverty, but for reasons very different from those held by Malthus.

The other major source of amelioration of poverty would come from the operations of the economic system envisioned by Du Pont whose growth and development along lines of broad-based and constant demand for consumer products would alleviate the sources of poverty that Du Pont interpreted as plaguing the British economy.

Du Pont's concluding position was that the ills that result from the misallocation of production and its attendant cyclical disruptions should not be attributed to the niggardliness of nature. Nature has given man the ability to err but also the faculty to recognize errors and the reason to correct them. It is natural law that assures man some minimum of happiness, regardless of his economic position, that keeps him from a life of idleness, and that leads him to be satisfied to labor for a low wage that leaves a profit to those who pay their wages, and thus makes possible a class of well-educated well-funded capitalists who follow an "invisible hand"[25] to invest where net social benefit is highest: predominantly in processes involving a high proportion of immediately agricultural products:

We must be grateful for all natural laws.——Those which are responsible for the fact that men, not entirely deprived of happiness, but having enjoyments, thinking, living, raising children, are nevertheless led by their own thoughts to be satisfied with receiving for their work a wage which leaves a profit to those who pay them, are among the most respectable, the most beneficial. It is those laws which have made it possible for agricultural, commercial and manufacturing enterprises to come into existence and which regulate them every day. Without them, the earth would have been populated only with a small number of hunters, wandering, bare, without shelter, subject to every deprivation, exposed to every danger.[26]

3. Du Pont's Critique of Say's Traité d'économie politique

Although the first edition of Say's *Traité d'économie politique* appeared in 1803, the second was delayed until the first resignation of Napoleon and did not appear until late in 1814, at the very time Du Pont was in the Provisional Government. There is debate over the question of which edition of Say's *Traité* is the best. The 1875 *Grand Dictionnaire Universel du XIXe Siècle*[27] considers the 1814 edition to be the definitive edition. Horace Say, Jean Baptiste's son, considered the third, 1817, edition to be even better, as it reflected Say's experiences upon visiting Britain in 1815 and observing the effects of the Napoleonic Wars on that industrializing nation's economy. Nevertheless, the 1814 edition that Du Pont read and commented on at length in his final book is, if not the definitive edition, still very close to the final form of Say's ideas as he left them to posterity. In this sense it is reasonable to treat Du Pont's comments on the 1814 edition as a reasonable evaluation of Say's matured thought.

The bulk of Du Pont's critique of Say's work was published as the third part of his *Examen* in 1817 and consists of a long letter written to Say in April 1815 upon Du Pont's reading of Say's recently printed second edition. This and four other letters in the series of correspondence between the two men, as well as marginal notes in Du Pont's hand in his copy of Say's *Traité*, provide the basis for an interpretation of Du Pont's critique of Say's system.

Du Pont's approach to his fellow French citizen was to reproach the younger man (Say was a mere 48 years of age in 1815, Du Pont already 75) for being unfaithful to the few remaining *économistes* in France such as Morellet (who lay dying at the time) and Du Pont. Thus, at first reading it would appear that Du Pont's comments are simply those of an old man who felt deserted by a wayward son, without hope of intellectual posterity. In fact, Du Pont did use the family analogy to describe the relationships among Quesnay, Smith, Turgot, Say, himself, and others:

> I see that it is not a student that we have, but a very strong Rival; who, being thirty or forty years younger, will contribute a great many most useful truths to humanity.
> You have almost all our principles and, if we make exception of what concerns public revenue, you get out of them exactly the same practical consequences.
> This idea that occurs to you to *reject* us, and which you do not hide well, my dear Say, does not do away with the fact that you are through the branch of Smith a grandson of *Quesnay*, a nephew of the great Turgot.[28]

This mock-serious rebuke was intended by Du Pont to serve as a polite conveyance of his very real objections to Say's approach to the methodology and substance of political economy. Du Pont's objections are grounded in critical differences in approach to the science and represent perhaps the last attempt by pre-Smithian political economists to reverse the direction of political economy toward a broader methodological framework encompassing politics and ethics.

Du Pont told Say that although he (Say) might not accept the fact, he did, in fact, hold almost all the physiocratic principles (as indeed Du Pont argued that Smith had held almost all of the physiocrats' principles) but was misled as to the uniqueness of original value in nature and consequently as to the methods of financing government activities.

Du Pont reproved Say for divorcing the study of government from the study of wealth and for discarding the former from his definition of political economy:

> How could you try to split in two this beautiful science in order to isolate that of wealth which is but a collection of calculations and developments apt to show the usefulness of conforming to the

LAW. The latter was, has always been, will always be and in its entirety within the RIGHT, which cannot be violated without injustice, without tyranny, without crime.[29]

The degree of emotional force in Du Pont's comments concerning the scope of political economy represents simply a reaction to Say's position, on the one hand, and an outcome of the development of Du Pont's own thought over the Revolutionary and Napoleonic periods, on the other. Ever since Du Pont's involvement in Turgot's abortive institutional reforms, if not indeed from Du Pont's pre-Quesnay poem addressed to Louis XV's finance minister in 1761, Du Pont had been concerned with discovering the form of government most likely to improve the condition of the people. This concern was heightened in the Revolutionary assemblies in which Du Pont was one of the few economists to participate, and culminated in 1814 in Du Pont's own brief term in the French Provisional Government, just before he read and commented on Say's *Traité*. Say's own words are clearly calculated to lay to rest the pre-Smithian definition of political economy that included politics as well as the study of the production and consumption of wealth,[30] and even to argue that "Dr. Smith's work is but a promiscuous assemblage of the soundest principles of Political Economy, supported by the clearest illustrations, . . . an ill-digested mass of enlightened views and valuable information."[31] Indeed, Du Pont complimented Say on his descriptions of the various occupations and industries and their interrelationships, on his chapters dealing with consumption, and on Say's view of private entrepreneurship.[32] However, because Say did not include the study of government in his scope of political economy as did Du Pont, it was inevitable that his treatment of public finance should be deficient in Du Pont's eyes. On this point Du Pont referred to his own *Table Raisonnée* as the correct outline of the subject matter of political economy and noted that it begins with the words: Table Raisonnée des Principes de l' Economie Politique, *"la sensibilité de l' homme, ses facultés, sa volonté,* premières et inalienables *propriétés,* qu'il tient de DIEU et de *la* NATURE."[33]

Arguing from this assumption that man's right to property is ordained by nature, Du Pont claimed that Say's chapter on taxation was wrongly founded because

> if even *representative* governments do not have the RIGHT, must not have the power, to interfere with the liberty involved in any type of work, to interrupt the operations of any trade, to attach the property of any citizen, of any man even a foreigner, you can see that the chapter would have to be rewritten in its entirety.[34]

In Say's own work is found a definition of the production and consumption of wealth that is pointedly different from the physiocratic use of the terms. The physiocrats meant by *production* the creation of an article of value directly from nature; its original value was increased only to the extent that labor (an indirect application of the food and natural substance contained in that labor) was applied to that *transformation* process through the cumulative remolding of the products of nature.[35] Similarly, Du Pont's physiocratic concept of consumption involved the physical products of nature, as described in detail in the section on Du Pont's economic system.[36] It is not surprising that Du Pont argued in favor of making more simple products with higher capital-labor ratios, for machines used, in his estimation, fewer agricultural products in their operation than did luxury goods fashioned by hand, since the machines, unlike the laborers, did not require three meals a day.[37] Say was careful to spell out his use of the words *production* and *consumption*, which are clearly in the midstream of the development of their classical meanings down to the present.[38]

Similarly, Say is consistent in his definition of the scope of political economy in stating that

> it would be foreign to the plan of this work, to enquire in whom the right of taxation is or ought to be vested. In the science of political economy, taxation must be considered as matter [*sic*] of fact and not of right; and nothing further is to be regarded, than its

nature, the source whence it derives the values it absorbs, and its effect upon the national and individual interests. The province of this science extends no further.[39]

Were it not for Say's view of political economy as compared to Du Pont's and for Say's rejection of the physiocratic dogma of the exclusive source of value to lie in nature, his notions on taxation would conceivably have been less noxious to Du Pont. Say argued that a tax, however levied, and wherever its burden fell, took once and for all an amount of value and potential from the economy, no matter how that tax was spent by the government:

> The object of taxation is, not the actual commodity, but the value of the commodity, given by the tax-payer to the tax-gatherer. . . . The moment that value is parted with by the tax-payer, it is positively lost to him; the moment it is consumed by the government or its agents, it is lost to all the world, and never reverts to, or re-exists in, society. . . . However the money levied by taxation may be refunded to the nation, its value is never refunded; because it is never returned gratuitously, or refunded by the public functionaries, without receiving an equivalent in the way of barter or exchange.[40]

Say went on to conclude with the general rule of thumb that taxation of goods containing a greater amount of primary-production material seemed to decrease the wealth and productive capacity of the nation more so than did taxation of luxury goods far removed from the state of primary production. Although this is not the place to analyze Say's unusual theory of value redistribution in taxation, it is nevertheless instructive of Du Pont's own critique of Say's theory of taxation to be aware, not only of the scope, but of the substance of Say's opinions concerning the effect of taxation on the production and value of wealth.

From this short description of Say's ideas on the subject, it is understandable not only that Du Pont reiterated his own opinion concerning the scope of political economy, particularly in reference to cases where government plays a direct role in affecting economic activity, but also that Du Pont took advantage of the fact that Say concluded from his general observations that taxes on goods containing a greater proportion of unworked primary products seemed to lower the stock of wealth to a greater extent than did taxes on highly worked goods. Du Pont neatly agreed with Say on this point, providing his own explanation for such a phenomenon. The closer a good is to the level of primary production, reasoned Du Pont, the more value, or the greater a net accumulation of wealth it represents to the economy. The more a good has been worked with wealth-consuming labor, the less net wealth it represents, and the less the value that can be lost from it through taxation. Yet Du Pont would not agree with Say's argument that value is necessarily lost to society through taxation: he would argue that the loss of value varies indirectly with the utility of the services government ultimately provides as a result of the taxation. Nevertheless, since Say's theory of value and taxation offers no clear-cut guide to an enlightened tax policy, it was more appropriate yet for Du Pont to propose his single tax, not on land or on primary production, but on the net product.

Because of the two men's fundamental differences on the larger issue of the proper scope of political economy, Du Pont restated his own views of the operation of the economy and offered his suggestions for taxation, already analyzed in the preceding section, that would in his view least interfere with and therefore most promote the increase of wealth in society; he capped his presentation with an appeal to Say to

> grant us a bit of integrity, my dear Say. We [i.e., the physiocrats] are neither fools nor idiots; we are extremely perceptive; we have not written and governed for fifty years, in countries with widely differing laws and customs, without learning anything.[41]

Du Pont's epistle ends with an exhortation to Say to rejoin the ranks of those who see that economic questions are inextricably intertwined with political and ethical ones, and to apply his genius not to the specific problems of any one country in a given period of history but to the common laws that bind mankind together in a community of moral, political, and economic relationships, none of which can be understood separately from the others.[42]

The letter published in Du Pont's 1817 *Examen* was itself the fifth in a series of eight letters exchanged between the two economists during the period April 5, 1814 to February 6, 1816.

The first letter,[43] from Say to Du Pont on April 5, 1814, just four days after Napoleon's loss of control of the city of Paris, was an appeal to Du Pont, who had just been appointed secretary-general of the Provisional Government, for a cabinet position in the government then being formed. Say noted that Napoleon had offered him a generous stipend and position as economic advisor if Say would rework his first (1803) edition of the *Traité* in a way favorable to Napoleonic reform, but that Say had refused.

There is no record of a direct reply from Du Pont concerning Say's request for a position in the new government. However, Du Pont wrote to him on June 20, 1814,[44] after they had both appeared before a meeting in which Du Pont had publicly praised the newly released second edition of Say's *Traité*. The letter contains preliminary versions of several of the criticisms that were to be published in the *Examen*, notably with respect to Say's characterization of the physiocratic school.[45]

Say's reply[46] of June 23 to Du Pont's letter contains an apology for characterizing Quesnay merely as a physician, reports Say's own vacillation on the question of whether men, by joining into society, actually procure for themselves any rights at all, and makes the point that Say's personal opinions on their political gains from joining into society in no way affected the economic theory he studied. He agreed that he differed with physiocrats on certain principles and called on Du Pont to recognize his parting with the physiocrats as the outcome of his own thinking, honestly arrived at, and only unjustly characterized as being misguided physiocracy. Three weeks later, on July 12, Say sent another letter[47] to Du Pont, thanking him for his annotations to Say's prefatory remarks in his second edition. Although the set of annotations actually sent by Du Pont has not been retained among Du Pont's papers, marginal notes in this section do appear in Du Pont's hand in the prefatory remarks in his copy of the *Traité*. Most of the more important comments in these marginalia were incorporated into his long letter, later published in the *Examen*. Two of these marginalia were never published. The first, recorded in a brief, emotional, and pointed form one would expect of marginal comments, reveals Du Pont's reaction to Say's interpretation of the scope of political economy, stripped of the veneer with which Du Pont composed his comments intended for publication in the *Examen:*

First some truths are uncovered, then they are coordinated, and later, Systems are formed. These Systems are deficient when not enough *truths* are known, or *when* errors are interpersed in them.

As soon as all truths or most of those which are of great importance are known, it will become obvious that they are bound into a beautiful system.

You yourself have said in several other places in this excellent work about diverse ideas that you bring up with good reason, *it's a false system, it is an absurd system*. But if there are false and absurd systems, it is only because there can be and there are systems that are true, just and reasonable.

Therefore one must not take the word *system* the wrong way when one has no reason to add to it a bad epithet but you did feel like decrying: and what about [duty?].[48]

The second marginal note is a clear objection to Say's comment in his *Traité* that statistics are the handmaiden of political economy in the same sense that history is the handmaiden of politics (or political science). To this Du Pont commented in the margin that

statistics represent a fairly interesting object of curiosity [;] as a matter of fact, statistics cannot influence *political economy* in any way. The former is not a science of *rights*, and no statistical fact can preclude the fact that a man is entitled to freedom of actions which are harmless and to dispose of his property as he wished, nor can it prove that one can hamper either of these freedoms without infraction or damage.[49]

In his letter of July 12, 1814[50] Say replied to Du Pont's annotations rather briefly, noting that he had studied them carefully and would correct his own work in accordance with the suggestions of Du Pont wherever they had changed his thinking.

Shortly thereafter, Say took advantage of the end of the Napoleonic Wars to spend several months traveling through England and Scotland, where he met "all those who are occupied with political economy."[51] On the first of February, 1815, Say sent Du Pont a note[52] indicating that he had presented himself at Du Pont's residence to discuss his observations on Britain and review the talks he had just had with the British economists, and was disappointed to have found Du Pont not at home. Apparently, the two men never did meet for such a discussion, for Napoleon reentered Paris on March 19, following his return from Elba. Du Pont, already engaged in preparing for his emigration to America, accelerated his departure plans and was on the high seas by April 22, the date of his long letter to Say, which was published in the *Examen*.

Say's reply to this letter, which may be taken as his comments concerning the contents of Du Pont's critique of his work in the *Examen*, was contained in his letter to Du Pont (now settled in America), written the fifteenth of November, 1815.[53] In that reply he warmly thanked Du Pont for his long letter, but upheld the necessity of maintaining his own honestly held opinions concerning the scope and nature of political economy. He countered Du Pont's objections about the ultimate source of value by pointing out that the amount of value in any object does not depend on the degree of participation of the mud of the land in its fashioning and that the value of an object fashioned by a craftsman might well exceed the value of primary products consumed in the fashioning process. As for the proper scope of political economy, he candidly observed that the physiocrats had been concerned with what ought to be, and he with what is. He begged Du Pont not to judge him by the standards established by physiocratic thinkers of a different age. Finally, in answer to Du Pont's comments on his section on taxation, Say argued that the work of man, machinery, and nature all produce wealth; consequently, they should all be taxed, rather than nature alone.

Du Pont's reply of February 6, 1816[54] to Say's letter of November 15, 1815, and the last in their exchange of correspondence, is a touching letter, for in it Du Pont sought forgiveness for having quarreled so with Say, but he explained that argument was the only sport in which he could engage at his advanced age. Although he attempted to restate some of his comments from his long letter of April 22, 1815, he pleaded that his health was failing, that he was mentally depressed over the social disruptions of the Napoleonic period, and, as a result that he no longer had the stamina to continue their spirited debate. He thanked Say for the copy of Say's 1815 *Catéchisme*,[55] which is a simplified version of the points made by Say in his *Traité*, but was never to comment on the work.

Thus, the bulk of Du Pont's comments on Say's work is evident from the one letter printed in his 1817 *Examen*. If there was any doubt as to whether Du Pont might have been influenced by Say's thoughts and letters, an investigation of the complete set of correspondence dispels that possibility. In the end, as in the beginning, Du Pont was unwilling to compromise a system that gave ontological as well as epistemological order to the moral, social, political, and economic elements of what he saw as one, inseparable, universe.

4. The Scope of Political Economy

Given Du Pont's view of the scope of political economy as revealed in his final writings, the parameters of politics are of interest to him in themselves. However, in spite of Du Pont's stated position, it must be said that he did not actually treat these parameters as variables within his economic system. Rather, he took a deep interest in the various "magnitudes" at which these parameters might be set and in the normative questions of what might be the "best" magnitudes.

For instance, if the effect of government is taken as a parameter of economic activity, then in any case in which the production, distribution, or consumption of scarce resources is examined (that is, in any typical modern economic question), some given effect is assumed about the operation of government. In reality, government is a strong influence on economic activity; but it may be assumed to have no influence on the economic question. On the other hand, it may be assumed to establish and operate, either neutrally or positively, a certain type of tax structure, or a certain form of monetary system, or to enforce a certain set of laws governing market operations. Government's fiscal role, its tax collecting and spending, may be treated as a parameter, which may be variously set by the economic scientist to observe the different possible outcomes. Or, alternatively, government may be construed as a variable.

However, the main tradition of economic thought (which begins at least with Smith and certainly includes Say and most modern economists) has held that government — insofar as it is a creature of society's noneconomic decision-making needs (that is, to the extent that it is influenced by human considerations other than the maximization of mankind's economic wealth through the efficient combination of scarce resources)—at least such noneconomic, though possibly controlling, government, is outside the scope of economics. This exclusion has held, even when certain economic functions of government are permitted to be treated as parameters or even as variables within an economic problem.

If there are those who argue today that exclusion of political factors renders an economic science insufficiently broad in scope for answering economic questions, because, for instance, increasingly important social costs cannot be measured within the traditional economic framework and therefore have effects on humans that are crucial to the economic question itself but that are also manifested by humans overwhelmingly in their noneconomic influence on government, then these persons would be in agreement with Du Pont that it is necessary to incorporate the study of government and its (in the modern sense, noneconomic) functions to obtain a true understanding of how to maximize people's happiness.

They would agree with Du Pont that wealth, as measured and studied by the modern economic method, and the method approved of by Say, is no longer of sufficient interest as to be important in a society where political and economic decisions are densely intertwined. Therefore, if any one person in modern society were to argue that the maximization of economic wealth through the efficient use of resources that can be utilized within a nongovernment framework, or a framework whose boundaries are merely outlined by government, is not only no longer sufficient to explain how that society sees that its wealth is best maximized, but that that kind of wealth is no longer of sufficient importance when compared to the kind of wealth in which social but noneconomic behavior plays an essential role in production, distribution, and consumption, then he would conclude that that kind of presently traditional economics might itself be relegated to the history of economic thought.

Such a person finds a supporter in Du Pont, who from his first writings saw the overall importance of government in its ability to produce the kinds of goods and services, such as transportation, that had broad social benefits and were unlikely to be produced for the efficient use of society without a broad social base to its costs. At the same time, he followed a strictly laissez-faire belief in government's proper role concerning the market place: government should uphold private property and guard against monopolistic control to enable the market to allocate resources efficiently where it can. However, he never became convinced that a useful science would develop from an exclusive concentration on the wealth provided only by the market place. He never felt that government should abrogate its responsibilities to provide social goods and services.

In that sense, then, Du Pont's view of the scope of political economy can be labeled neither "right" nor "wrong." It can only be characterized as a view broader than that held by Smith and the classical and neoclassical traditions, yet one whose usefulness may in the future, as public goods come to overshadow private goods in men's minds, once again come into prominence.

The normative content of his broadly based political economy is deserving of comment. Modern economists generally argue that economic theory treats of what is possible under whatever normative conditions may have been set by society. If economic scientists try to study the ways in which scarce natural resources are combined to maximize wealth, but then define the scope of economic science in a way that no longer includes the variables that in fact cause wealth to be maximized, their science will become less and less able to answer the questions they ask. If they limit the definition of wealth to what is no longer considered important by society, then it no longer answers questions important to mankind.

Du Pont argued that whatever is considered important should be investigated, and, moreover, that what should be considered important can itself be known from natural laws that ultimately limit mankind's maximizing behavior. If modern men argue that no such laws in fact exist, then they simply disagree with Du Pont on principles. But if modern men argue that it does not matter whether such laws exist or what they are, then modern men must accept the consequences that their economic theory may or may not be serving a useful purpose and that, even if it was serving a useful purpose at one time, it may no longer be useful as the factors excluded from that theory change; and they must be prepared to change the basis of their economic theory. Such was Du Pont's argument when he called for the inclusion of what he saw as ascertainabe basic laws, the knowledge of which, he thought, when incorporated into economic theory, would always assure the relevance of that theory. "Vous voyez, mon cher Say," Du Pont ended his letter to the younger economist, "que notre science a beaucoup d'étendue, qu'elle embrasse un bien grand nombre d'objets. Pourquoi la restreindre à celle *des richesses* . . . ?"[56]

Thus, even to the end of his life Du Pont was convinced that physiocratic economic theory, part of a much broader view of society as a whole, founded in natural law, was the only correct way to study the economy. Consequently, he maintained to the end that economics was by its very nature a normative tool as well as a positive theory and saw not conflict but rather the ultimate strength from such a combination of scientific analysis and moral action.

Notes for Chapter VII

1. DPDN, ed., *Oeuvres de Turgot,* 9 vols. (Paris: Belin, 1811 [vol. 1]; Delance, 1808–10 [vols. 2–9]).
2. Eugène Daire, ed., *Oeuvres de Turgot* (Paris: Guillaumin, 1833). Daire published a new edition in 1844.
3. DPDN, *Oeuvres de Turgot,* 3: 309–11.
4. Ibid., pp. 312–15.
5. Ibid., p. 315.
6. Ibid.
7. Ibid., p. 316.
8. Ibid., pp. 329 ff.
9. Eugène Daire, ed., *Oeuvres de Turgot,* Nouvelle édition avec les notes de Dupont [sic] de Nemours, augmentée par Eugène Daire et Hippolyte Dussard et précedée du'une Notice sur la vie de Turgot, 2 vols. (Paris: Guillaumin, 1844).
10. August Oncken, "Turgot als Staatsmann, Turgot als Theoretiker," *Hand-und Lehrbuch der Staatswissenschaften,* 1 Ab., 2 Band i. Teil (1902), cited in Robert Perry Shepherd, *Turgot and the Six Edicts,* Columbia University Studies in the Social Sciences, no. 47 [1903] (New York: AMS Press, 1970).
11. Robert L. Meek, "Smith, Turgot, and the 'Four Stages' Theory," *History of Political Economy 3,* no. 1 (Spring 1971): 9–27.
12. Thus, a luxury good into whose shaping went a large quantity of labor, cost society much wealth, consumed by workers who had to eat as they labored. The price of such a luxury good grossly overstated the net wealth it represented for society, because much useful wealth was consumed, and payment made to capital, in the creation of the luxury good.
13. This mechanism is discussed below under "Economic Growth." It should be pointed out that the remarks concerning elasticities of demand and supply schedules are not meant to suggest that Du Pont used these terms, but rather that his writings reflected an understanding of their operation that may correctly be interpreted in this more modern terminology.
14. See, for instance, DPDN, *Examen,* pp. 4–7, where Du Pont counters the argument of Malthus that the use of moral constraint by the working class would

result in higher wages: Du Pont argues that in an open economy competition from lower wages in other countries where moral constraint is not practiced would, through the competitive forces of international trade as well as through outright immigration, wipe out any such wage increases.

15. Ibid., p. 28.

16. Ibid., pp. 124 ff.

17. Ibid., p. 124.

18. Ibid., p. 126.

19. Ibid., p. 6.

20.

These precautions will not keep the population from reaching the subsistence level, which would be neither possible nor desirable to prevent. But, as we have just observed, they will not be any less precious, since they will be able to spread among families more common sense and morality, these two contributing the most to domestic happiness, and decreasing adversity the most.

We must speak of a third cause for constant improvement, for a perpetual betterment and always increasing in the condition of men grouped into a society. It is the fruit of that progress in the sciences and in the arts which tremendously helps form investment capital, which is itself a result of the *competition* between the working classes. it is because with every passing day, slowly but visibly, the latter obtain a great deal of small enjoyments, in their lodging, their clothing, their furniture, their food, the comforts of life, which they did not know before, and which the wealthy were unaware of in days gone by. As these little pleasures of life, very real although not costly, become accessible to people in general, they enter the realm of common right, no one could or would dare deprive anybody of them. They represent a type of wealth accessible to the poor. They make up a sizable proportion of the capital of civilized nations. [Ibid., p. 36]

21. The reader will recall that rent and interest are distinguished only in particular cases, and that the earner of profit is generally included in the same class as the rent- and interest-earning capitalists.

22.

The due respect for property, without which men would plunder one another's possessions, without which the fruit of their work could hardly be kept, without which there would be no crops, without which consequently provisions would be scarcer and the population unhappier yet, and more restrained, this respect so necessary to the whole society, is responsible for the fact that in all countries and under all governments, there is inevitably a class of men who because of this find themselves on the fringes of poverty and are stopped in their desire to raise a family. [DPDN, *Examen*, p. 4]

23. Ibid., pp. 5–6.

24. The quotation from Du Pont on this point appears in fn. ref. 19 above.

25. Du Pont continued to share, of course, the physiocrats' disagreement with Adam Smith's view that the "invisible hand" guides investment to the optimal social allocation in a nonphysiocratic society. See Adam Smith, *Wealth of Nations*, ed. Edwin Cannan (New York: Random House, 1937).

26. DPDN, *Examen*, p. 37.

27. *Grand Dictionnaire Universel du XIXe Siècle* (Paris, 1875), vol. 14, p. 305.

28. DPDN, *Examen*, p. 118. Du Pont's italics.

29. Ibid., p. 120. Du Pont's italics.

30. Say's own view of the scope of political economy, to which Du Pont reacted with such vehemence, may be usefully quoted from the English-language translation of his *Traité:*

For a long time the science of *Politics*, confined in strictness, to the investigation of the principles which lay the foundation of the social order, was confounded with *Political Economy,* which unfolds the manner in which wealth is produced, distributed and consumed. Wealth, nevertheless, is essentially independent of political organization. Under every form of government, a state, whose affairs are well administered, may prosper. Nations have risen to opulence under absolute monarchs, and have been ruined by popular councils. If political liberty is more favourable to the development of wealth, it is but indirectly; in the same manner that it is more favourable to general education.

In confounding in the same researches the essential principles of good government with those on which the growth of wealth, either public or private, depends, it is by no means surprising that authors should have involved these subjects in obscurity, instead of elucidating them. Stewart [*sic*] who has entitled his first chapter "Of the Government of Mankind" is liable to this reproach. The Sect of 'Economists' of the last century, throughout all their writings, and J. J. Rousseau in the article "Political Economy" in the Encyclopédie, lie under the same imputation.

It is only, it appears to me, since the time of Adam Smith, that these two very distinct inquiries have been uniformly separated; the term *Political Economy* being now confined to the science which treats of wealth, and that of *Politics,* to designate the relations existing between a government and its people, and the relations of different states to each other. [*Treatise,* pp. xix–xx. Italics in original.]

31. Jean Baptiste Say, *Treatise on Political Economy,* 2d American ed., trans. C. R. Prinsep, ed. Clement C. Biddle (Boston, 1824), p. xxi. The "Preliminary Discourse" from which this quotation is taken had been omitted from the British edition but restored to the second American edition. It appeared in the second French edition read by Du Pont.

32. Du Pont wrote in the *Examen:*

Everything has been covered by the admirable developments that you have given to the various reports on the various uses that are made of wealth; and by the more than admirable chapter on *consumption* and *private administration,* in which you had the reasoning power of Aristotle, the spirit of Socrates, the ingenious grace of Franklin. I am going to have my grandchildren copy it. [P. 121]

33. Ibid., p. 122. Du Pont's memory of this 1773 publication was innacurate. It actually begins: "Table Raisonnée des Principes de l'Economie Politique, les sensations de l'homme, ses facultés, sa volonté, lui appartiennent, exclusivement par le Décret de la Providence qui le fait être lui. Posséder quelque chose exclusivement et justement, c'est avoir un Propriété. . . ."

34. Ibid. Du Pont's italics.

35. In fact, the French word *productions* is roughly equivalent to the English phrase, "agricultural commodities and minerals."

36. Although a luxury good might be fashioned only by the application of much labor, the very application of large amounts of labor to the good is an indication that much food and other natural resources that supported the laborers in the work on the luxury good was consumed in the transformative process. The resulting high market value of that good can fall to nearly nothing when tastes and fashions change, although the fashioning of that luxury good has actually consumed a large quantity of the fruits of nature through labor.

37. Nor is it surprising that the only nonpolitical and non-French contemporary work on philosophy among the books carried across the ocean on either of his two trips to America was *Esprit de Leibniz* (source: "Catalogue of Books Listed According to Size," EMHL Document no. W2-5130, p. 1). If Du Pont's obstinacy that with the exception of nature itself no wealth could be created except there be a loss of wealth from whatever went into that process, as in Leibniz's philosophy of the

transmission of ideas, it is, then, all the more paradoxical that Du Pont was willing to accept the proposition that the operation of capital goods, i.e., machinery, did not entail a consumption of stored-up wealth.

38. Say wrote the following clear definitions in his *Treatise:*

> My reader will have seen from the explanation [earlier in the work], that, in like manner as by production is meant the creation, not of substance, but of utility, so by consumption is meant the destruction of utility, and not of substance, or matter. When once the utility of a thing is destroyed, there is an end of the source and basis of its value;—an extension of that, which made it an object of desire and of demand. It thenceforward ceases to possess value, and is no longer an item of wealth.
>
> Thus, the terms, to *consume,* to *destroy* the *utility,* to *annihilate* the *value* of any thing, are as strictly synonymous as the opposite terms, to *produce,* to *communicate utility,* to *create value,* and convey to the mind precisely the same idea. Consumption, then, being the destruction of value, is commensurate, not with the bulk, the weight, or the number of the products consumed, but with their value. [P. 124. Say's italics.]

39. Ibid., p. 193.
40. Ibid., p. 193.
41. DPDN, *Examen,* p. 123.
42.
You see, my dear Say, that our science is broad in scope, that it embraces many subjects. Why do you limit yourself to that *of wealth,* which is only one branch, only a thin chapter? Get up from your counting table and take a walk in the country. . . .

Your talent is vast: certainly do not imprison it in the ideas, the tongue, the books, the rules, and the prejudices of the English. . . .

The task is noble and grand. . . . Such is our calling, my dear Say. . . . Will you give me your hand? . . . We have much to do, you and I, and at my age, my time is growing very short. Make your decision. [Ibid., pp. 152–59. Du Pont's italics.]

43. Say to DPDN, April 5, 1814, EMHL Letter no. W2-4064.
44. DPDN to Say, June 20, 1814, EMHL Letter no. W2-1232.
45. In it he advises Say to reexamine Du Pont's comments in the fifth volume of his *Oeuvres de Turgot,* concerning Turgot's correspondence with Smith, in which Du Pont expresses regret for not having a more complete set of replies from the Scottish economist. In this letter is an explanation of what Du Pont was referring to in the *Examen* when he spoke of the retractions in Smith's *Wealth of Nations,* book 5. In Du Pont's view Smith made, in the first four books, the best and wisest commentary on the maxims of the French physiocrats, but then had thought again about the possibly unfavorable reaction of the British Parliament to his comments and had disfigured the end of his work with a recantation, that he had already refuted in the earlier sections of his work, concerning laissez-faire.
46. Say to DPDN, June 23, 1814, EMHL Letter no. W2-4131.
47. Say to DPDN, July 12, 1814, EMHL Letter no. W2-4136.
48. Marginal notes in hand of DPDN in his personal copy of the 2d (1814) ed. of Say's *Traité,* vol. 1, pp. xvi–xvii, Rare Book Collection, EMHL. The final word in this quotation appears as "dev" which I take to mean *devoir,* or duty.
49. Ibid., p. xix. Du Pont's italics.
50. Say to DPDN, July 12, 1814.
51. Say to DPDN, February 1, 1815, EMHL Letter no. W2-4164.

52. Ibid.
53. Say to DPDN, November 15, 1815, EMHL Letter no. W2-4241.
54. DPDN to Say, February 6, 1816, EMHL Letter no. W2-1362.
55. Jean Baptiste Say, *Catéchisme d'économie politique* (Paris: Crapelet, 1815).
56. DPDN, *Examen*, pp. 152–53. Du Pont's italics.

VIII.
Summary and Conclusions

A. Summary

With the exception of a memorandum in verse submitted to Finance Minister Choiseul when Du Pont was twenty-one, there is only one economic writing by Du Pont from the period before he first came into contact with the physiocratic school through Mirabeau. This single example of his pre-Mirabeau thought was the pamphlet *Réflexions sur l'écrit intitulé: Richesse de l'Etat.* In it Du Pont exhibited a disposition toward government aid to agriculture, a strong predilection for a shifting of the tax burden from peasants to landowners, and a general disapproval of trade duties.

Du Pont came to these conclusions on the basis of his observations of social conditions, from his general education, and perhaps from whatever ideas circulating at that time that fitted his preconceived views. There is no suggestion of an awareness on his part of the ideas of physiocracy. Du Pont stated in his autobiography that he was unaware of Quesnay's articles, "Fermiers" and "Grains," in the *Encyclopédie.* Thus, Du Pont's earliest thought, before he was introduced to Mirabeau and the physiocratic school, reveals a disposition for free trade, improvement of agriculture, and a shifting of taxation from the peasantry to the land-owning class.

In the period between Du Pont's discovery by Mirabeau and Du Pont's introduction to Quesnay, the only change in Du Pont's position as revealed by his single publication of this period is a reinforced emphasis on free international trade in, and a call for higher and stabler prices of, grain. Mirabeau's *Théorie de l'impôt* and Quesnay's *Encyclopédie* articles to which Du Pont was introduced during this period only led him to reaffirm the arguments that he had expressed in his earliest pamphlet.

By Du Pont's own admission, Quesnay's ideas, both in their embryonic form in the *Encyclopédie* articles and as presented in Mirabeau's *Théorie de l'impôt* (which contained a simplified version of the *tableau économique*), constituted the strongest of doctrinal "conversions" in its effect on Du Pont. His reaction could have been no stronger had he independently arrived at the conviction that God must surely have offered salvation to mankind by sacrificing Himself in human form, and Du Pont had then been introduced to the Bible and Book of Common Prayer. What more perfect a proselyte could a missionary ask for than one who believed already? The physiocratic school became Du Pont's church, Quesnay his Peter, and its doctrine his catechism. It is no wonder that in his last years Du Pont was to bemoan Say's own *Catéchisme* based on the economic doctrines of Adam Smith, whom Du Pont saw as a revisionist, or to maintain the metaphor, a British Luther.

The dozen years between Du Pont's entrance into the physiocratic school and his assumption of duties as assistant to Turgot during the latter's term as finance minister contained the peak and the decline of the school's activities. Du Pont's energies were expended during the greater part of this period in editing, and writing many of the contents of, the *Journal de l'Agriculture* and the *Ephémérides du Citoyen*. In the hundreds of articles turned out by Du Pont during this period he defended physiocracy against its detractors and rephrased the ideas of Quesnay in nearly every possible combination of words and clauses contained in the French language.

Perhaps his greatest achievement during this period, as judged by the criterion of economic analysis, was his indefatigable communication of the ideas of physiocracy both in his journals and books and in his correspondence. He edited, for instance, Quesnay's *Physiocratie*, which probably would not have seen the light of day without Du Pont's editorial efforts. He wrote a popular interpretation of Mercier de la Rivière's highly theoretical synthesis of physiocracy, *L'Ordre naturel et essentiel des sociétés politiques*. His books on transportation policy and monopoly, *De l'administration des chemins* (1767) and *Du commerce et de la Compagnie des Indes* (1769), contain brilliant applications of physiocratic theory to policy topics of pre-Revolutionary France. But perhaps his greatest contribution to the history of economic policy was to convince politically important persons of the advantages of agricultural and tax reforms and to convince himself of the absoluteness of the truths of physiocracy, which built within him a firm faith in its correctness. He carried this faith with him throughout Turgot's administration, his own later service to the *ancien régime*, his activities in the Revolution, and even to the end of his life in 1817.

Du Pont's theory of knowledge during the period 1763–72, and indeed throughout his life, was posited on the acceptance of Quesnay's doctrine of natural law. If all phenomena, both in nature and in society, were under the control of natural laws, then men could observe which of their actions were in accordance with these laws by noting the good or bad, efficient or inefficient, and productive or unproductive issue of behavior in particular cases and in general. Society in general and the economy in particular could be arranged to reflect the universal laws of nature, and the resulting arrangement would be none other than the physiocratic system outlined by Quesnay.

Du Pont's theory of value during this period reflected a recognition that wealth is produced by nature and given its valuation in the market place. Its proper value, however, is determined by its conditions of production. In general, Du Pont did not pursue the determinants of market demand to arrive at any general theory of value in use. His theory of value differs from Quesnay's only in Du Pont's greater emphasis on exchange value. Du Pont felt that the prices set by the market place must be considered as influencing a good's value, but in the absence of any inquiry by him into the relative strengths of the forces determining value, he developed no theory of use-value and was satisfied to accept the cost of production as the true measure of the value of goods beyond the primary-production stage.

His views on commerce and industry were distinctly physiocratic. His views on government policy, however, went beyond those of other physiocrats in his enthusiastic support of direct government assistance to transportation and to other industries that could not be operated efficiently or free of monopoly without government support. Du Pont's attitude of economic activism on the part of the government comes not from physiocracy but from his own views developed before his introduction to the doctrine. His views on government policy are distinctly non-Colbertist and are generally laissez-faire. Although agriculture admittedly constituted the vast majority of activities in the economy, government support was definitely to be limited to the encouragement of capital improvements in agriculture and to the construction of a more efficient transportation network to lower the freight costs and speed the allocation of agricultural products. Thus, government was to maintain a strictly hands-off policy concerning industry and commerce in general, except to assure the absence of monopoly forces.

All in all, although Du Pont's writings were voluminous during these "years of high (physiocratic) theory," it cannot be said that Du Pont succeeded in providing any breakthroughs in the theory, or even in isolating its weaknesses as points for improvement by his fellow physiocrats. Indeed, his writings and those of all the other physiocratic disciples, including the theoretician Mercier, were only refinements of the general system set forth by Quesnay. Du Pont's major contribution in this period was to communicate and to clarify the physiocratic position.

Having accepted the theory of physiocracy as Truth, Du Pont was disturbed by the failure of physiocracy to be accepted by the general (educated) public. In his scheme of things an intelligent man who considered all knowledge and observed the universe well could come ultimately to no other conclusion than that society would prosper under a physiocratic political and economic system. Because physiocracy had in fact been the system that put all Du Pont's own personal views of the world into order, and because others did not see physiocracy as a truly correct social order, he therefore concluded that what was required of him was not repeated broadcasting of the physiocratic doctrine to a public that had come to consider its adherents to be a group of boring dogmatists. Rather, he felt that he could be more effective through active involvement in the one institution he felt could succeed in effecting social change in France, namely, the government.

The year 1773 forms the dividing line between Du Pont as the theoretical scribbler and Du Pont as the policy formulator. As a theoretician Du Pont's mind was stunted from applying the aggressive inquiry of which it was capable to physiocracy itself. Physiocracy was the very basis of his analytical framework. As a policy formulator Du Pont was a comparatively competent and honest man in government service, an administrator and representative who used effectively the physiocratic theory that drove his analysis of economic problems.

The trend of his writings on economic policy reveals that he gradually learned the political lesson that the more specific his suggestions and the less couched in physiocratic theoretical justification, the more likely they were to be acted upon. However, the analysis of his policy writings reveals that his proposals were always based on a firm physiocratic foundation. What is significant is that Du Pont was the first professional economist to make the transition from theoretical discussion to active public policy-making.

Following the Revolution Du Pont did not have much opportunity to try to effect reform. The Revolution had brought so much reform that some of his earlier proposals were actually instituted, but the entire social environment in which he had developed had been altered by the Revolution and the ascendancy of Bonaparte. The old *économiste* was truly, in Margaret Mead's phrase, an "immigrant" in an unfamiliar social setting. Only in his last years did Du Pont return to economic thought, where he was also by now an "immigrant" in a changed world. New ideas were growing up with the Industrial Revolution. Du Pont had been isolated from this revolution and from recent events in British economic thought by Napoleon and by his own prejudices. There are hints in his final correspondence with Say that he was beginning to understand at least some of the reasons why Say and the rising classical school were not satisfied to use physiocracy as a framework for viewing the changed world. But the physical, social, cultural, and intellectual isolation of his last years kept Du Pont from pursuing the blossoming events in British economic thought. He died before they came to full bloom.

Du Pont's final writings are valuable as a source for the historian of economic thought. His writings and his preserved correspondence cover many fascinating details of the physiocratic school's inception, rise, and decline, as well as useful commentaries on the efforts of its adherents before, during, and after the Revolution to apply its economic tenets to the political realities of those later years.

Another point of interest in his final writings consists of his arguments with members of the English classical school. His correspondence with Say after the fall of Napoleon keenly reveals the differences in methodology as well as assumptions that cut a gorge between Du Pont's physiocracy and Say's Smithite economics; and his correspondence also reveals that, despite these differences, their systems shared many similarities. In his final book Du Pont applied his theory to the model of population growth envisioned by Malthus to demonstrate that the physiocratic system could offer a bright alternative to the gloomy outcome portended for mankind by the Englishman.

Du Pont's economic writings and his life reveal the strengths and weaknesses of acting on the basis of theory.

Physiocracy gave Du Pont the confidence and the necessary analytical tools to propose sage economic reforms that, if fully implemented, could have aided the overwhelmingly agricultural French economy in that stage of its development. But Du Pont's absolute faith in his theory kept him from questioning it. The closest he ever came to a crisis of faith was after the rise of Napoleon, but this crisis involved not Du Pont's faith in physiocracy but rather his faith in mankind's ability to govern itself. He felt no need to test the truths of his theory or to question its assumptions. This faith and his mild anglomania led him to approve of Smithite economic doctrine only insofar as that doctrine in turn agreed with physiocratic views. Du Pont had fortified himself intellectually within a system that had strong powers of analysis but that, like all theories, prevented him from turning his naturally keen critical powers against the theoretical framework itself. Physiocracy, like any theory, provides useful explanations of the operation of economic phenomena only insofar as the theory is correct. As economic society became less agricultural and more industrial, the analytical powers of physiocracy weakened, and other theory that better explained industrial society came to be more useful than physiocracy for analyzing economic activity during the industrialization of the West in the nineteenth century.

B. Conclusion

Du Pont's contributions to economics may be divided into several areas of emphasis. While the physiocratic school was active, Du Pont's writing talents and indefatigable energy proved him to be a major link in communication between the school and its contemporaries as well as between the school and later students of economic thought. His writings during this period resulted in the greatest quantity and the clearest exposition of physiocratic ideas to come from any member of the school. Over and above the ideas of his fellow *économistes*, Du Pont evolved a strong conception of the responsibilities of government in directing social investment. This conception and his decision to turn from writing to political action resulted in the first important case of a professional economist turned government policy maker, a tradition in which he would be followed by others down to the present.[1]

His final, and most dramatic, contribution was his demonstration in his final work that the popularly rejected physiocratic theory could still serve as an engine of economic analysis to challenge the ideas of the early classical school. His major disagreement with the classical economists, as manifested in his debate with Say, over the appropriate scope of economic science, remains today an alternative view worthy of contemplation by those who find the scope of contemporary economic analysis deficient.

Altogether, then, the economic writings of Du Pont de Nemours are a fruitful source for the historian and sociologist of economic thought as well as a provocative perspective from which to view the development and progress of contemporary economic thought.

Notes to Chapter VIII

1. Turgot and Ricardo represent the reverse direction of migration: from the world of economic policy to that of economic theory. Keynes seems to have been at home in both worlds. Smith, minor government positions aside, never left the academic world. Many other, often unsung, economists never leave the world of economic policy.

Bibliography

Beccaria, César. "Discours prononcé le neuf Janvier 1769, par M. le Marquis César Beccaria Bonesana à l'ouverture de la nouvelle Chaire d'Economie Politique, fondée par S. M. l'Impératrice Reine dans les Ecoles Palatines de Milan." *Ephémérides du Citoyen* 6 (1769): 57–152.

Bosher, J. F. *French Finances, 1770–1795: From Business to Bureaucracy.* New York: Cambridge University Press, 1970.

Cantillon, Richard. *Essai sur la nature du commerce en général.* 1755. Edited with an English translation and other material by Henry Higgs. Reissued for the Royal Economic Society. London: Cass, 1959.

"Catalogue of Books Listed according to Size." 1799[?]. Eleutherian Mills Historical Library, Greenville, Delaware (hereafter EMHL). Document no. W2-5130.

Daire, Eugène, ed. *Oeuvres de Turgot.* Paris: Guillaumin, 1833.

──────, ed. *Oeuvres de Turgot.* Nouvelle édition avec les notes de Dupont [*sic*] de Nemours, augmentée par Eugène Daire et Hippolyte Dussard et précédée d'une Notice sur la vie de Turgot par Eugène Daire. 2 vols. Paris: Guillaumin, 1844.

──────. *Physiocrates.* 2 vols. Paris: Guillaumin, 1846.

Donaghay, Marie Martenis. "The Role of Physiocratic Thought in the Anglo-French Commercial Treaty of 1786." Master's thesis, University of Virginia, 1967.

Dubois, A., ed. Notice to *De l'origine et des progrès d'une science nouvelle,* by Pierre Samuel Du Pont de Nemours. Paris: Paul Geutner, 1910. Pp. v–ix.

Du Pont de Nemours, Pierre Samuel. "Analyse de *Canaux navigables* par Linguet." *Ephémérides du Citoyen* 3 (1769): 79–125.

_____. "Analyse de l'*Encyclopédie économique ou Système général d'économie rustique* par la Société d'Economie Politique de Berne." *Ephémérides du Citoyen* 9 (1771): 59–144.

_____. "Analyse de 'Rétablissement de l'impôt dans son ordre naturel.'" *Ephémérides du Citoyen* 8 (1769): 136–63.

_____. "Analyse des *Dialogues* de Galiani." *Ephémérides du Citoyen* 11 (Supplement [1769]): 193–247.

_____. "Analyse des *Saisons*." Pt. 3. *Ephémérides du Citoyen* 6 (1771): 163–246.

_____. *Analyse historique de la législation des grains, depuis 1692, à la quelle on a donné la forme du Rapport à l'Assemblée Nationale.* Paris: Petit, 1789.

_____. "Aperçu de la valeur des' récoltes du royaume." In *L'Administration de l'Agriculture,* edited by Henri Pigeonneau and Alfred de Foville, pp. 140–48. Paris: Guillaumin, 1882.

_____. "Catalogue des écrits composés suivant les principes de la science économique." *Ephémérides du Citoyen* 2 (1768): 191–202.

_____. *Compagnie d'Amérique: Mémoire qui contient le plan des opérations de la Société.* An 7 (1799).

_____. "Comparaison de l'état de l'agriculture en Angleterre avec celui de la France, d'après le mémoire de M. de Lazowski." In *L'Administration de l'Agriculture,* edited by Henri Pigeonneau and Alfred de Foville, pp. 255–64. Paris: Guillaumin, 1882.

_____. "Comparaison entre le prix de l'argent et celui des denrées dans le siècle dernier et dans le commencement de celui-ci."*Ephémérides du Citoyen* 7 (1770): 43–76.

_____. *De l'administration des chemins.* Paris: Merlin, 1767.

_____. *De la lotterie.* Paris: Imprimerie Nationale, March 1791.

_____. *De la manière la plus favorable d'effectuer les emprunts, qui seront nécessaires, tant afin de pourvoir aux besoins du moment, que pour opérer le remboursement des dettes de l'Etat, dont les intérêts sont trop onéreux. . . .* Paris: Baudouin, 1789.

_____. *De la véritable et la fausse économie dans les dépenses publiques d'une nation.* Paris: Imprimerie Du Pont, 1792.

_____. *De l'exportation et de l'importation des grains.* Soissons et Paris, 1764.

_____. *De l'origine et des progrès d'une science nouvelle.* Paris: Desaint, 1768.

_____. *De l'origine et des progrès d'une science nouvelle.* 1768. Edited by A. Dubois. Paris: Geuthner, 1910.

_____. *De quelques améliorations dans la perception de l'impôt et de l'usage utile qu'on peut faire des employés réformés.* Paris: Imprimerie Nationale, January 6, 1791.

_____. "Des courbes politiques." Related in a letter from DPDN to Carl Ludwig von Baden, n.d. [1774]. In *Carl Friedrichs von Baden Brieflicher Verkehr mit Mirabeau und Du Pont,* edited by Carl Knies. 2 vols. Heidelberg, 1892. 2: 289–300.

_____. "Des divers moyens que l'on peut employer dans l'état actuel de l'Europe, pour procurer la construction et l'entretien des grands canaux de navigation." *Ephémérides du Citoyen* 10 (1771): 43–61.

_____. *Discours prononcé á l'Assemblée Nationale sur l'état et les ressources de nos finances (avec pièces justificatives).* Versailles: Baudouin, September 4, 1789.

_____. *Discours sur la Caisse d'escompte; imprimé sur l'ordre de l'Assemblée sous ce titre: Discours prononcé à l'Assemblée Nationale par M. Du Pont sur les banques en général, sur la caisse d'escompte en particulier, et sur le projet du premier ministre des finances, relativement à cette dernière.* Paris: Baudouin, November 14, 1789.

_____. *Discours sur les biens ecclésiastiques.* Paris: Baudouin, October 24, 1789.

_____. *Du commerce et de la compagnie des Indes.* Paris, 1769.

_____. *Du Pont de Nemours on the Dangers of Inflation: 1790.* Translated by Edmond E. Lincoln. Foreword by Pierre Samuel du Pont II. Boston: Baker Library, Harvard Graduate School of Business Administration, 1950.

_____. Editorial postscript to "Réponse à la lettre de Mr. M. [Baudeau] insérée dans le journal de mars dernier, par l'auteur des *Ephémérides du Citoyen* [i.e., Le Trosne]." *Journal de l'Agriculture* 5 (June 1766, pt. 3): 57.

_____. *Effet des assignats sur le prix du pain.* Paris, September 10, 1790.

_____. *L'Enfance et la jeunesse de Du Pont de Nemours.* Paris: [private edition], 1906.

_____, ed. *Ephémérides du Citoyen, ou Bibliothèque Raisonnée des Sciences Morales et Politiques.* Paris, Vols. 6 (1768)–3 (1772).

_____. *Examen du livre de M. Malthus sur le Principe de population; auquel on a joint la traduction de quatre chapitres de ce livre supprimés dans l'édition française; et une lettre à M. Say sur son Traité d'économie politique.* Philadelphia: Lafourcade, 1817.

_____. *Examen et parallèle des différents projets de droits sur les boissons.* . . . Paris[?], n.d. [1790?].

_____. Footnotes to "Discours prononcé le neuf Janvier 1769, par M. le Marquis César Beccaria Bonesana. . . ." *Ephémérides du Citoyen* 6 (1769): 57–152.

_____. Footnotes to Forbonnais's "Observations sur le mémoire qui traite des lois prohibitives du commerce étranger." *Journal de l'Agriculture* 4 (January 1766, pt. 1): 46–149.

_____. "Fragment d'un ouvrage intitulé: *Elements de philosophie économique* par l'auteur des *Ephémérides.*" *Ephémérides du Citoyen* 7 (1771): 50–70.

_____. "Grande et coûteuse charité, très dangereuse parce qu'elle est mal entendu en un point." *Ephémérides du Citoyen* 4 (1770): 186-201.

_____. "Histoire abrégée des grains depuis cent ans jusqu'à nos jours." *Ephémérides du Citoyen* 1 (1769): 37–69.

_____, ed. *L'Historien.* Paris: Du Pont. Daily, October 26, 1795–September 5, 1797. Nos. 1–654.

_____. "Idées sur le Département de l'Agriculture et sur les avantages qui peuvent résulter de la bonne administration de ce département." *L'Administration de l'Agriculture,* edited by Henri Pigeonneau and Alfred de Foville, pp. 148–54. Paris: Guillaumin, 1882.

_____. *Idées sur les secours à donner aux pauvres malades dans une grande ville.* Paris, 1786.

_____. "Instruction sur la culture du lin." *L'Administration de l'Agriculture,* edited by Henri Pigeonneau and Alfred de Foville, pp. 95–96. Paris: Guillaumin, 1882.

_____, ed. *Journal de l'Agriculture, du Commerce et des Finances*. Paris, Vols. 3–18 (September 1765–November 1766.)

_____. Letter to Carl Friedrich von Baden, February 12, 1778. In *Carl Friedrichs von Baden Brieflicher Verkehr* . . . , edited by Carl Knies. 2 vols. Heidelberg, 1892. 1:192–99.

_____. Letter to Carl Ludwig von Baden, January 15, 1773. In *Carl Friedrichs* . . . , edited by Carl Knies. 2 vols. Heidelberg, 1892. 2:25–31.

_____. Letter to Carl Ludwig von Baden, n.d. [1773]. *Carl Friedrichs* . . . , edited by Carl Knies. 2 vols. Heidelberg, 1892. 2:32–34.

_____. Letter to Carl Ludwig von Baden, n.d. [1773]. *Carl Friedrichs* . . . , Edited by Carl Knies. 2 vols. Heidelberg, 1892. 2:99–107.

_____. Letter to A. N. Isnard, December 28, 1773. EMHL. Letter no. W2-27.

_____. Letter to Jean-Baptiste Say, April 5, 1814. EMHL. Letter no. W2-4064.

_____. Letter to Jean-Baptiste Say, June 20, 1814. EMHL Letter no. W2-1232.

_____. Letter to Jean-Baptiste Say, February 6, 1816. EMHL Letter no. W2-1362.

_____. *Lettre à la Chambre du Commerce du Normandie; Sur le Mémoire qu'elle a publié relativement au Traité de Commerce avec Angleterre*. Rouen [?] and found in Paris: Moutard, 1788.

[_____.] Mr. C. "Lettre aux auteurs, etc. au sujet du cabotage des grains." *Journal de l'Agriculture* 6 (July 1766, pt. 1): 177–206.

_____. "Lettre de M. Dupont [*sic*] de Nemours, sur l'ouvrage de M. Malthus, intitulé: Essai sur le principe de population." *Notice des travaux de l'Académie du Gard pendant l'année 1810*, by the Académie de Nimes. Nîmes: Blachier-Belle, 1811. Pp. 212–38.

_____. "Lettre de M. H. à l'auteur des *Ephémérides*: Sage arrêt du Parlement de Paris." *Ephémérides du Citoyen* 8 (1768): 193–97.

_____. "Lettre de Mr H. à l'auteur des *Ephémérides du Citoyen*, sur la marche naturelle des erreurs et des vérités." *Ephémérides du Citoyen* 2 (1770): 6–15.

_____. Manuscript of an unpublished fourth edition of *Philosophie de l'univers*. [1814]. EMHL Rare Book Collection.

_____. Marginal hand written notes in Du Pont's personal copy of *Traité d'économie politique*, by Jean-Baptiste Say. 2d ed. 2 vols. Paris, 1814. 1:xvi–xvii. EMHL Rare Book Collection.

_____. "Mémoire sur la différence qui existe et qui doit exister entre l'Assemblée d'Administration de l'Agriculture et la Société d'Agriculture de Paris." *L'Administration de l'Agriculture*, edited by Henri Pigeonneau and Alfred de Foville, pp. 199–202. Paris: Guillaumin, 1882.

_____. "Mémoire sur les dîmes." *L'Administration de l'Agriculture*, edited by Henri Pigeonneau and Alfred de Foville, pp. 223–31. Paris: Guillaumin, 1882.

_____. "Mémoire sur les municipalités." *Carl Friedrichs. . . .*, edited by Carl Knies. 2 vols. Heidelberg, 1882. 1:244–83.

_____. *Mémoires sur la vie et les ouvrages de M. Turgot*. Paris, 1782.

_____. *Mémoires sur la vie et les ouvrages de M. Turgot*. Philadelphia, 1788.

_____. *National Education in the United States*. Translated by B. G. du Pont. Newark, Del., 1923.

_____. "Notice abrégée des différents écrits modernes qui ont concouru en France à former la science de l'économie politique." *Ephémérides du Citoyen* 1:xi–li; 2:iii–xlviii; 3:iii–xix; 4:iii–xxiv; 5:iii–lvii; 6:5–52; 7:5–38; 9:5–78 (all 1769).

_____. *Objections et réponses sur le commerce des grains et des farines*. Amsterdam [?] and found in Paris, 1769.

_____. "Observations sur la lettre précedente," *Journal de l'Agriculture* 5 (May 1766, pt. 2): 40–120.

_____. *Observations sur les effets de la liberté du commerce des grains, et sur ceux des prohibitions*. Basel [?] and found in Paris, 1770.

_____. "Observations sur l'effet du dérangement des saisons depuis cinq années." *Ephémérides du Citoyen* 1 (1771): 68–88.

_____. "Observations sur l'état des défrichements publié au volume précédent." *Ephémérides du Citoyen* 8 (1770): 41–52.

_____. "Observations sur une lettre de M. le comte de*** à l'auteur des *Ephémérides* sur les canaux de navigation." *Ephémérides du Citoyen* 9 (1771): 44–73.

_____, ed. *Oeuvres de Turgot.* 9 vols. 1: Paris: Belin, 1811; 2–9: Paris: Delance, 1808–10.

_____. *On Economic Curves: A Letter Reproduced in English Translation with the Original Diagram.* Edited by Henry W. Spiegel. Reprints of Economic Tracts. Baltimore, Md.: The Johns Hopkins University, 1955.

_____. *Opinion . . . sur le projet de créer pour 1,900 millions d'assignats monnoie sans intéret.* Paris[?], September 25, 1790.

_____. *Opinion . . . sur le revenu public produit par la vente du tabac.* Paris: Baudouin, April 23, 1790.

_____. *Opinion . . . sur les assignats.* Paris: Baudouin, April 15, 1790.

_____. *Philosophie de l'univers.* 1st ed. Paris: Du Pont, 1796.

_____. "Préface." *Journal de l'Agriculture* 2 (September 1765, pt. 1): iii–xlii.

_____. *Principes et opinion de M. du Pont* [*sic*] *. . . sur le disposition que doit faire l'Assemblée Nationale de biens ecclésiastiques en générale, et de ceux des ordres religieux en particulier.* Paris: Baudouin, December 17, 1789.

_____. "La question des dîmes." *L'Administration de l'Agriculture,* edited by Henri Pigeonneau and Alfred de Foville, pp. 32–34. Paris: Guillaumin, 1882.

_____. "La question des dimês ecclésiastiques." *L'Administration de l'Agriculture,* edited by Henri Pigeonneau and Alfred de Foville, p. 26. Paris: Guillaumin, 1882.

_____. "Rapport fait à l'Assemblée Nationale au nom du Comité des Subsistances, par M. du Pont [*sic*], Député de Bailliage de Nemours, le 4 juillet 1789." *Procès-verbal des séances de l'Assemblée Nationale de France, tenues en l'année 1789 et suivantes; précédé du récit des séances des députés de communes, depuis 5 mai jusqu'au 12 juin suivant; de procès-verbal des conferences pour la vérification des pouvoirs; et de procès-verbal des séances des députés des communes, 12 jusqu'au 17 juin 1789.* Paris: Imprimerie Nationale, 1791. Pp. 180–210.

_____. *Rapport fait au nom du Comité de l'Imposition . . . sur les impositions indirectes en générale et sur les droits, à raison de la consommation des vins, et des boissons en particuliers.* Paris: Baudouin, October 29, 1790.

_____. *Rapport fait au nom du Comité des Finances à l'Assemblée Nationale . . . sur la répartition de la contribution, en remplacement des grandes gabelles, des gabelles locales et des droits de marque de cuirs, des marques des fers, de fabrications sur les amidons, de fabrication et de transport, dans l'intérieur du royaume, sur les huiles et savons.* Paris: Baudouin, August 14, 1790.

_____. *Rapport fait au nom du Comité des Finances sur les moyens de remplacer la gabelle et de rétablir le niveau entre les recettes et les dépenses ordinaires de l'année 1790.* Paris[?], March 11, 1790.

_____. *Rapport sur les taxes, vulgairement nommées droits à l'entrée des productions et des marchandises dans les villes fait au nom du Comité de l'Imposition.* "Annexe" attached. Paris[?], 1790.

_____. "Réflexions sur le commerce de pure industrie." *Journal de l'Agriculture* 3 (October 1765, pt. 1): 31–36.

_____. *Réflexions sur l'écrit intitulé: Richesse de l'Etat.* Paris, 1763.

_____. *Replique de M. Du Pont à M. Didelot au sujet des droits d'aides sur les boissons. . . .* Paris: Imprimerie Nationale, [December 25, 1790] 1791.

_____. "Réponse à la lettre de M. N., ingénieur des ponts et chaussées sur l'ouvrage de M. Du Pont qui a pour titre: *De l'administration des chemins.*" *Ephémérides du Citoyen* 8 (1769): 93–135.

_____. *Réponse demandée par Monsieur le Marquis de*** à celle qu'il a faite aux Réflexions sur l'écrit intitulé: Richesse de l'Etat.* London, 1763.

_____. "Révolution dans le commerce de l'Inde." *Ephémérides du Citoyen* 7 (1769): 276–82.

_____. "Supplément à l'article des *Critiques raisonnées.*" *Ephémérides du Citoyen.* Supplement to vol. 11 (1769), pp. 193–247.

_____. *Table raisonnée des principes de l'économie politique.* Karlsruhe, Ger.: Maklot, 1775.

_____. *Troisième rapport fait au nom du Comité des Finances . . . sur le remplacement de la gabelle et des droits sur les cuirs, les fers, les huiles, les savons et les amidons.* Paris: Baudouin, October 8, 1790.

Dutot, [Charles de Ferrare?] *Réflexions politiques sur les finances et le commerce.* Paris, 1738.

Grand dictionaire universel du XIXe siècle. Paris, 1875.

Greenlaw, Ralph W., ed. *The Economic Origin of the French Revolution: Poverty or Prosperity?* Boston: Heath, 1958.

Heimann, Eduard. *History of Economic Doctrines: An Introduction to Economic Theory.* New York: Oxford University Press, 1964.

Higgs, Henry. *The Physiocrats.* New York: Macmillan, 1897.

Hume, David. *Political Discourses.* Edinburgh, 1752.

Isnard, Achylle-Nicolas. *Traité des richesses.* 2 vols. London, 1781.

Jaffé, William. "A N. Isnard, Progenitor of the Walrasian General Equilibrium Model." *History of Political Economy* 1, no. 1 (1969): 19–43.

Knies, Carl, ed. *Carl Friedrichs von Baden Brieflicher Verkehr mit Mirabeau und Du Pont.* 2 vols. Heidelberg: Carl Winter, 1892.

Kuczynski, Marguerite, and Meek, Ronald, eds. *Quesnay's Tableau Économique.* London: Macmillan for the Royal Economic Society and the American Economic Association, 1971.

Leibniz, Gottfried Wilhelm von. *Esprit de Leibnitz.* 2 vols. Paris, 1772.

Letwin, Wiliam. *The Origins of Scientific Economics: English Economic Thought, 1660–1776.* London: Methuen, 1963.

McDonald, Joan. *Rousseau and the French Revolution, 1762–1791.* University of London Historical Studies, 18. London: The Athlone Press of the University of London, 1965.

Malthus, Thomas Robert. *Essai sur le principe de population.* 3 vols. Translated from the 2d English edition by Pierre Prévost. Paris: J. J. Paschoud, 1809.

———. *Principle of Population.* 2d ed. London, 1803.

Meek, Ronald L. *The Economics of Physiocracy: Essays and Translations.* Cambridge, Mass.: Harvard University Press, 1963.

———. "Smith, Turgot, and the 'Four Stages' Theory." *History of Political Economy* 3, no. 1 (1971): 9–27.

Melon, Jean François. *Essai politique sur le commerce.* Paris, 1734.

Mercier de la Rivière, Paul Pierre. *L'Ordre naturel et essentiel des sociétés politiques.* Paris, 1767.

Mirabeau, Victor Riqueti Marquis de. *L'Ami des hommes.* Paris, 1756.

_____. *L'Ami des hommes, ou Traité de la population.* 2 vols. 2d rev. ed. Paris, 1760.

[_____, assumed author.] *Réponse par Monsieur le Marquis de*** à l'auteur des Réflexions sur un écrit intitulé: Richesse de l'Etat.* Paris, 1763.

_____. *Théorie de l'impôt.* Paris[?], 1760.

Montesquieu, Charles de Secondat, Baron de La Brède et de. *L'Esprit des Loix.* Paris[?], 1748.

New Cambridge Modern History. 12 vols. New York: Cambridge University Press, 1957–70.

Ogg, David. *Europe in the Seventeenth Century.* 8th ed. New York: Collier, 1962.

Oncken, August. "Turgot als Staatsmann, Turgot als Theoretiker." *Hand-und Lehrbuch des Staatswissenschaften.* 1 Ab., 2 Band. i. Teil (1902), cited in *Turgot and the Six Edicts,* by Robert Perry Shepherd. Columbia University Studies in the Social Sciences, no. 47. 1903. New York: AMS Press 1970.

Phillips, A. W. "The Relationship between Unemployment and the Rate of Change in Money Wage Rates in the United Kingdom, 1862–1957." *Economica,* November 1958, pp. 283–99.

Pigeonneau, Henri, and de Foville, Alfred, eds. *L'Administration de l'Agriculture au contrôle général des finances (1785 à 1787): Procès-verbaux et rapports.* Paris: Guillaumin, 1882.

Quesnay, François. "Extract from 'Corn.'" In *The Economics of Physiocracy,* by Ronald L. Meek. Cambridge, Mass.: Harvard University Press, 1963, pp. 72–87.

_____. "Extracts from 'Men.'" In *The Economics of Physiocracy,* by Ronald L. Meek. Cambridge, Mass.: Harvard University Press, 1963, pp. 88–101.

_____. "Fermiers." In *François Quesnay et la physiocratie,* edited by Alfred Sauvy et al., pp. 427–58. 2 vols. Paris: Institut National d'Etudes Démographiques, 1958.

_____. "Grains." *François Quesnay et la physiocratie,* edited by Alfred Sauvy et al., pp. 459–510. 2 vols. Paris: Institut National d'Etudes Démographiques, 1958.

_____. "Hommes." *François Quesnay et la physiocratie,* edited by

Alfred Sauvy et al., pp. 511–78. 2 vols. Paris: Institut National d'Etudes Démographiques, 1958.

Rousseau, Jean Jacques. *Du contrat social; ou, Principes du droit politique.* Amsterdam: Marc Michel Ray, 1762. EMHL copy contains copious marginal notes in Du Pont's hand in first volume only.

Roussel de la Tour. *Richesse de l'état.* Paris, 1763.

Saricks, Ambrose. *Pierre Samuel Du Pont de Nemours.* Lawrence, Kan.: University of Kansas Press, 1965.

_____. "Pierre Samuel Du Pont de Nemours and the French Revolution." Ph.D. dissertation, University of Wisconsin, 1950. Microfilm.

Say, Jean Baptiste. *Catéchisme d'économie politique.* Paris: Crapelet, 1815.

_____. Letter to Pierre Samuel Du Pont de Nemours [hereafter DPDN], July 12, 1814. EMHL. Letter no. W2-4136.

_____. Letter to DPDN, June 23, 1814. EMHL. Letter no. W2-4131.

_____. Letter to DPDN, February 1, 1815. EMHL. Letter no. W2-4164.

_____. Letter to DPDN, November 15, 1815. EMHL. Letter no. W2-4241.

_____. *Traité d'économie politique.* 2d ed. Paris, 1814.

_____. *Treatise on Political Economy.* 2d Am. ed. Translated by C. R. Prinsep. Edited by Clement C. Biddle. Boston, 1824.

Schelle, Gustave. *Du Pont de Nemours et l'école physiocratique.* Paris: Guillaumin, 1888.

Schumpeter, Joseph A. *History of Economic Analysis.* New York: Oxford University Press, 1954.

Sée, Henri. *Economic and Social Conditions in France during the Eighteenth Century.* New York: Crofts, 1927.

Shepherd, Robert Perry. *Turgot and the Six Edicts.* Columbia University Studies in the Social Sciences, no. 47. 1903. New York: AMS Press, 1970.

Smith, Adam. *The Wealth of Nations.* 1776. Edited by Edwin Cannan. New York: Random House, Modern Library, n.d.

Spengler, Joseph J. "Physiocratic Thought." *International Ency-clopedia of the Social Sciences.* Edited by David L. Sills. New York: Macmillan and the Free Press, 1968. Vol. 4, pp. 443–46.

Turgot, Anne Robert Jacques. *Reflections on the Formation and the Distribution of Riches.* 1770. Reprints of Economic Classics. New York: Kelley, 1963.

Vauban, Sébastien Le Prestre Marquis de. *Dîme royale.* Paris, 1707.

Weulersse, Georges. *Le mouvement physiocratique en France de 1756 à 1770.* 2 vols. Paris: Félix Faulcon et Guillaumin, 1910.

Index